WAR MAPS

The Macdonald Illustrated Books
Division

Managing Editor   Robin Cross
Editor   Martin Mulligan
Designer   Keith Anderson
Production   John Moulder
Cover art   Jerry Goldie

WAR MAPS

World War II, from September 1939 to August 1945, air, sea and land, battle by battle.

SIMON GOODENOUGH

St. Martin's Press
New York

WAR MAPS: World War II, from September 1939 to August 1945, air, sea, and land, battle by battle.
Copyright © 1982 by Macdonald & Co. Ltd. All rights reserved.
Printed in the United States of America. No part of this book may be used or reproduced in any manner whatsoever without written permission except in the case of brief quotations embodied in critical articles or reviews. For information, address St. Martin's Press, 175 Fifth Avenue, New York, N.Y. 10010.

ISBN 0-312-85584-2

First published in Great Britain by Macdonald & Co. Ltd.

First U.S. Edition

10 9 8 7 6 5 4 3 2 1

Contents

Foreword

by
David G. Chandler

Head of Dept. of War Studies,
R.M.A. at Sandhurst.

In *Biography for Beginners*, E. C. Bentley wrote:

'Geography is about maps,
But biography is about chaps.'

For the reader of military history no such clear distinction can be drawn, for both men and maps are inextricably involved in the prosecution and in the study of modern wars. Supply and demand have not always coincided in either case. General Sir Ian Hamilton reputedly had to begin planning the ultimately disastrous Gallipoli campaign of 1915–16 with the sole aid of an outdated tourist guide. A generation later Field-Marshal Sir William Slim wryly noted that in his experience most battles were fought in the dark, uphill, in the rain and at a spot that was inevitably at the corner of four separate map-sheets. As for the student of warfare seeking information from the printed word, there are still too many books which include inadequate supporting cartography and sometimes none at all. This volume of maps, diagrams and supporting text will prove particularly useful to the reader studying the dramatic events of the Second World War, whether for the first time or with some considerable experience behind him.

No map or diagram, however carefully designed and executed, can give more than a very generalized idea of the military events portrayed. The bold sweep of a coloured arrow over a broad tract of country can give scant idea of the destruction, death and horror, the din, dust and smell, or the alternating human emotions of terror, elation and boredom, that go to make up the complexity of modern war. Everything on a campaign or battle map appears straightforward. However, as Clausewitz wrote in his celebrated study, *On War*: 'Everything is very simple in War, but the simplest thing is difficult. These difficulties accumulate and produce a friction which no man can imagine exactly who has not seen War.'

Continued overleaf

On the other hand the careful examination of a book of this kind can give some appreciation of the sweep of a huge struggle, its ebb and flow over continents and oceans, and through the air-space over them. The participant rarely sees much of the overall game, and finds it particularly hard to relate one event to another many hundreds of miles away. Winston Churchill was exceptional in his ability to diagnose the great turning points of the Second World War. On 22 June 1941 – the date on which Hitler launched *Operation Barbarossa*, the invasion of the Soviet Union – the British Prime Minister claimed that he realized we would not lose the war. Just over five months later – on 7 December 1941, which saw the Japanese attack on Pearl Harbor and the entry of the United States into the war – he became convinced that we would win it. The enlargement of the war area in June and the subsequent drawing in of the vast manpower and industrial resources of the USA were the two critical events in the struggle, and although a number of great triumphs still awaited the arms of the Axis in the long term they were doomed to defeat providing the Allied resolve and determination held firm – as indeed it was to do. All must hope that the world is never required to face such an overall ordeal – made all the more terrible by nuclear weaponry – again.

Introduction

This atlas of the main military and naval events of the Second World War has been divided into sections representing the general theatres of the war. Each theatre is followed to its conclusion through the text, which explains and amplifies briefly the details given in the maps. The various theatres did not, of course, exist in isolation, though to the majority of combatants at ground and sea levels it must have appeared that they did. Events in one theatre of war naturally affected events and decisions in other theatres. These events must be assessed in parallel if the many pressures that influenced their course and outcome are to be appreciated fully.

For example, the war in North Africa and, later, in Italy, as well as the need for garrisons in western Europe, siphoned off reserves which were urgently required on Hitler's Russian front. Similarly, his need of troops and equipment in Russia eroded Hitler's commitment to Rommel in North Africa. Wavell also suffered in this respect: many of his own troops were drawn off by the Allied need for reinforcements in Greece. Hitler's ultimate problem came with the Allied invasion of north-west Europe, when he was confronted by simultaneous pressures from east, west and south.

The Allies themselves were not in complete agreement about the overall strategy of the war. The Americans favoured an early landing in France but the British were determined to attack the 'soft underbelly' of Europe, through North Africa and Italy. Although the Americans were at first persuaded to adopt the British approach, the Italian campaign was eventually hampered by taking second place to the preparations for the Normandy landings. The British maintained that a determined advance through Italy would have enabled the Allies to reach Vienna before the Russians and, perhaps, to have anticipated the Russian drive through eastern Europe. But the Americans did not wish to become embroiled in European political rivalries. Even when they had the opportunity to reach Berlin before the Russians, they held their advance on the Elbe, so as not to provoke Stalin. The Russians seized their chance and the scene was set for future strife.

The war in the Orient remained on the whole a completely separate struggle, though inevitably it acted as a drain on Allied resources which might otherwise have been deployed in Europe. Japan had invaded China in 1937 and by 1939 held substantially the richest areas of China. It was the Japanese attack on Pearl Harbor in 1941 and the declaration of war by America that committed Germany and Italy in turn to declare war on America in support of their Axis partner. Thus America was drawn into both theatres simultaneously. These theatres actually impinged on each other's territory only in the Indian Ocean, with Japanese threats to Ceylon and Madagascar. Control of the Indian Ocean would have given the Japanese a base from which to attack Allied sea routes from Suez to the Far East and Australia; it would also have had a serious bearing on events in North Africa. Paradoxically, it was the Russians who gained most in the east, though they kept out of the war until the very end. They invaded Manchuria on the same day that the bomb was dropped on Nagasaki and over-ran the country in nine days, completing their conquest after the cease-fire came into force between Japan and the Allies.

With these examples of overlapping influences in mind, it is worth putting the various theatres in proper perspective by presenting the events briefly in overall chronological sequence. The war in Europe began with Hitler's invasion of Poland in September 1939, the invasion of Denmark and Norway in April 1940, and the invasion of France and the Low Countries in May 1940. Italy did not enter the war until June, when the fall of France seemed certain.

The North African theatre opened up as soon as Mussolini took his stand beside Hitler; so did the war in the Balkans. The Italians invaded Egypt in September 1940, and, impatient for success, advanced into Greece in October. These were the months of the Battle of Britain and Hitler's plan for Operation Sealion. Having failed on that front, Hitler turned his attention to plans for the invasion of Russia. Meanwhile the Italians had been thrown out of Greece and held by Wavell in Egypt. Between December 1940, and February 1941, Wavell achieved brilliant successes against the Italians in Libya and began his Ethiopian campaign but it was in February, too, that Rommel arrived in North Africa. By April 1941, Rommel had recovered Cyrenaica. In the same month, Hitler invaded Yugoslavia and Greece, swiftly making up for the earlier Italian failure. In May, the Germans over-ran Crete. For the next three years, the Allies had to resort to short, sharp raids by Combined Operations as their chief means of offensive in Europe.

With the Balkans secured, Hitler unleashed Operation Barbarossa on an ill-prepared Russia in June 1941. While the fortunes of the protagonists in North Africa swept to and fro during the remainder of that year, the Germans burst through the inadequate Russian defences. By November, they were on the outskirts of Moscow, while in North Africa the Crusader battles raged around Tobruk. By the end of the year, German forces in both theatres were temporarily halted.

On December 7, 1941, the Japanese attacked Pearl Harbor and the Americans entered the war. The Japanese conquest of the Pacific Islands and of Malaya and Burma was startlingly swift. The government of the Dutch East Indies surrendered on March 8, 1942. The last remaining forces in Bataan and Corregidor, in the Philippines, surrendered on April 9 and May 6 respectively. By May 15, British forces in Burma had withdrawn behind the River Chindwin. But there were signs of hope as well. Between May 3 and 8, the first Japanese attempt to seize Port Moresby was stopped in the Coral Sea. On June 4, the Japanese suffered another severe setback in the Battle of Midway.

On June 28, 1942, Hitler's summer offensive on the Russian front began with renewed vigour. Stalingrad itself was under attack by August. In North Africa, Rommel seemed unstoppable. Tobruk fell to him in June. In July, Auchinleck barely managed to hold him in the first Battle of El Alamein. Hitler was on the verge of great triumphs. The Arctic convoys bringing vital supplies to the Russians were under heavy attack. In July, Convoy PQ-17 was virtually wiped out by German U-boats and bombers. The story was similar in the Mediterranean, where the Malta convoys were essential to the survival of the island fortress that still threatened Rommel's supply route. In August, the exhausted remains of the Pedestal convoy barely got through to sustain Malta during the months of extreme crisis. In the Far East, US marines were struggling to obtain a foothold on the island of Guadalcanal.

The German situation was very different by the end of that year. Between the night of October 23–24 and November 4, Montgomery inflicted a signal defeat on Rommel at the second Battle of El Alamein. Four days later, the Americans landed in North Africa. On November 19, the Russians began their own counter-attack at Stalingrad and Paulus was forced to surrender the remains of VI Army at the end of January 1943. Manstein made several brilliant attempts to hold the Russians, as they fought to retrieve the ground they had lost the previous year. He could not do so for long. In June, the Germans lost the tank battle of Kursk. By the end of the year, the Russians had established bridgeheads across the Dniepr.

On May 13, not long before Kursk, the remaining Axis forces in North Africa surrendered. The Allies invaded Sicily in July; in September, they landed in southern Italy. Their drive to Rome was halted by Kesselring's inspired defence and by December the stalemate at Monte Cassino had begun. Meanwhile, in the Pacific, the Americans were fighting their way from atoll to atoll. From June 1943, they were battling for the central Solomons. They over-ran the Gilbert Islands in November and the Marshall Islands in February 1944. On the mainland, the second Arakan campaign was opened by the British in December 1943, but in March 1944, the Japanese launched their attacks on Imphal and Kohima.

In January 1944, Leningrad had at last been relieved, after a long and often terrible siege. Sebastopol was retaken by the Russians in May and the Ukraine was over-run. In mid-May, Monte Cassino fell at last and on June 4 the Americans entered Rome, just two days before the Allies landed on the Normandy beaches. Kohima and Imphal were relieved in the same month and in the Pacific the Battle of the Philippine Sea ensured the safety of the American landings on the Marianas.

While the Allies fought through the hedgerows of north-west France, the Russians advanced on Poland. Forward units of the Soviet army crossed the Bug and entered Poland in mid-July. They had reached the Vistula by the end of the month. In August, the Germans entered Czechoslovakia. By the end of August, the Allies had liberated Paris and the Russians were within reach of Warsaw. They paused for breath, while the gallant Polish uprising in Warsaw during August and September was crushed by the Germans. The Poles in Warsaw surrendered on October 2, as the Allies advanced towards the Rhine. On October 20, the Americans returned to the Philippines and landed at Leyte.

Hitler's last fling in the west was the Ardennes offensive in December 1944. He lost the so-called Battle of the Bulge, with the Russians applying constant pressure on the opposite front, as they advanced to the Oder, which they reached on January 31, 1945. The months of February and March, in the Far East, saw the American Marines fighting a bloody battle on Iwo Jima and Slim's 14th Army brilliantly recapturing Meiktila and Mandalay in Burma. On March 6, Hitler tried a last fling on his own eastern front but he failed to retain the Lake Balaton oil fields. On March 7, the Allies made their first crossing of the Rhine, over the bridge at Remagen. On April 1, the Americans landed at Okinawa; the final preliminary to the isolation of the Japanese homeland. American forces in Europe reached the Elbe on April 12 and stopped. Vienna fell to the Russians on April 14. On April 16, two Soviet fronts began their final advance on Berlin. The Reichstag fell on April 30. By the end of the first week in May, victory in Europe was assured.

Victory in the east had still three months to wait. Rangoon was retaken by the Allies on May 3, 1945, only a few days before the German surrender in the west. Final resistance on Okinawa did not end until the third week in June. There were further mopping-up operations in the Philippines until the end of the war. Preparations began for the assault on the main islands of Japan itself. Operation Olympic was scheduled for November 1945, for an assault on Kyushu. Operation Coronet was scheduled for March 1946, for the attack on Honshu. The atomic bombs dropped on Hiroshima on August 6 and on Nagasaki on August 9 cut sharply across these plans. Anxious to seize what territory they could before the Japanese surrendered, the Russians invaded Manchuria on the same day as the Nagasaki bomb fell. The final Japanese surrender was signed on September 2, aboard the USS *Missouri*. The war, in all its theatres, was over at last.

War in Europe

There were many who believed that the conflict of 1914–18 had been the 'War to end all Wars'. Marshal Foch was not among those optimists. 'This is not peace,' he said, after the Treaty of Versailles; 'it is an Armistice for twenty years.' He read the German mood correctly. Unable to understand how she had lost the war, bowed beneath the weight of reparations, stripped of her colonies, isolated from her western neighbours by the demilitarized zone of the Rhineland and disarmed, Germany required only a leader who could exploit and direct her sense of bitterness and frustration.

It was not just *Lebensraum* to the east that Hitler wanted; it was German leadership of the whole of Europe. He would

Europe on the eve of war. Britain is allied with France, Poland, and Turkey and has an understanding with the USA. Germany is allied with Italy, and has an understanding and non-aggression pact with the USSR.

seize by force if necessary what Germany had been cheated of in 1914–18. Building on the real hardship experienced by the people in the Depression of 1931–32, Hitler's Nazi Party quickly obtained a majority in the Reichstag and in 1933 Hitler became Chancellor. Two years later he repudiated the disarmament terms of the Treaty of Versailles and in 1936 he put the nerve of the western powers to the test and marched into the Rhineland. There was no reaction. Anxious for peace at any price, the western powers preferred to ignore all the obvious signs of impending conflict.

Encouraged by their lethargy, Hitler annexed more than six million Austrian Germans in March 1938. In September he annexed three million more Germans in the Sudetenland. Bohemia and Moravia were occupied in March 1939 and the state of Slovakia was effectively isolated. In the same month, Memel was annexed, with its high German population. Hitler then looked towards Danzig and the Polish Corridor to the Baltic, which stood between Germany and East Prussia.

At last the western powers had begun to re-arm. Hitler saw that he must make his move at once if he was to maintain his advantage. On August 23, 1939, he signed the Moscow Pact, to protect his move into Poland. On September 1, he invaded Poland and two days later Britain declared war on Germany.

Blitzkrieg in Poland

Hitler's invasion of Poland on September 1, 1939, was the first full-scale demonstration of the swiftness and power of *Blitzkrieg* tactics. Weak points in the Polish defence were quickly penetrated and units of resistance were isolated as German armour moved rapidly forward. There was little chance for co-ordinated counter-attacks.

Without waiting to declare war, Germany invaded under cover of a pre-dawn air attack aimed at cities and soldiers alike. General von Brauchitsch's plan was a double pincer movement. The inner pincer (IV, VIII and X Armies) was to meet on the Vistula at Warsaw, while the outer pincer (III and XIV Armies) was to meet on the Bug at Brest Litovsk (map 1). The *Luftwaffe* had complete control of the sky by the second day of the campaign. By September 5, the Germans had broken through the cordon defence and over-run the Polish Corridor (map 2). As the inner pincer moved on Warsaw (map 3), a Polish counterblow on the River Bzura failed to stop the Germans (map 4). Rundstedt routed Kutrzeba's Polish divisions in a fierce battle on a narrow front.

Farther east, Guderian's armoured corps reached Brest Litovsk on September 14 and completed the outer pincer with Kleist's armour from the south (map 5). Three days later the Red Army intervened from the east, destroying the last Polish hopes. Warsaw surrendered on September 27 and the last organized resistance collapsed in the first week in October. The speed of the invasion had been partly prompted by Hitler's desire to complete it before the French attacked him in return. In the event, both the French and British remained wholly inert.

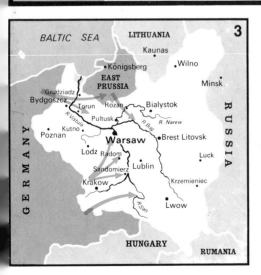

1. Alignment of the forces on September 1, 1939. The double pincer movement was to meet on the Vistula and the Bug.

2. The first five days saw the break through the Polish defence and the X Army mechanized drive towards Warsaw.

3. From September 6–10, the pincers from north and south were closing on Warsaw.

4. The Battle of the Bzura: the failure of the only large-scale counterblow.

5. The outer pincer closes on Brest Litovsk and the Red Army intervenes. Warsaw held out for ten more days after the Soviet involvement.

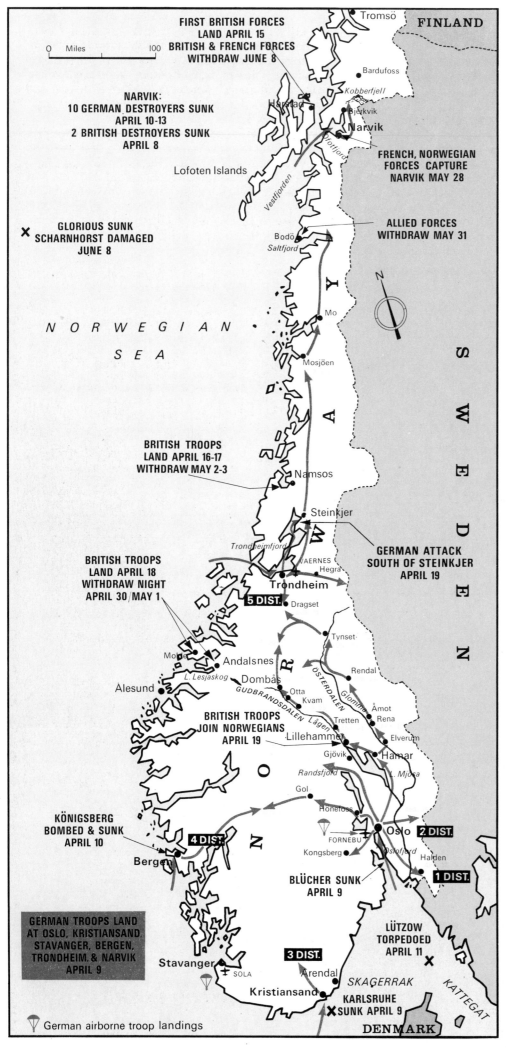

The map

FINLAND

Tromsö

FIRST BRITISH FORCES
LAND APRIL 15
BRITISH & FRENCH FORCES
WITHDRAW JUNE 8

Bardufoss

Kobberfjell

NARVIK:
10 GERMAN DESTROYERS SUNK
APRIL 10-13
2 BRITISH DESTROYERS SUNK
APRIL 8

Harstad

Bjerkvik

Narvik

Ofotfjord

FRENCH, NORWEGIAN
FORCES CAPTURE
NARVIK MAY 28

Lofoten Islands

Vestfjord

GLORIOUS SUNK
SCHARNHORST DAMAGED
JUNE 8

Bodö
Saltfjord

ALLIED FORCES
WITHDRAW MAY 31

N O R W E G I A N

S E A

Mo

N

S W E D E N

Mosjöen

BRITISH TROOPS
LAND APRIL 16-17
WITHDRAW MAY 2-3

Namsos

Steinkjer

Trondheimfjord

GERMAN ATTACK
SOUTH OF STEINKJER
APRIL 19

VAERNES
Hegra

Trondheim

5 DIST.   Dragset

BRITISH TROOPS
LAND APRIL 18
WITHDRAW NIGHT
APRIL 30/MAY 1

Tynset

Molde

Andalsnes

Rendal

Alesund

L. Lesjaskog   Dombås

GUDBRANDSDALEN

ÖSTERDALEN

Otta
Kvam

Glomma

Åmot

Lågen   Tretten

Rena

BRITISH TROOPS
JOIN NORWEGIANS
APRIL 19

Lillehammer

Elverum

Gjövik

Hamar

Randsfjord

L. Mjösa

Gol

KÖNIGSBERG
BOMBED & SUNK
APRIL 10

Honefoss

FORNEBU

Oslo   2 DIST.

4 DIST.

Kongsberg

Oslofjord

Halden

Bergen

1 DIST.

BLÜCHER SUNK
APRIL 9

GERMAN TROOPS LAND
AT OSLO, KRISTIANSAND,
STAVANGER, BERGEN,
TRONDHEIM, & NARVIK
APRIL 9

LÜTZOW
TORPEDOED
APRIL 11

3 DIST.

Stavanger

SOLA

Arendal

SKAGERRAK

Kristiansand

KARLSRUHE
SUNK APRIL 9

KATTEGAT

German airborne troop landings

DENMARK

0   Miles   100

The Invasion of Norway

Norway was important to Hitler as a springboard for aerial attack against Britain and against the British naval blockade which threatened the route of his vital supply ships bearing iron-ore from Sweden through the port of Narvik.

Germany invaded Denmark and Norway without warning. On April 8, 1940, British warships encountered German vessels escorting transports towards Kristiansand, Stavanger, Bergen, Trondheim and Narvik. Landings were achieved at all these ports on April 9 but there was resistance at Oslo, where the cruiser *Blücher* was sunk and the pocket battleship *Lützow* damaged before paratroopers captured the city. Denmark was over-run on April 9.

Between April 10 and 13, British warships destroyed the German naval force that had convoyed troops to Narvik and on April 15 the Allies landed near Narvik. Between April 16 and 18, they also landed north and south of Trondheim but had to evacuate on May 1 and 2 as the Germans swept inland to control the country. Narvik was captured by the Allied force on May 28 but was kept under constant pressure and had to be evacuated on June 8 and 9 because of events in France. In the withdrawal, the carrier *Glorious* was sunk and both the German battle-cruisers *Scharnhorst* and *Gneisenau* were badly damaged.

Above: British prisoners captured near Trondheim.

Below: Sinking vessel in Narvik harbour, photographed through a German periscope.

The Military Balance in the West

After September 1939, six months of inactivity ensued on the western front. This was the 'phoney war' or *Sitzkrieg*. The Allies thought a blockade would check Hitler. He was in fact content to regroup after his victory in Poland, preparing for his invasion of Norway and Denmark and the spring offensive.

By May 1940, 2,350,000 Germans stood along the border from the North Sea to Switzerland, facing 2,862,000 Allied troops. The Allies had more tanks (about 3,000 against 2,700), many superior to their opponents, but these were tied down among the infantry divisions. The German tanks, combining greater speed with firepower, were organized into independent armoured divisions. In the air the Germans had the advantage (3,200 aircraft against 1,700).

This was to be decisive.

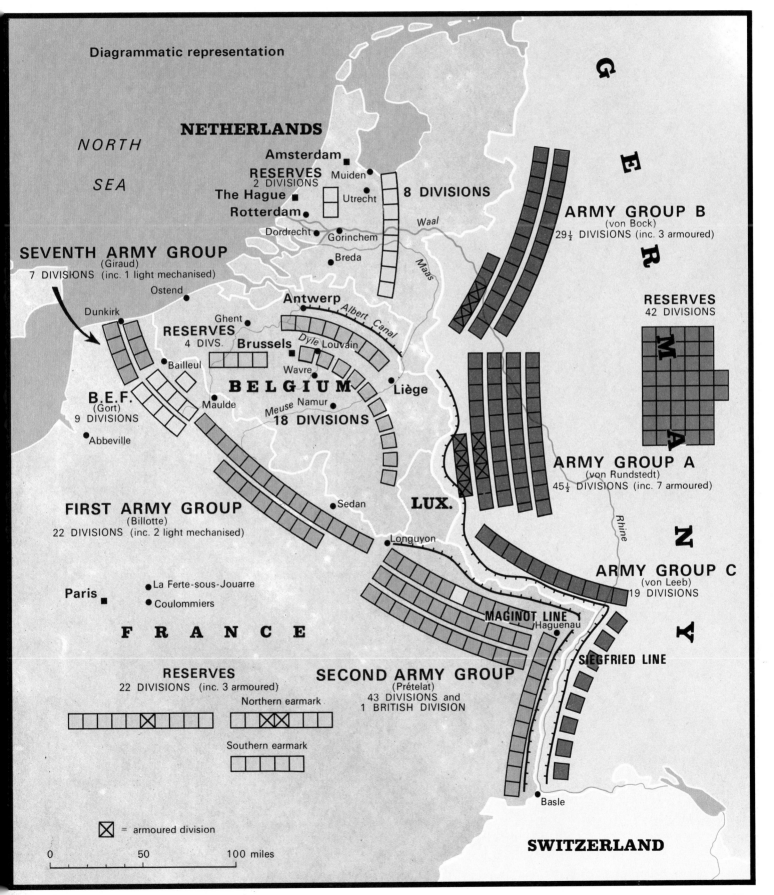

The Battle of the River Plate

The invasion of Poland had demonstrated to an apathetic Europe Hitler's might on land and in the air. In the same month, his warships flexed the Reich's muscles at sea. The German High Seas fleet had been scuttled at Scapa Flow at the end of the First World War. Hitler, therefore, was able to build a new fleet with modern, fast and powerful ships; the majority of the British capital ships were designed and built during or even before the First World War. Instead of attempting a full-scale surface battle, the Germans used their U-boats and pocket-battleships as formidable raiders on the sea lanes along which the vital maritime commerce of Britain flowed.

Two pocket battleships, the *Deutschland* and the *Admiral Graf Spee*, were ordered into the Atlantic in August, 1939, before hostilities opened against Poland. The *Deutschland* achieved only limited success but the *Graf Spee* conducted a spectacular campaign, sinking nine merchantmen in two months. Her first victim was the *Clement*, sunk off Pernambuco on September 30. In the first three weeks of October, she sank four more ships in the South Atlantic: the *Newton Beach*, *Ashlea*, *Huntsman* and *Trevanion*. With five Allied hunting groups searching for her, she sailed around the Cape of Good Hope and sank the *Africa Shell* on November 15 and stopped the *Mapia* the next day. Three more victims followed in the first week of December: the *Doric Star*, *Tairoa* and, finally, the *Streonshalh*. The *Graf Spee* was back in the South Atlantic and heading for the River Plate.

Commodore Harwood, in command of Force G, based on the Falkland Islands, was waiting with three of his cruisers off the mouth of the Plate. He sighted the *Graf Spee* on December 13 and divided his force, attacking the *Graf Spee* from two directions. Captain Langsdorff first engaged the heavy cruiser *Exeter*, which received a terrible pounding from the *Graf Spee*'s 11-inch guns. Langsdorff then switched targets to the light cruisers *Ajax* and *Achilles*, fearing an attack by their torpedoes. Both ships received considerable damage until, surprisingly, Langsdorff broke off the action and headed towards the safety of Montevideo. He reached the port at midnight and determined to make repairs but was then tricked into believing that a strong force had gathered to wait for him outside territorial waters. Langsdorff scuttled the *Graf Spee* on December 17 and shot himself shortly afterwards. The hunt and the kill had captured the attention of the whole world.

Above: The supply ship **Altmark** *(left) guards the captured* **Huntsman** *before she is sunk by the* **Graf Spee**.

Left: The pocket-battleship **Admiral Graf Spee** *was the product of the restrictions imposed by the Treaty of Versailles, which forbade Germany to build ships of more than 10,000 tons. She was therefore light and fast but heavily armoured and well armed.*

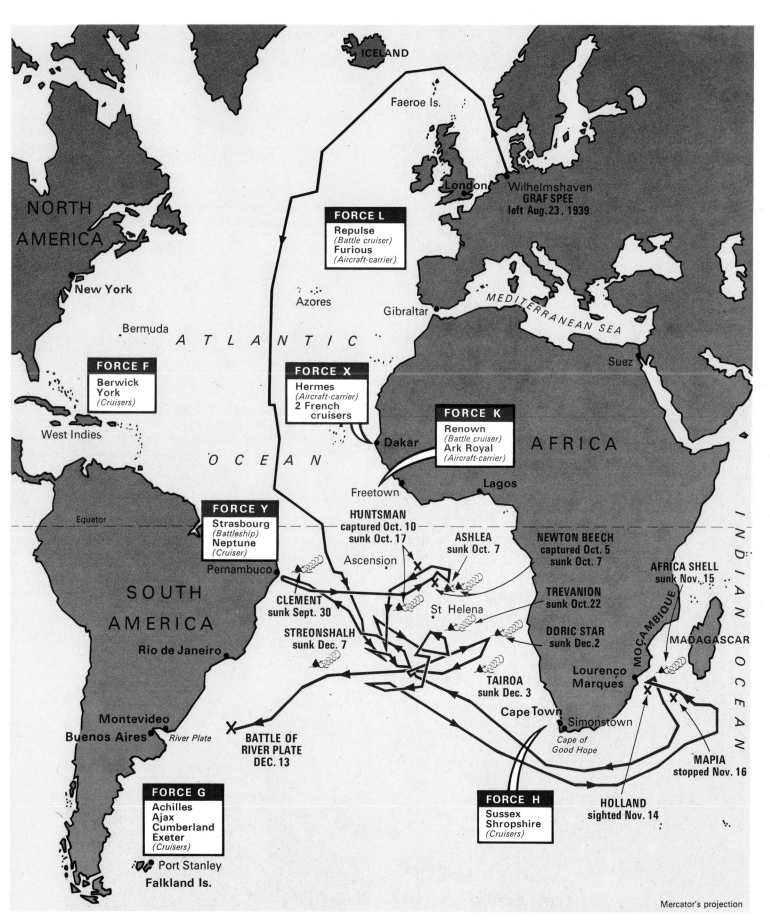

ICELAND

Faeroe Is.

London Wilhelmshaven
GRAF SPEE
left Aug. 23, 1939

FORCE L
Repulse
(Battle cruiser)
Furious
(Aircraft-carrier)

NORTH
AMERICA

New York

Bermuda

A T L A N T I C

M E D I T E R R A N E A N   S E A

Azores

Gibraltar

Suez

FORCE F
Berwick
York
(Cruisers)

West Indies

FORCE X
Hermes
(Aircraft-carrier)
**2 French
cruisers**

FORCE K
Renown
(Battle cruiser)
Ark Royal
(Aircraft-carrier)

AFRICA

Dakar

O C E A N

Freetown

Lagos

Equator

FORCE Y
Strasbourg
(Battleship)
Neptune
(Cruiser)

Pernambuco

HUNTSMAN
captured Oct. 10
sunk Oct. 17

Ascension

ASHLEA
sunk Oct. 7

NEWTON BEECH
captured Oct. 5
sunk Oct. 7

AFRICA SHELL
sunk Nov. 15

SOUTH
AMERICA

CLEMENT
sunk Sept. 30

St Helena

TREVANION
sunk Oct.22

DORIC STAR
sunk Dec.2

I N D I A N   O C E A N

MADAGASCAR

STREONSHALH
sunk Dec. 7

Rio de Janeiro

MOÇAMBIQUE

Montevideo
Buenos Aires   *River Plate*

TAIROA
sunk Dec. 3

Cape Town

Lourenço
Marques

**BATTLE OF
RIVER PLATE
DEC. 13**

Simonstown

Cape of
Good Hope

**MAPIA
stopped Nov. 16**

FORCE G
**Achilles
Ajax
Cumberland
Exeter**
(Cruisers)

FORCE H
**Sussex
Shropshire**
(Cruisers)

**HOLLAND
sighted Nov. 14**

Port Stanley
Falkland Is.

Mercator's projection

The voyage of the **Graf Spee**, from Wilhelmshaven to the River Plate, between August and December 1939. The German pocket-battleship was launched at Wilhelmshaven on New Year's Day, 1934, and took part in the Coronation Naval Review at Spithead in 1937. She was ordered out into the Atlantic by Admiral Raeder, commander-in-chief of the German navy, in anticipation of the opening of hostilities against Poland, so as to be in readiness to cause the maximum possible disruption among Allied shipping and to dislocate Allied hunting groups in the South Atlantic. She was eventually trapped in the neutral port of Montevideo, after a determined and courageous battle by the outgunned British cruisers under Harwood's command. Langsdorff finally proved to be indecisive in action and scuttled the **Graf Spee** when he could well have escaped to wreak yet more havoc in the Atlantic and Indian Oceans.

17

Blitzkrieg in the West

The Allies expected any attack to come through Belgium, on their left flank, as it had in 1914. Their right flank was protected by the Maginot Line and they regarded the Ardennes, in the centre, as impassable. Manstein's plan (map 1) gave them what they expected, an advance by Army Group B through Holland into Belgium to draw the Allied left flank forward. At the same time Army Group A made a surprise attack through the unprotected Ardennes, cutting the Allied armies in two and advancing towards Calais to pinch the Allied left between Army Groups A and B.

The offensive was launched on May 10, 1940 (map 2). Air attacks against major Dutch and Belgian airfields were followed by paratroop drops into the heart of Holland. A daring raid on the strong Belgian fort of Eben Emael opened the Albert Canal for troops to cross into Belgium. On May 14, Rotterdam was heavily bombed and Holland surrendered. The BEF and French 1st Army moved up to reinforce the Belgians between Namur and Antwerp but were soon forced back.

Meanwhile Army Group A had forced its way through the Ardennes, sweeping aside French resistance and reaching the Meuse on May 12 (map 3). Three bridgeheads were established across the river in the next two days and a 50-mile front was driven west between Sedan and Dinant (map 4). Stopping only briefly to take stock of their success, the leading German tanks reached the Channel at Noyelles on May 20 (map 5). The Allies were by then completely split and their left flank was attempting to fall back from Belgium, with their rear now threatened by Guderian's Panzers.

On May 21, the retreating BEF, with French assistance, counter-attacked at Arras, attempting to join up with the French armies farther south. The attempt failed. Guderian and the leading German tanks then turned north to cut off the BEF from the Channel ports but he was temporarily stopped by Hitler and von Rundstedt who were themselves surprised by the speed of the advance and feared a setback. The excuse given for the halt was to allow Goering's *Luftwaffe* the chance to destroy the trapped forces from the air.

The net continued to tighten. Boulogne fell on May 25 (see next page) and Calais fell on May 26. Two days later, Belgium capitulated and thus exposed more than 300,000 French and British caught at Dunkirk to increased pressure from the surrounding Germans.

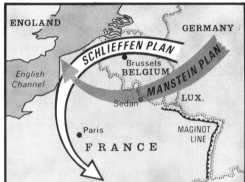

Above: (1) The Allies expected Germany to repeat the Schlieffen Plan of 1914 and attack through Belgium. Manstein's Plan caught them by surprise and quickly penetrated what the Allies had thought to be the impassable Ardennes, between their defences on the Maginot Line and those along the Belgian border.

Left (2) The German offensive on May 10, 1940. The attack by Army Group B in the north held the attention of the Allied left, enabling Army Group A to reach the Meuse against insignificant opposition. The Belgian fort of Eben Emael held a strong position defending the Albert Canal, an important barrier between Germany and Belgium. German paratroops captured Eben Emael on May 11.

Above: German stormtroopers strike at the Albert Canal in Belgium.

Right: (3) German Panzer divisions break through the Ardennes and head for Dinant, Monthermé and Sedan to obtain crossings on the River Meuse.

Far right: (4) The breakthrough is made at Sedan and the French 9th Army is forced back.

Below: (5) German tanks speed across France to the sea before turning north towards Boulogne and Calais, breaking between the French 9th and 2nd Armies. De Gaulle's armour counter-attacked on May 17, the BEF on May 21. Both failed.

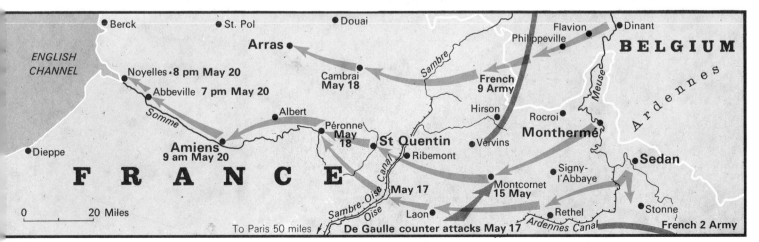

Dunkirk and the Fall of France

The delay imposed by Hitler and von Rundstedt on the advance of the Panzer Divisions up the Channel coast, as well as the necessity for the Germans to secure the Channel ports of Boulogne, Calais and Gravelines (map 1), gave the BEF the momentary breathing space that was required for the miracle of Dunkirk to get under way. The garrison at Calais, under the command of Brigadier Nicholson, put up especially brave resistance. Called on to surrender, Nicholson replied, 'The answer is No. It is as much the British Army's duty to fight as it is the German Army's.' He was forced to surrender on May 26–27.

While Calais was making its stand, Operation Dynamo, the evacuation of Dunkirk, began under the brilliant direction of Admiral Ramsay and with the help of many small civilian craft. When it started on May 26, it was thought that at best a two-day operation might pull off 30–40,000 troops. The evacuation lasted nine days and rescued 338,000 British, French and Belgian soldiers. Their defensive perimeter was steadily driven in by the surrounding ground forces and strafed by the *Luftwaffe* (maps 2 and 3). Much of the effect of this strafing was softened by the sand and, not for the last time, Goering's boast that he would destroy the enemy proved hollow. On June 5, the Germans overwhelmed the remains of the French 1st Army, who had been bravely screening the evacuation.

The second phase of the invasion of France began smoothly on the same day, June 5 (map 4). General Weygand had hoped to regroup behind the Somme, the Aisne and the Maginot Line but his defences were quickly broken through in several places and his troops proved lacking equally in equipment and morale. By June 10, the first German tanks had crossed the Seine. On the same day, Mussolini began to advance into southern France, confident by then that France was on the losing side. The French Government withdrew to Bordeaux and Paris fell to the Germans on June 14.

As French resistance disintegrated and the remaining French armies were trapped against the Maginot Line, the German columns spread west, south and east (map 5). Rejecting Churchill's offer of an 'indissoluble union' of France and Britain, Prime Minister Reynaud resigned and was replaced by Marshal Pétain who at once asked for an armistice, on June 17. The Armistice was signed on June 22 and 400,000 French soldiers belonging to the three French armies in the east surrendered. On June 24, a French delegation in Rome signed an armistice with Italy, despite the embarrassing fact that a mere six French divisions had held up Mussolini's 32 Italian divisions in the south. The capital of the French Government was established at Vichy, in the Unoccupied Zone.

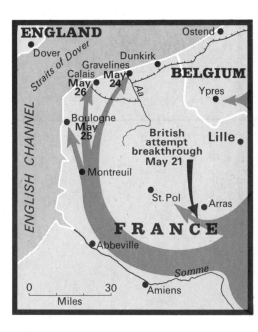

Above: (1) Three-pronged Panzer sweep north towards Boulogne, Calais and Gravelines, before the noose is tightened on Dunkirk.

Bottom left and below: (2 and 3) The Germans close on Dunkirk in the last days of May and the beginning of June, 1940.

Bottom right: Ships of the armada prepare to evacuate the BEF.

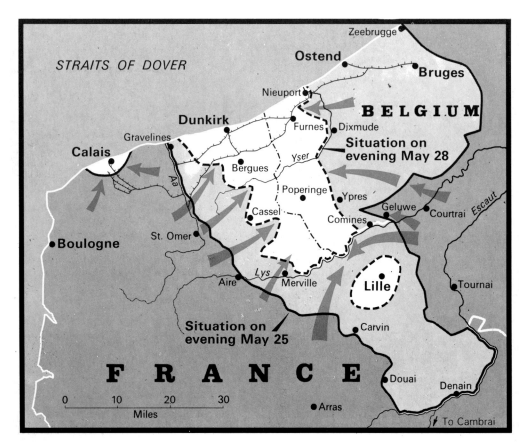

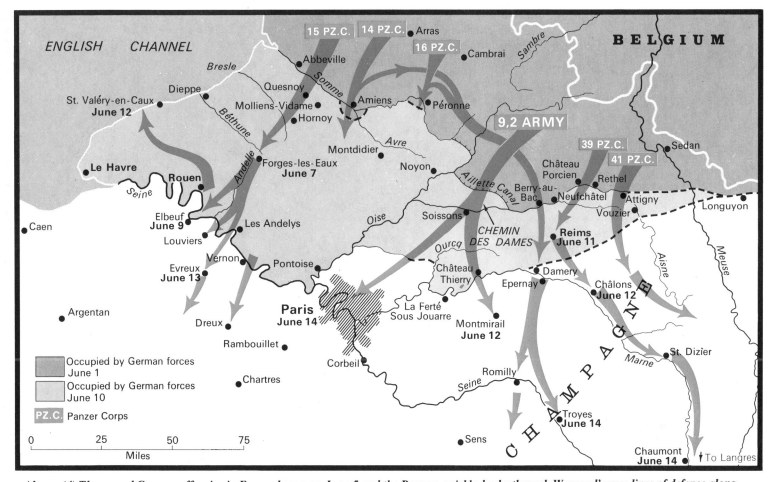

Above: (4) The second German offensive in France began on June 5 and the Panzers quickly broke through Weygand's new lines of defence along the Somme and the Aisne.

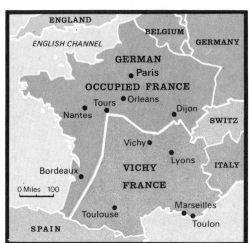

Above: (6) After the Armistice, France was divided into two zones: Occupied France under the Germans and Unoccupied France under Marshal Pétain's Vichy Government.

Left: (5) The last few days of Hitler's invasion of France were a rout. Only in the south-east was there any successful resistance, against the Italian advance over the Alpes Maritimes.

Operation Sealion

With the fall of France, Hitler was confident that the war in the west was won and he could turn his attention to Soviet Russia. When it became clear, by mid-July 1940, that Britain would reject all overtures of peace, he began to consider plans for an invasion (map 1), for which reports had already been prepared at the end of 1939. The first date set by Hitler was September 15 but Operation Sealion was beset with problems. Service chiefs could not agree about the exact shape of the invasion; the British navy remained a threat; the British army was still intact after Dunkirk, requiring a large German invasion force and a vast armada of troop barges; above all, Goering's *Luftwaffe* failed to gain air superiority, without which the invasion was impossible and with which it was unnecessary since Britain would then supposedly capitulate.

The invading force was kept in readiness at ten days' notice throughout most of September but the date was put back to September 21, then the 24th, then the 27th. Hitler ordered limited dispersal on October 2. On October 12, Sealion was postponed until 1941. It was not until March 1942, that it was virtually abandoned by being put on a year's notice. Hitler had turned his attention to Russia, hoping to demoralize Britain by a swift victory in the east.

The Battle of Britain

Control of the air was essential to the success of Operation Sealion. For nearly two months, the fate of Britain depended on the courage of its airmen, the technical superiority of its fighters and the efficiency of its ground control and radar. The *Luftwaffe* had nearly 3,000 bombers, fighters and fighter-bombers ranged against an initial 600–700 fighters of Fighter Command under Air Chief Marshal Dowding (map 2).

From August 1, the *Luftwaffe* turned its attention to the airfields of south-east England and subsequently to other inland airfields. Fighter Command was very nearly destroyed but on September 7 Hitler switched his attack to the capital, partly in retaliation for a raid by the RAF on Berlin on August 24–25. This change was a fatal error which gave Fighter Command time to recuperate. The battle over London was at its height between September 7 and 15. By the end of the month, the battle was won. Daylight raids stopped on October 5 and Operation Sealion was postponed on October 12. More than 1,700 German planes had been shot down.

Night raids against London and other major cities followed during November and December. Coventry was devastated by 500 bombers on November 14–15. The 'blitz' did not end until May, 1941. By then, more than 40,000 British civilians had been killed and 50,000 had been seriously wounded.

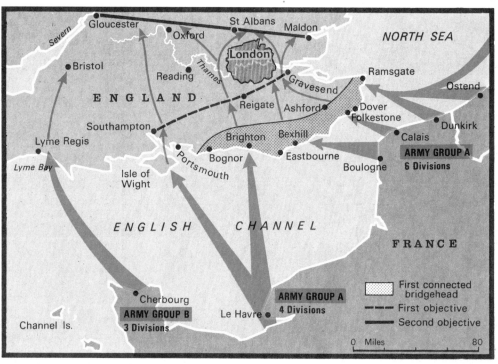

Left: (1) The plan for Operation Sealion. The 'short' route across the Channel was favoured over the longer route across the North Sea, which might have been less exposed to counter-attack but which presented insuperable logistical problems.

*Right: (2) The **Luftwaffe** was divided into three **Luftflotte** for the aerial attack on Britain. Hitler's mistake was to switch the attacks from the fighter bases to the capital on September 7. The invasion was called off on October 12 but provincial cities still had to endure their own night-time 'blitz'.*

*Below left and right: Airmen wait on RAF and **Luftwaffe** bases in instant readiness for take-off. They share the same air of nonchalance, similar pipes and clothing.*

R.A.F. Fighter Command
- ◯ Command Headquarters
- ⊕ Group Headquarters
- ● Sector station
- ◌ Fighter base
- + Low-level radar station
- ✛ High-level radar station
- ♨ Towns bombed

German bases
- ○ Fighter
- ● Twin-engined Me.110
- + Bomber
- St (Stuka) Dive-bomber

0   50   100
Miles

Glasgow

NORTHUMBER-
LAND

LUFTFLOTTE 5
from Norway and
Denmark

Newcastle

FIGHTER
COMMAND
GROUP 13

Sunderland

Belfast

Middlesbrough

NORTH   SEA

YORKSHIRE
Driffield

Hull

Range of High-level Radar

Liverpool
Mersey-
side

Manchester
Sheffield

FIGHTER COMMAND GROUP 12

Nottingham

Range of Low-level Radar

Norwich

Amsterdam

NETHERLANDS
Rotterdam

Birmingham
Coventry

Ipswich   Martlesham

Debden

Stanmore
London
Northolt
Uxbridge
Croydon
Biggin Hill
Kenley

North Weald
Hornchurch
Rochford
Rochester
Eastchurch
Manston
Canterbury

Antwerp

Ghent

Swansea
Cardiff

Bristol

FIGHTER
COMMAND
GROUP 11

Andover
Middle Wallop
Worthy Down

West Malling
Detling

Hawkinge
Lympne

Calais

Lille

BELGIUM

LUFTFLOTTE 2

FIGHTER
COMMAND
GROUP 10

Exeter

Southampton
Portsmouth

Tangmere

Ventnor

+St

Portland

Plymouth

ENGLISH

Cherbourg

Le Havre

Amiens

+St

CHANNEL

LUFTFLOTTE 3

Paris

+St

F R A N C E

Rennes

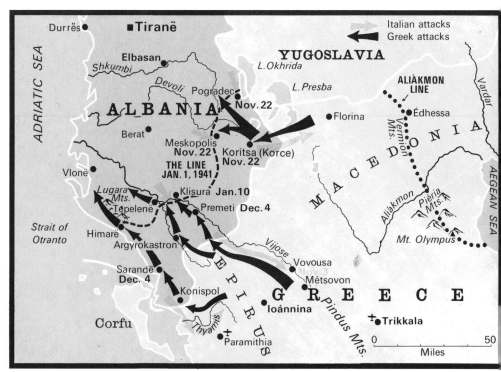

Above: (2) The main Italian attacks on Greece were down the valleys of the Thyamis and the Vijose. Mussolini invaded on October 28 and was stopped within five days. He was then steadily driven back by determined Greek counter-attacks.

Above: (1) Italy had a foothold in the Balkans after her victory in Albania in 1939. Mussolini saw the conquest of Greece as an obvious and prestigious step that would quickly restore his flagging reputation.

The Italian Attack on Greece

During the spring and early summer of 1940, Hitler restrained Mussolini from opening another front in the Balkans, while Germany concentrated on western Europe and prepared for the invasion of Russia. But Mussolini was jealous of Hitler's triumphs in the west and was looking for a quick victory of his own. He thought he saw that opportunity in Greece (map 1).

In August 1940, Mussolini ordered Greece to renounce the guarantees of her independence made by Britain in 1939. He then concentrated an army of 162,000 on Greece's Albanian border. On October 28, he demanded the passage of Italian troops to unspecified points in Greece. Without further warning, he advanced across the border and down the valleys towards Metsovon (map

2). General Papagos quickly mobilized his forces in a determined and skilful resistance and the initial Italian advantages were abruptly reversed.

Within a few days, the Greeks had defeated the crack III Alpini Division, caught in the Pindus Mountains, and captured 5,000 men. On November 22, the Greeks captured Koritsa, together with large amounts of Italian equipment, and defeated the fully mechanized IX Army. By the end of the year, they had advanced well into Albania and by March 1941 almost half Albania was in

Greek hands and the British were bombarding the Italian-held port of Vlone from the sea.

Hitler had been preparing to support the Italians as early as January, when it was clear that things had got out of hand, but he was persuaded by Mussolini that the enterprise was not yet lost and that the Italians still wanted the glory of victory. By March, Hitler was once again preparing to step in to help his ineffectual ally. Plans were drawn up for an advance on Greece through Yugoslavia and Bulgaria.

Left: Italian dead. Defeat was a personal humiliation for Mussolini and, despite his losses, he continued to explain to Hitler that there was nothing of importance to report from the Greek front.

Below: A captured Italian colonel and his ADC in a sidecar, taken prisoner by the Greeks for questioning during the Italian fiasco of 1940–41.

Above: (1) The Axis advances in North Africa and the Balkans stretched the Allied resources to the limit.

Right: (2) The main attack on Yugoslavia came from List's XII Army from Bulgaria, which was also responsible for sweeping down into Greece. The German advances from north, east and south-east were accompanied by an Italian advance down the Dalmatian coast towards Dubrovnik.

Below: (3) Hitler pressed Rumania into conceding territory to her neighbours – Russia, Hungary and Bulgaria.

The States in Yugoslavia

Right: German infantry in Yugoslavia, with rifles and dicebeakers, commandeer a maintenance car to speed their advance.

The Punishment of Yugoslavia

Hitler's advance on the Balkans was motivated by a desire to protect his southern flank before the invasion of Russia, rather more than any wish to help his Italian allies. In autumn 1940 he peacefully secured his hold on the Rumanian oil-fields (map 3) and in March 1941 he compelled Bulgaria to join the Tripartite Pact (signed by Germany, Italy and Japan). Yugoslavia also joined the Pact, under pressure, in March but a coup led by General Simovic overthrew the regime of Prince Paul on March 27 and rejected the German alliance. The coup was encouraged by the movement of nearly 57,000 British troops to Greece (map 1).

Hitler ordered an immediate attack on Yugoslavia and Greece. Operation Punishment was a masterpiece of organi-zation and the Yugoslavs stood little chance against German efficiency and armament. The invasion began on April 6, 1941, with heavy bombing by the *Luftwaffe* of the major cities, especially Belgrade. The Yugoslav air force was quickly destroyed. German armour and infantry then attacked from several directions (map 2): from the north (II Army from Germany and Hungary), from the east (Kleist's I Panzer Group from Rumania) and from the south-east (List's XII Army from Bulgaria to cut Yugoslavia off from Greece). The 28 Yugoslav divisions, which were strung out along the frontier with only one division in reserve, faced 33 German divisions, six of which were armoured.

The attack went exactly to plan and the campaign lasted only ten days. Belgrade was seized on April 12 and Yugoslavia surrendered unconditionally on April 17.

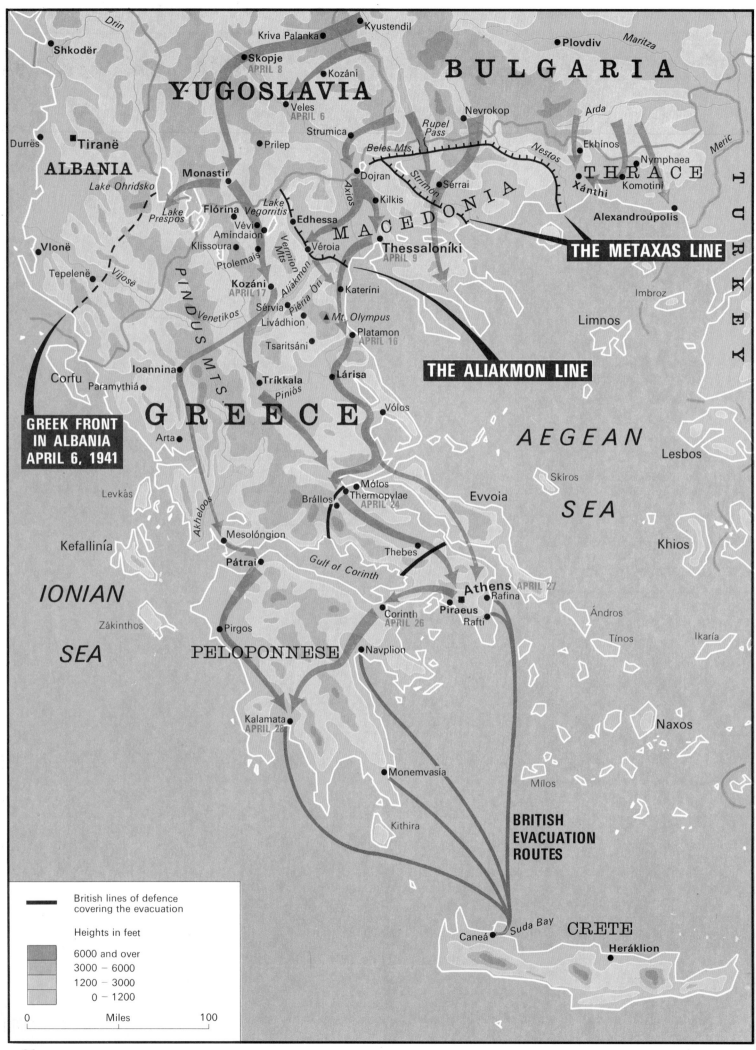

SHKODËR

DURRËS
TIRANË
ALBANIA

VLONË

TEPELENË

Drin

Kriva Palanka

SKOPJE
APRIL 8

YUGOSLAVIA

Prilep

Veles
APRIL 6

Monastir

Lake Ohridsko

Lake
Prespos

Florina
Vévi
Amíndaion
Klissoura
Ptolemaís

Kozáni
APRIL 17

Kyustendil

Kozáni

Strumica

PINDUS MTS.

Lake
Vegorritis

Edhessa

Véroia

Vermion
Mts

Aliakmon

Sérvia
Livádhion

Tsaritsáni

Venetikos

Corfu
Paramythiá

GREEK FRONT
IN ALBANIA
APRIL 6, 1941

Ioannina

Arta

Trίkkala

Piniós

Lárisa

BULGARIA

Plovdiv

Maritza

Nevrokop

Rupel
Pass

Beles Mts.

Dojran

Kilkis

Axiós

Strimón

Sérrai

MACEDONIA

Thessaloníki
APRIL 9

Katerίni

Piérra Óri

▲ Mt. Olympus

Platamon
APRIL 16

Arda

Ekhínos

THRACE

Xánthi

Komotiní

Nympha ea

Meric

Alexandroúpolis

THE METAXAS LINE

THE ALIAKMON LINE

Imbroz

Limnos

Vólos

GREECE

AEGEAN

Lesvos

Skíros

SEA

Levkás

Akheloos

Mesolóngion

Brállos

Mólos
Thermopylae
APRIL 24

Evvoia

Khios

Kefallinía

Pátrai

Gulf of Corinth

Thebes

IONIAN

Zákinthos

Pirgos

Navplion

Corinth
APRIL 26

Athens APRIL 27
Rafina

Piraeus
Rafti

Ándros

Tínos

Ikaría

SEA

PELOPONNESE

Kalamata
APRIL 28

Monemvasía

Kithira

Mílos

BRITISH
EVACUATION
ROUTES

Naxos

Caneá

Suda Bay

CRETE

Heráklion

British lines of defence
covering the evacuation

Heights in feet

6000 and over

3000 – 6000

1200 – 3000

0 – 1200

0   Miles   100

26

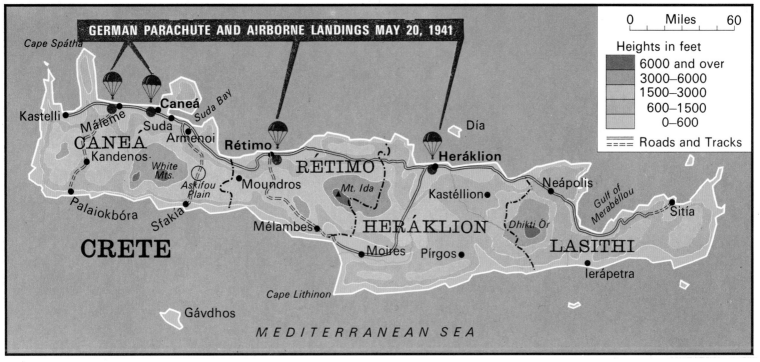

Above: (2) The German airborne landings on Crete. It was only at Máleme that they gained a foothold on the first day.

Left: (1) The German advance through Greece, April 1941.

The Invasion of Greece and Crete

The Germans invaded Greece on April 6, 1941 (map 1). The majority of the Greek forces still faced the Italians on the Albanian Front; the remaining Greek, British and Commonwealth troops held the Metaxas and Aliákmon Lines. List's XII Army advanced through the Rupel Pass and the Monastir Gap, forcing the surrender of the Greek troops in the east and pushed Wilson to the Thermopylae Line.

The Greek 1st Army, in the west, surrendered on April 23. Wilson withdrew into the Peloponnese. British warships withstood *Luftwaffe* attacks, moving 43,000 men before Kalamata was captured on April 28.

Major-General Freyburg was then given the task of holding Crete against General Student. On May 20, heavy aerial bombardment began. Parachute drops were made at Máleme, Rétimo and Heráklion (map 2). The Germans were rebuffed at Rétimo and Heráklion, establishing a foothold near Máleme airfield, on May 21 (map 3). Reinforcements forced the steady withdrawal of Freyburg's defence.

The British evacuated nearly 15,000 men; the remaining 18,000 surrendered on May 31. Student's VII Air Division was exhausted. Hitler was horrified at the losses. There were no more air operations like it.

Below: (3) The fight for Máleme airfield was the key to Crete.

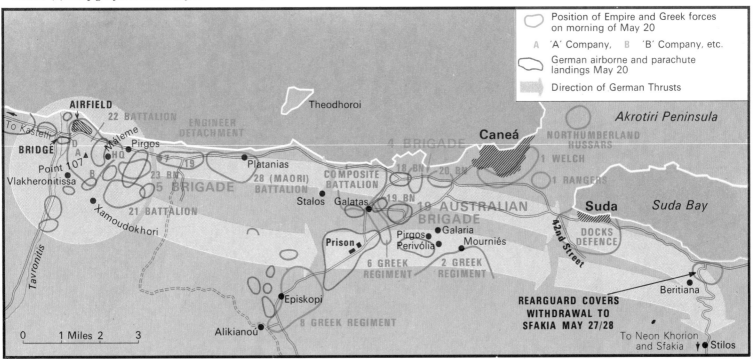

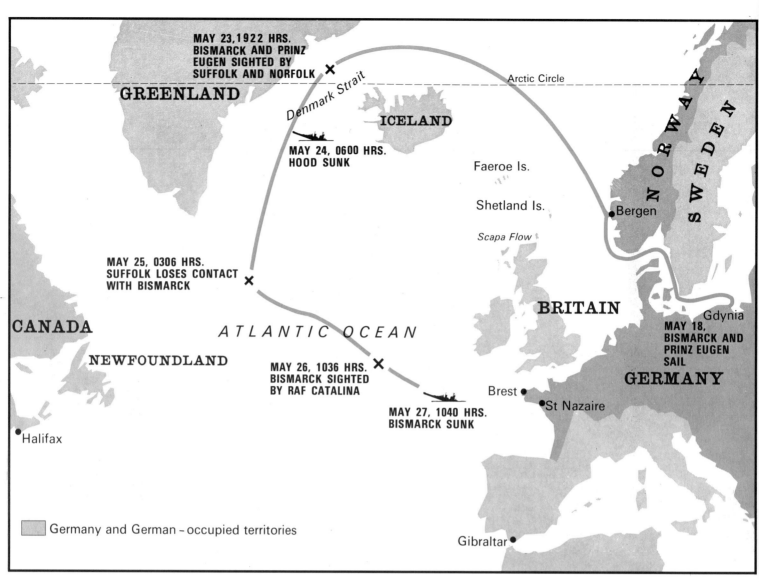

MAY 23, 1922 HRS.
BISMARCK AND PRINZ
EUGEN SIGHTED BY
SUFFOLK AND NORFOLK

GREENLAND

Arctic Circle

Denmark Strait

ICELAND

MAY 24, 0600 HRS.
HOOD SUNK

Faeroe Is.

Shetland Is.

Scapa Flow

Bergen

MAY 25, 0306 HRS.
SUFFOLK LOSES CONTACT
WITH BISMARCK

CANADA

ATLANTIC OCEAN

NEWFOUNDLAND

BRITAIN

Gdynia

MAY 18,
BISMARCK AND
PRINZ EUGEN
SAIL

GERMANY

MAY 26, 1036 HRS.
BISMARCK SIGHTED
BY RAF CATALINA

Brest

St Nazaire

MAY 27, 1040 HRS.
BISMARCK SUNK

Halifax

Germany and German – occupied territories

Gibraltar

Above: (1) The route of the Bismarck, from Gdynia to her Atlantic grave.

Right: (2) The break-out routes from German waters that might be taken by the German ships and which had to be covered by the Home Fleet.

Below: (3) The Battle in the Denmark Strait and the sinking of the Hood. An important troop convoy was on its way south of Iceland at the time.

GREENLAND

Denmark Strait

NORWEGIAN SEA

ICELAND

ATLANTIC OCEAN

Faeroe Is.

Shetland Is.

Bergen

Orkney Is.

Scapa Flow

NORTH SEA

HOME FLEET
King George V
Prince of Wales
(Battleships)
Hood
(Battle-cruiser)
Victorious
(Aircraft-carrier)
4 Cruisers
9 Destroyers

Below: (4) The hunting groups close in as the Bismarck turns east towards home.

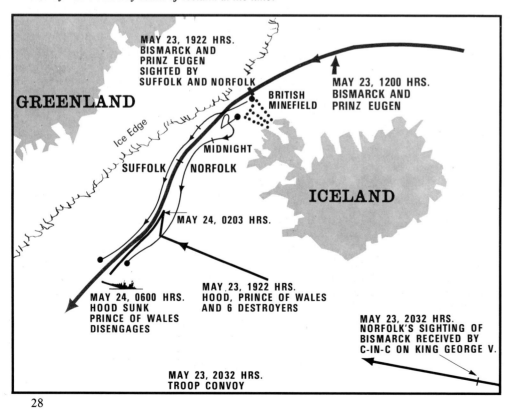

MAY 23, 1922 HRS.
BISMARCK AND
PRINZ EUGEN
SIGHTED BY
SUFFOLK AND
NORFOLK

GREENLAND

Ice Edge

MAY 23, 1200 HRS.
BISMARCK AND
PRINZ EUGEN

BRITISH
MINEFIELD

MIDNIGHT

SUFFOLK   NORFOLK

ICELAND

MAY 24, 0203 HRS.

MAY 24, 0600 HRS.
HOOD SUNK
PRINCE OF WALES
DISENGAGES

MAY 23, 1922 HRS.
HOOD, PRINCE OF WALES
AND 6 DESTROYERS

MAY 23, 2032 HRS.
NORFOLK'S SIGHTING OF
BISMARCK RECEIVED BY
C-IN-C ON KING GEORGE V.

MAY 23, 2032 HRS.
TROOP CONVOY

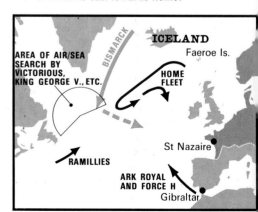

AREA OF AIR/SEA
SEARCH BY
VICTORIOUS,
KING GEORGE V., ETC.

BISMARCK

ICELAND

Faeroe Is.

HOME
FLEET

St Nazaire

RAMILLIES

ARK ROYAL
AND FORCE H

Gibraltar

Left: The Bismarck (circled), spotted by an RAF reconnaissance plane in a Norwegian fjord on May 21. The Home Fleet at Scapa Flow was immediately alerted and prepared to pursue and to intercept the Bismarck and Prinz Eugen before the two ships escaped into the Atlantic through the Denmark Strait. The ships had already been spotted by a Swedish ship on May 20, on their way toward Bergen.

Below: The Bismarck fires a salvo at the Hood in the short and disastrous engagement in the Denmark Strait. It was a hit from the Bismarck's fifth salvo that exploded the magazine of the British battle-cruiser and sealed her fate after only eight minutes of action. Both ships had eight 15-inch guns. The Bismarck was the strongest warship of her time, displacing more than 50,000 tons against the Hood's 40,000 tons. But the Hood had been the pride of the Royal Navy and its most impressive capital ship when she was launched twenty years before the Bismarck. Her great weakness was lack of adequate armour.

The Pursuit of the Bismarck

May 1941 saw not only the German airborne attack on Crete in the Mediterranean but also a dramatic chase in the North Atlantic, when the brand-new battleship *Bismarck* made her first and only foray of the war. Admiral Raeder had intended to break out the *Bismarck* and *Prinz Eugen* from the Baltic and the *Gneisenau* and *Scharnhorst* from Brest simultaneously to form a powerful strike force in the Atlantic that could take on the most strongly escorted convoy. *Gneisenau* and *Scharnhorst* were delayed by enemy action and refitting but Raeder determined to go ahead with the *Bismarck* and *Prinz Eugen* (map 1).

The two ships sailed from Gdynia on May 18, under the command of Admiral Lutjens (map 2). They were photographed by an RAF reconnaissance aircraft in a fjord near Bergen on May 21 and they sailed again the same day. Admiral Tovey, C-in-C Home Fleet, aboard the *King George V* at Scapa Flow, was alerted and detached the battle-cruiser *Hood* and the battleship *Prince of Wales* to join the cruisers *Suffolk* and *Norfolk* in the Denmark Strait (map 3). The *Suffolk* sighted the *Bismarck* on May 23 and Force H (*Renown*, *Ark Royal* and *Sheffield*) was ordered to sail north from Gibraltar to join the chase. The *Hood* and the *Prince of Wales* engaged the *Bismarck* and the *Prinz Eugen* early in the morning of May 24. Eight minutes after the action started, a shell from the *Bismarck* penetrated the weak deck armour of the *Hood*, struck one of her magazines and blew her in half. She sank immediately. Three men survived from a complement of 1,400.

After suffering several direct hits and scoring one hit on the *Bismarck*'s oil tanks, the *Prince of Wales* broke off the action.

Lutjens determined to press on into the Atlantic (map 4). It was only after a torpedo attack by Swordfish from the *Victorious* that he prepared to turn back towards St Nazaire. Meanwhile, *Prinz Eugen* had slipped away to the south; she returned safely to Brest on June 1. The *Suffolk* and *Norfolk* continued to shadow the *Bismarck*, even after losing contact.

On the morning of May 26, the *Bismarck* was spotted by an RAF Catalina flying boat and the chase continued. A torpedo from one of *Ark Royal*'s Swordfish struck the *Bismarck*'s steering gear and forced her to drop speed. Harried by a flotilla of destroyers, the demoralized crew could do little but await their fate. The *King George V* and *Rodney* closed in on the morning of the 27th and silenced her guns. The cruiser *Dorsetshire* sank her with torpedoes. There were 110 survivors from a complement of more than 2,300.

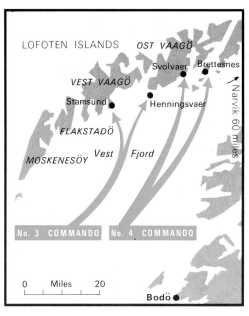

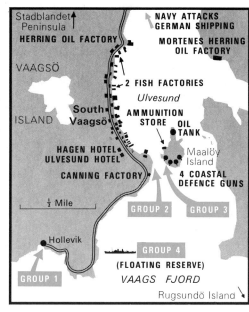

(1) The first major combined operations,
aimed at distracting German forces.

(2) The Lofoten Islands raid, March 1941,
destroyed fish oil factories and shipping.

(3) The Vaagso raid, December, 1941,
increased Hitler's obsession with Norway.

The Early Raids

Expelled from western Europe by the summer of 1940 and, by May 1941, from Greece and Crete as well, the Allies resorted to quick commando raids intended to restore morale and distract German troops. The first major combined operations attacked installations in the Lofoten Islands, Spitzbergen and Vaagso (map 1). They occupied German troops in Norway, which, as the war progressed, Hitler needed badly in the east.

Light raids in June and July 1940, near Boulogne and on Guernsey, were followed by a large-scale commando raid on targets in the Lofoten Islands in March 1941 (map 2). Two converted cross-Channel steamers were used to convey 600 men under the command of Brigadier Haydon, escorted by a flotilla of destroyers. The attack on March 4 was a success. The fish oil factories were destroyed, 11 ships were captured, 200 Germans were taken prisoner and 300 Norwegian volunteers

were taken off, all for the loss of one commando.

On August 25, 1941, a combined operations raid under Rear-Admiral Vian destroyed the coal installations in the Spitzbergen archipelago, worked since 1931 by a Soviet company (map 1). The raid was agreed between Russia, Norway and Britain, to prevent the coal falling into German hands. More than 500,000 tons were burnt, plus 275,000 gallons of fuel oil, petrol and grease.

Lord Louis Mountbatten then replaced Admiral Keyes as head of Combined Operations and brought new energy and imagination to the task. He launched his first major raid at Vaagso Island on December 27, with a subsidiary raid on Maaloy Island (map 3). Rear-Admiral Hamilton's force employed nearly 600 men to destroy the garrison, fish oil factories and shipping. This success fed Hitler's obsession with the need to garrison Norway heavily.

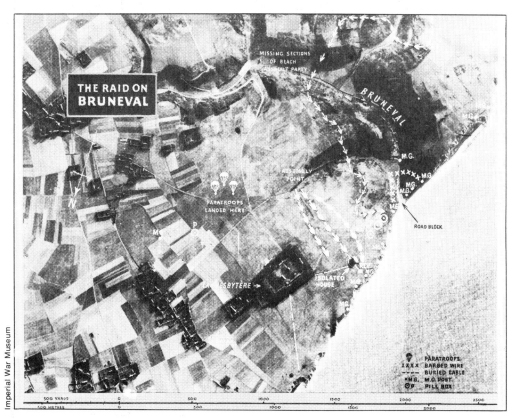

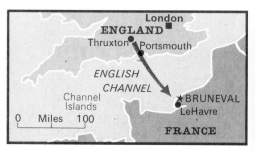

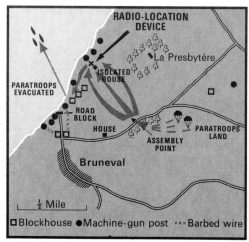

The Raid on St Nazaire

The Normandie Dock at St Nazaire was the only dock large enough, outside German waters, to accommodate the new battleship *Tirpitz*. In the opening months of 1942, the *Tirpitz* was in a Norwegian port but it was feared that she would break out into the Atlantic and mount powerful surface raids on Allied shipping, using the dock facilities at St Nazaire when necessary. Without those facilities, she would be seriously hampered. It was essential to destroy the Normandie Dock, as well as the valuable submarine pens at St Nazaire.

An old US destroyer, the *Campbeltown*, was stripped of excess weight, so that she could navigate the Loire, and loaded with explosives in her bow. She was to ram the dock gates. The explosives would blow up on a delayed fuse to destroy the gates completely. Operation Chariot was accompanied by troops in sixteen motor launches and one MTB, which, with the troops on the *Campbeltown* herself, were to carry out further destruc-

tion in the dock area. Commander Ryder was in charge of the naval force; Colonel Newman commanded the 600-man shore force.

The force and its escort left Falmouth on March 26 (see inset map 6). Early on March 28, the *Campbeltown* made her way up the Loire under cover of dark (map 6). Caught by German searchlights and subjected to heavy fire, she struck the dock gates at 0134 hours and lodged there. The surviving commandos raced ashore to carry out their other demolition work. The launches, meanwhile, had come under fire and most of the flimsy craft were destroyed. Only two returned safely to England. One-quarter of the men were killed; many were left ashore and went into prison camps. Some time after 1000 hours that morning, the charges on the *Campbeltown* blew up, smashing the lock gate. The water rushed in and the *Campbeltown* was carried half way along the Normandie Dock, which was not used again by the Germans. The *Tirpitz* never sailed in the Atlantic.

The Raid on Bruneval

Mountbatten planned another combined operation in February 1942. This time the target was a German radio-location site at Bruneval, on the coast of France, not far from Le Havre (maps 4 and 5). Reconnaissance photographs from the air indicated that there was an early-warning radio device located in a pit half way between an isolated house and the cliffs. The house itself stood about 100 yards from the cliff edge. It was believed that the device was already responsible for locating British bombers in raids over the coast and in enabling the Germans to destroy many aircraft.

A force of six officers and 113 men from the 1st Airborne Division, under the command of Major Frost, was parachuted in on February 27, with the task of capturing the radio station, taking away parts of the device for later examination and destroying the rest. The raiders overcame limited resistance, achieved their objectives and, after a last-minute gun battle on the cliffs, were taken off by navy craft which had been delayed by the need to avoid German destroyers and E-boats. Casualties were three dead and seven wounded.

Far left: RAF reconnaissance photograph of the Bruneval area. Compare with map 5.

Left, above: (4) Bruneval was well-placed to provide early warning of Allied planes.

Left, below: (5) The route taken by the raiders after their parachute drop.

Right: (6) The attack on St Nazaire. The Campbeltown *struck home dead on target, after surviving intensive enemy fire.*

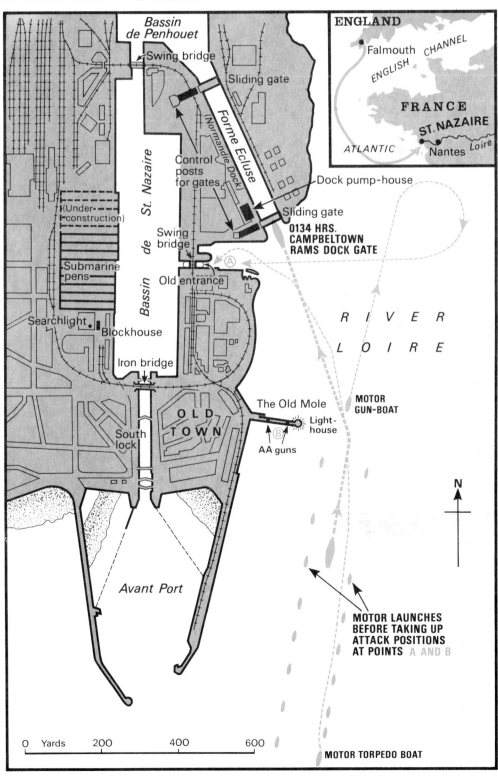

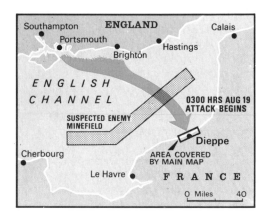

Left above: (1) The 'fleet' that sailed to attack Dieppe departed from four south coast ports on the night of August 18, arriving without mishap off the coast of France just before dawn.

Left below: (2) The attack on Dieppe, August 19, 1942. The only real success was on the right flank, where No 4 Commando silenced the Hess battery, west of Dieppe.

Right: A German soldier helps one of the few men who managed to leave the beach and enter the town.

Below: The attackers left all their equipment behind them when they finally withdrew in confusion. They left their dead also and prisoners for the Germans.

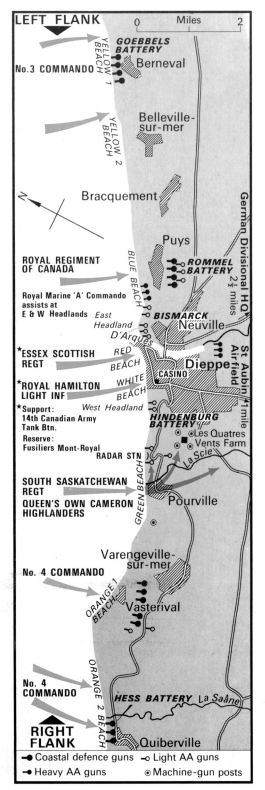

The Dieppe Disaster

According to Winston Churchill, Operation Jubilee, the raid on Dieppe, was intended to be a 'reconnaissance in force . . . to discover what resistance would have to be met in the endeavour to seize a port'. The raid was also intended to provide battle experience for the troops. More than half did not live to use that experience. The attack against a strongly-held sector of the French coast proved to be ill-conceived and over-optimistic. It turned into a full-scale disaster for the Allies. Despite this, much was learnt about German defensive methods that was put to good use at the time of the Normandy landings in June 1944.

The raid was on a much greater scale than anything previously attempted. Major-General Roberts commanded troops from the 2nd Canadian Division, with commando units whose job it was to destroy coastal batteries on either side of the attack. The 6,000 men were carried in nine landing ships and escorted by eight destroyers. They crossed the Channel on the night of August 18–19, 1942 (map 1). The attack went in at dawn on August 19 (map 2).

On the extreme left, No 3 Commando was to destroy the Goebbels battery; on the inner left, the Royal Regiment of Canada was to destroy the heavy battery Rommel and attack Bismarck. In the centre, the Essex Scottish Regiment and the

Royal Hamilton Light Infantry were to land at Dieppe itself. On the inner left, the South Saskatchewan Regiment and the Queen's Own Cameron Highlanders of Canada were to capture Les Quatres Vents Farm, attack Hindenburg from the rear and then St Aubin airfield, while on the inner left No 4 Commando was to destroy Hess battery. This last assault was almost the only success of the operation. No 4 Commando achieved its aim swiftly and by 0730 hours was on its way back to England.

On the other flank, the story was very different. No 3 Commando failed to silence Goebbels battery and the attack on Rommel was pinned down. So were the central attacks on Dieppe. The Germans poured in a murderous storm of fire on the landing craft and the few tanks that got off the beach were not able to break through the German defences. Approximately three hours after the first assault, the reserves were committed but they, too, were pinned down. At 0830 hours, the Royal Marine 'A' Commando was sent in to renew the assault in the centre but was forced back. Success was clearly impossible. Men were killed even before they landed and could not move forward once on the shingle beach. The decision to withdraw was taken at 0900 hours but it was another three or four hours of continued slaughter before the last of the survivors were taken off, leaving behind the dead and those who were to be taken prisoner.

The Canadians lost 215 officers and 3,164 men; the Commandos lost 24 officers and 223 men. The total military cost was 494 officers and 3,890 men killed, wounded and missing. All the vehicles and equipment landed were lost, including 28 tanks. The Royal Navy lost 81 officers, 469 men and 34 ships, including the destroyer *Berkeley*, which had to be torpedoed to prevent it falling into enemy hands. The RAF lost 190 men and 106 aircraft. German casualties were approximately 600 men.

The Cockleshell Raid
In summer, 1942, small and fast German merchantmen evaded the Allied blockade to bring valuable supplies into Bordeaux. Major Hasler and the small-boat commandos of the Royal Marine Boom Patrol Detachment were ordered to sink these ships. Five cockles, with two men each, were launched from the submarine Tuna *off the Gironde estuary at 2100 hours, December 7 (map, left). Only two cockles reached their target. Hasler and Sparks in* Catfish *attached limpet mines at Bordeaux; Laver and Mills in* Crayfish *mined ships at Bassens. The cockles were scuttled and the men escaped inland. Only Hasler and Sparks reached England. One large cargo ship was destroyed and four others were forced to remain in dry dock for the rest of the war. The shipping in Bordeaux was no longer secure.*

Left: French civilians collect the dead.
Below: Only 28 tanks were successfully landed. All were lost.

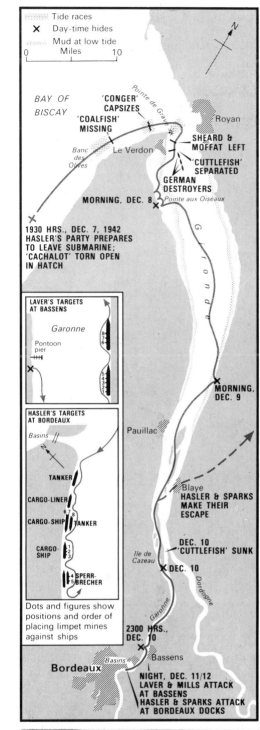

The War in North Africa

The Axis plan was to advance east along the Mediterranean coast of North Africa and then to sweep northwards and to seize the oil-fields of the Middle East. The Allies and the Axis both suffered from problems of supply in their battle for North Africa, as their lines stretched from their bases at Tripoli and Alexandria respectively. The conflict raged to and fro across Libya, with victories going first to Wavell and O'Connor, then to Rommel, next to Auchinleck, then Rommel again and finally to Alexander and Montgomery.

As Hitler became preoccupied with his commitment to the Russian front and the Allies invested greater resources in preparing the way for an attack on the 'soft underbelly' of Europe, Rommel's hold weakened and, with the arrival of the Americans, eventually slipped. Besides opening the way to Italy, the North African campaign also gave the Allies invaluable experience for the coming battle in Normandy.

Insurrection in Iraq and Syria

The oil-fields in the Middle East at which Hitler aimed were vital to both sides, as was strategic control of the eastern Mediterranean. The opening encounters in Libya and Ethiopia (see following pages) preceded events in Iraq and Syria by a few months but these events are best dealt with first.

On May 2, 1941, Rashid Ali, prime minister of Iraq, ordered an attack on the British garrisons at Basra and Habbaniyah, threatening oil supplies. Hitler sent munitions to support the insurrection, which had been fomented by the Nazis for some time, but Wavell replied with troops from Palestine, who occupied Baghdad (map 1). An armistice was agreed in the last days of May.

The Nazis also stirred up the pro-German Vichy French forces in Syria. Wavell committed troops from Palestine and Iraq, together with Free French forces. Damascus was captured on June 21 (maps 2 and 3), the French commander in Syria surrendered in early July.

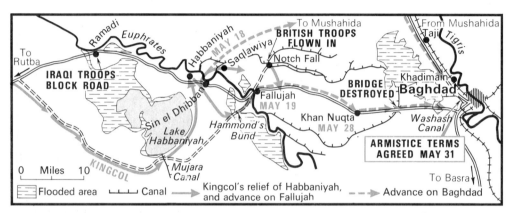

Above: (1) The advance on Baghdad. The British air base at Habbayinah held out against Rashid Ali's initial attack and was quickly relieved by Wavell's forces from the west.

Below: (2) Successful defence of the Allied oil interests in Iraq was only the prelude to the fierce campaign against the Vichy French in Syria. Troops from India were also used against Baghdad.

Above: (3) The Allied offensive in south-west Syria, which resulted in the capture of Damascus on June 21, 1941.

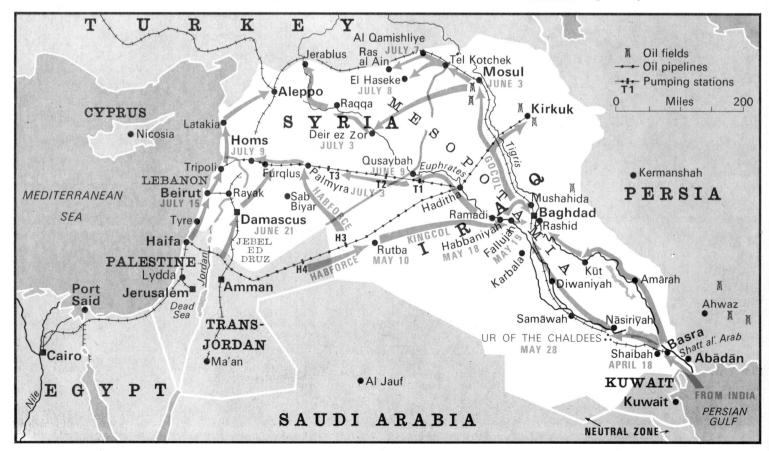

Wavell's Libyan Offensive

The first victory in the North African campaign went to Wavell, who achieved brilliant success against considerable Italian odds in Cyrenaica (map 1). Five Italian divisions, commanded by Marshal Graziani, advanced into Egypt in September 1940 and occupied Sidi Barrani on September 16. Wavell's Western Desert Force, commanded by Major-General O'Connor, began their counter-attack at the end of the first week in December and reached Piccadilly on December 8 and Nibeiwa on December 9 (map 2). Assisted by a naval bombardment and a small coastal force, they retook Sidi Barrani on December 10.

Mussolini then sent a special message to the commandant of Bardia, General Bergonzoli, nicknamed 'Electric Whiskers', to 'stand at whatever cost' but the fortress surrendered to 6th Australian Division on January 5, 1941, after a heavy naval bombardment (map 3). Bergonzoli escaped to Tobruk, which was taken on January 22, with the help of an air and naval

bombardment (map 4). Derna was occupied on January 30 and, by February 9, 7th Armoured Division had reached El Agheila, at which point they were halted. The remaining Italians surrendered unconditionally.

The operation had been hampered by Churchill's insistence that Wavell turn his attention to Greece and by the withdrawal of 4th Indian Division to the Sudan (replaced by 6th Australian Division). O'Connor had also run into the problem of over-stretched supply lines, which was to harass both sides throughout the war. But in just two months Wavell and O'Connor had achieved a remarkable victory. Nine Italian divisions had been destroyed and 130,000 prisoners had been taken in a fine demonstration of fast movement and concentrated fire, which had advanced the front by 500 miles. On the Allied side, there had been only 2,000 casualties with a total of 500 dead. Whatever reputations were to fall later in the desert, this was a memorable and complete triumph.

(1) In autumn 1940 Libya threatened Egypt and the Suez Canal.

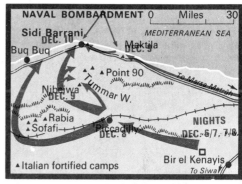

(2) First objective: the Sidi Barrani forts.

General Bergonzoli goes into captivity.

(3) Advance to Bardia, Tobruk and Derna.

(4) Wavell's Western Desert Force, commanded by O'Connor, reached El Agheila in two months.

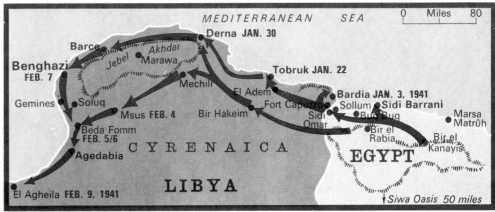

The Ethiopian Campaign

It was not only in Libya that Wavell had to tackle the Italians. In the summer of 1940, they had an empire in East Africa that consisted of Ethiopia, Eritrea and Italian Somaliland. This empire threatened the Sudan to the north, Kenya to the south and British Somaliland to the east, as well as the entrance to the Red Sea. French Somaliland had passed to the Vichy Government with the collapse of France. At this time, the Italians were greatly superior in numbers to the British, who were ill-coordinated and not fully prepared for an offensive.

The Duke of Aosta, in command of all Italian forces in Ethiopia, invaded British Somaliland on August 3, 1940 (maps 1 and 2). One half of the invading force moved north to seal off French Somaliland from possible British influence. The other half, commanded by General de Simone, entered British Somaliland, heading for Berbera, and immediately ran into fierce resistance by the Somaliland Camel Corps. De Simone did not reach Berbera until August 19 and Italian losses were heavy. The surviving garrison was evacuated.

Wavell's counter-offensive did not get under way for another five months. He planned a double attack on Ethiopia: one from the Sudan under Lieutenant-General Platt and the other from Kenya under Lieutenant-General Cunningham (map 3). At first both sides moved cautiously, each over-estimating the strength of the opposition. Platt advanced from Kassala on January 19, 1941, crossed into Eritrea, defeated one Italian force at Agordat on January 31 and pressed the Italians back to the heavily defended fortress defile of Keren, which fell on March 27 after heavy fighting (map 4). Platt was then able to advance to Asmara and Massawa and complete his victory in Eritrea before turning south towards Amba Alagi.

Meanwhile Cunningham had advanced rapidly from Kenya across the border into Italian Somaliland. By February 25 he had reached Mogadishu. Deciding that it would be better to move at once into Ethiopia before completing the conquest of Italian Somaliland, Cunningham turned north from Mogadishu and made a remarkable advance to Jijiga, which he reached on March 17. At the same time a small Allied force advanced through British Somaliland from Aden. Cunningham then moved west to Harar and Addis Ababa. The Ethiopian capital fell on April 6, having been abandoned by the Italians two days earlier, and the Duke of Aosta withdrew to the mountainous retreat of Amba Alagi to join the Italian forces that had been pushed out of Eritrea. The remaining Italians in Ethiopia he divided into two forces of resistance, one based on Gondar in the north and one south-west of Addis Ababa.

Cunningham moved north through Dessie to tackle Amba Alagi. The battle for the pass lasted two weeks and, when finally the Duke of Aosta surrendered on May 19, he was accorded full honours (map 5). In the south-west, Jimma was entered on June 21 and shortly afterwards the remaining Italians in that area surrendered. The last Italian resistance in Ethiopia ended at Gondar on November 27, when 22,000 Italians under General Nasi laid down their arms. The Emperor Haile Selassie had already returned to Ethiopia at the beginning of May 1941, five years after he had been forced to flee from his country by the Italian conquest of 1936. The Italian Empire in East Africa was finished.

Above: (2) De Simone's march on Berbera.
Left: (1) Italian East Africa, showing attacks on British Somaliland and Kassala.
Opposite, top: (3) The Ethiopian Campaign.
Opposite, bottom left: (4) Battle of Keren.
Opposite, bottom right: (5) Battle of Amba Alagi.

Below: The Emperor Haile Selassie returns in triumph to Addis Ababa.

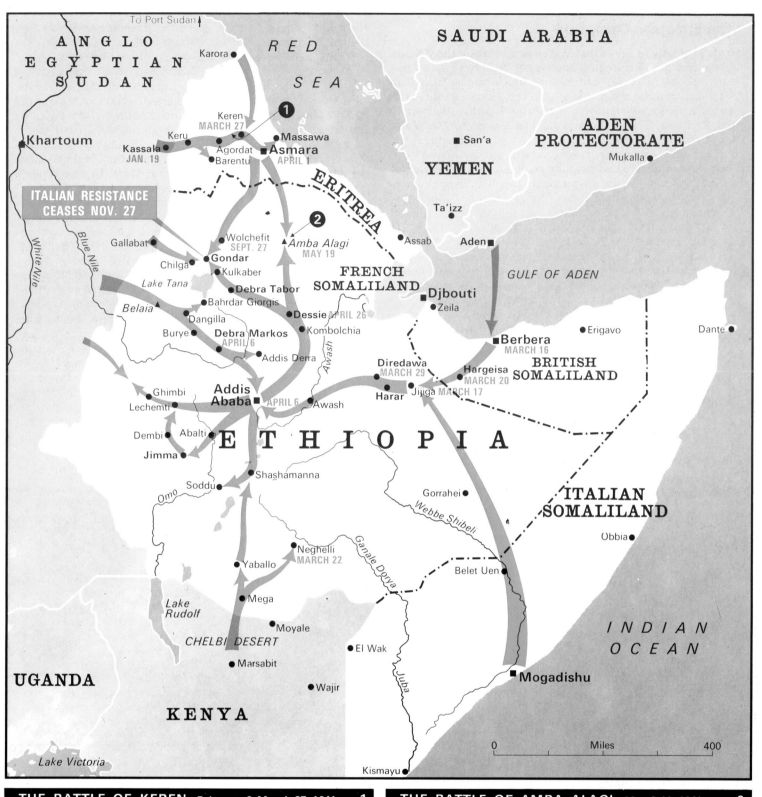

Map Labels (Main Map)

ANGLO EGYPTIAN SUDAN

To Port Sudan

RED SEA

SAUDI ARABIA

Karora

Khartoum

Kassala
JAN. 19

Keru

Keren
MARCH 27

Agordat

Barentu

Massawa

Asmara
APRIL 1

①

ERITREA

San'a

YEMEN

ADEN PROTECTORATE

Mukalla

Ta'izz

ITALIAN RESISTANCE CEASES NOV. 27

Assab

Aden

② *Amba Alagi*
MAY 19

White Nile

Blue Nile

Gallabat

Wolchefit
SEPT. 27

Chilga

Gondar

Kulkaber

Lake Tana

Belaia

Debra Tabor

Bahrdar Giorgis

Dangilla

Burye

Debra Markos
APRIL 6

Dessie APRIL 26

Kombolchia

Addis Derra

Awash

FRENCH SOMALILAND

Djibouti

Zeila

GULF OF ADEN

Berbera
MARCH 16

Erigavo

Dante

Diredawa
MARCH 29

Hargeisa
MARCH 20

BRITISH SOMALILAND

Ghimbi

Lechemti

Addis Ababa
APRIL 6

Awash

Harar

Jijiga MARCH 17

Dembi

Abalti

ETHIOPIA

Jimma

Omo

Soddu

Shashamanna

Gorrahei

Webbe Shibeli

ITALIAN SOMALILAND

Ubbia

Neghelli
MARCH 22

Yaballo

Ganale Dorya

Belet Uen

INDIAN OCEAN

Mega

Lake Rudolf

Moyale

CHELBI DESERT

Marsabit

El Wak

Juba

UGANDA

Wajir

Mogadishu

KENYA

Lake Victoria

Kismayu

0   Miles   400

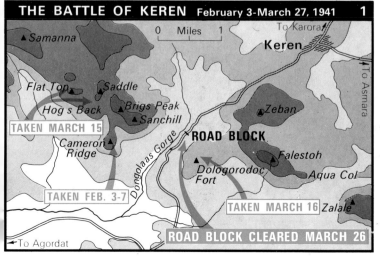

THE BATTLE OF KEREN February 3–March 27, 1941 ①

To Karora

Samanna

Keren

0   Miles   1

Flat Top   *Saddle*

Hog's Back   *Brigs Peak*

Sanchill

Zeban

To Asmara

TAKEN MARCH 15

Cameron Ridge

Dongolaas Gorge

ROAD BLOCK

Falestoh

Dologorodoc Fort

Aqua Col

TAKEN FEB. 3-7

TAKEN MARCH 16 *Zalale*

To Agordat

ROAD BLOCK CLEARED MARCH 26

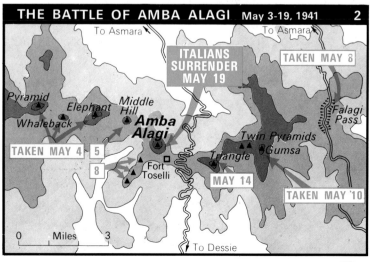

THE BATTLE OF AMBA ALAGI May 3-19, 1941 ②

To Asmara

To Asmara

ITALIANS SURRENDER MAY 19

TAKEN MAY 8

Pyramid   *Elephant*

Middle Hill

Whaleback

Amba Alagi

Falagi Pass

TAKEN MAY 4 5

8

Fort Toselli

Twin Pyramids

Gumsa

Triangle

MAY 14

TAKEN MAY 10

0   Miles   3

To Dessie

The Attack on Taranto

The Mediterranean played a key role in the battle for North Africa. British forces had initially to contend with the Italian navy, as well as with the Italian army in Libya and Ethiopia. The convoy route from Gibraltar to Alexandria was protected by Force H at Gibraltar and the British Mediterranean Fleet at Alexandria, under the command of Admiral Cunningham (map 1). With France out of the war and with Italy as an enemy, determined to cut off his lifeline, Cunningham had a difficult task. Each half of his split force was inferior in strength to the total Italian fleet. Italian ships, moreover, had better and more modern equipment than that of their British counterparts. Cunningham required great skill to preserve his sea lane.

It was impossible for the two British fleets to be joined, since to do so would have meant abandoning one or other end of the Mediterranean, on either side of the narrow, 30-mile channel between Cape Bon and the small Italian island of Pantelleria. It was just to the east of this channel that Malta occupied such a vital place in Britain's lifeline, as a base for attacks on Axis communications between Italy and North Africa. Cunningham's task was to reduce the Italian naval strength and so

take some of the pressure off Allied shipping passing through the Mediterranean. One of his main problems was to bring the Italians to battle in the first place.

A number of indecisive actions occurred between Italian and British ships during the summer and autumn of 1940. It was not until November that Cunningham was able to make his first substantial blow. For some time, plans had been laid for an air attack on the harbour of Taranto (map 2). Air reconnaissance photographs had been taken of net, boom and balloon defences. On November 11, it was observed that all six of the Italian battleships were in the harbour. 'All the pheasants had gone home to roost,' wrote Cunningham later.

The first wave of 12 Swordfish from *Illustrious* was on course for Taranto by 2100 hours on November 11 and arrived, on target, two hours later. They discharged their torpedoes and bombs. A second wave of nine planes arrived over the target at midnight. Both waves each lost one plane but the rest were safely back aboard the *Illustrious* by 0300 hours on November 12. For this small loss, three Italian battleships and two cruisers were crippled. It was a remarkable success which gave a great boost to Allied morale and freed two of the British battleships in the Mediterranean for vital duties in the Atlantic.

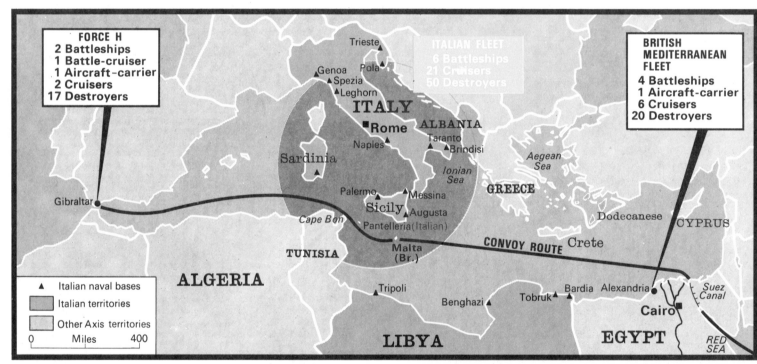

FORCE H
2 Battleships
1 Battle-cruiser
1 Aircraft-carrier
2 Cruisers
17 Destroyers

ITALIAN FLEET
6 Battleships
21 Cruisers
50 Destroyers

BRITISH MEDITERRANEAN FLEET
4 Battleships
1 Aircraft-carrier
6 Cruisers
20 Destroyers

▲ Italian naval bases

Italian territories

Other Axis territories

0 Miles 400

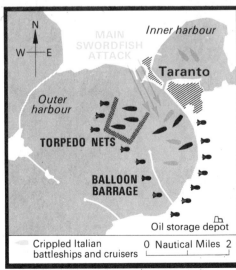

Above: (1) June 1940. The Italian battle fleet outnumbered either one of the British fleets that protected the convoy route through the Mediterranean. The Italian weakness lay in the lack of aircraft carriers, for which Mussolini at first saw little use in the Mediterranean.

Left: (2) The raid on Taranto, November 11, 1940. The three crippled battleships, Littorio, Caio Duilio and Conte di Cavour, lay in the outer harbour; the two crippled cruisers lay in the inner harbour.

Far left: Admiral Cunningham, C-in-C of the British Mediterranean Fleet.

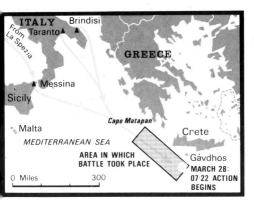

ITALY — Brindisi
From La Spezia — Taranto
GREECE
Messina
Sicily
Malta
MEDITERRANEAN SEA
Cape Matapan
Crete
Gávdhos
AREA IN WHICH BATTLE TOOK PLACE
MARCH 28: 07·22 ACTION BEGINS
0 Miles — 300

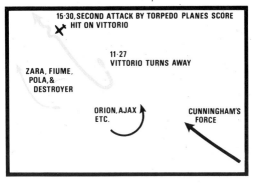

15·30, SECOND ATTACK BY TORPEDO PLANES SCORE HIT ON VITTORIO
11·27 VITTORIO TURNS AWAY
ZARA, FIUME, POLA, & DESTROYER
ORION, AJAX ETC.
CUNNINGHAM'S FORCE

Above: (3) **Vittorio Veneto** *is hit by a torpedo and turns for home.*

Right: (4) The night action in which **Pola,** **Fiume** *and* **Zara** *were eventually sunk.*

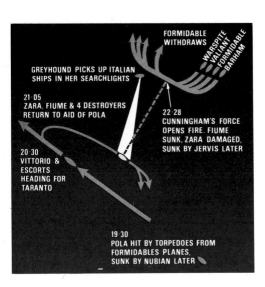

FORMIDABLE WITHDRAWS
WARSPITE VALIANT FORMIDABLE BARHAM
GREYHOUND PICKS UP ITALIAN SHIPS IN HER SEARCHLIGHTS
21·05 ZARA, FIUME & 4 DESTROYERS RETURN TO AID OF POLA
22·28 CUNNINGHAM'S FORCE OPENS FIRE. FIUME SUNK, ZARA DAMAGED, SUNK BY JERVIS LATER
20·30 VITTORIO & ESCORTS HEADING FOR TARANTO
19·30 POLA HIT BY TORPEDOES FROM FORMIDABLES PLANES, SUNK BY NUBIAN LATER

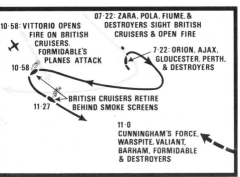

10·58: VITTORIO OPENS FIRE ON BRITISH CRUISERS. FORMIDABLE'S PLANES ATTACK
07·22: ZARA, POLA, FIUME, & DESTROYERS SIGHT BRITISH CRUISERS & OPEN FIRE
7·22: ORION, AJAX, GLOUCESTER, PERTH, & DESTROYERS
10·58
BRITISH CRUISERS RETIRE BEHIND SMOKE SCREENS
11·27
11·0 CUNNINGHAM'S FORCE, WARSPITE, VALIANT, BARHAM, FORMIDABLE & DESTROYERS

Top: (1) The track of the Italian fleet en route to intercept the Allied convoys from Alexandria to Greece.

Above: (2) The first engagement between the cruisers and the **Vittorio Veneto.**

Below: HMS Warspite, *one of the battleships in Cunningham's force. Her first salvo of 15-inch shells struck the* Fiume *at close range.*

The Battle of Matapan

After the attack at Taranto, Mussolini became increasingly cautious about committing his ships to battle. But in March 1941, the Germans persuaded him to launch an attack against British ships convoying reinforcements to Greece in a build-up of strength to counter the Axis invasion of the Balkans. Mussolini reluctantly agreed, with the promise of German air cover, but Cunningham had anticipated interference south of Gávdhos and was ready for trouble.

The Italian force included the 35,000-ton brand-new battle-ship *Vittorio Veneto*, with nine 15-inch guns, as well as eight cruisers and nine destroyers. Three of the Italian cruisers were sighted by an RAF Sunderland flying boat at 1230 hours on March 27; they were 75 miles east of Sicily and steering for Crete (map 1). That night, Cunningham took his three battle-ships (*Warspite*, *Valiant* and *Barham*), with the carrier *Formidable* and a destroyer escort, out from Alexandria to join his four cruisers already at sea. The Italian and British cruiser forces met at 0722 hours on March 28. The British cruisers attempted to draw the Italians onto the guns of Cunningham's advancing force, while at the same time keeping out of range of the *Vittorio Veneto*. When aircraft from the *Formidable* made contact with the enemy, the Italian cruisers turned away together with the *Vittorio Veneto* (map 2). Cunningham's force continued in pursuit. At 1530, *Formidable*'s torpedo bombers made a second attack on *Vittorio Veneto* and achieved a hit, which slowed down the battleship (map 3), but she continued on course for Taranto, protected by her cruisers and destroyers.

The action lasted into the night (map 4). At 1930 hours, the cruiser *Pola* was also struck by a torpedo and stopped. Unaware that Cunningham was still on their heels, the Italians sent back the cruisers *Zara* and *Fiume*, with four destroyers, to help the stricken *Pola*. The rescue ships were picked up by the *Greyhound*'s searchlights and at 2228 hours Cunningham's battle-ships opened up on the Italian cruisers at close range. The action lasted only four-and-a-half minutes, before the battle-ships turned away, harassed by the destroyers and the guns of the crippled cruisers. The destroyer *Jervis* was left to deal with the victims, while the search continued for the *Vittorio Veneto*. The *Fiume* had already sunk; the *Jervis* finished off the *Zara* and *Pola*. Two destroyers were also sunk. The *Vittorio Veneto* escaped. Despite this disappointment, Cunningham had ensured that the Italian fleet was not able to interfere with British warships and transports when, in the ensuing months, the time came to evacuate troops from Greece and Crete.

Rommel Recovers Cyrenaica

Rommel arrived in North Africa on February 12, 1941, only three days after the British reached El Agheila at the end of Wavell's Libyan offensive (map 1). Rommel's Afrika Korps was to have two Panzer divisions but XV Panzer Division did not arrive until the end of May and XXI Panzer Division (also known as V Light Division) was not complete until mid-April, although it began to arrive on February 14. The Allies were equally stretched. Wavell had to withdraw a substantial number of men to Greece, leaving only a covering force under General Neame.

On March 24, Rommel attacked with XXI Panzer and two Italian divisions, driving the British out of El Agheila (map 2). He was at Agedabia by April 2. The Italian column then advanced along the coast through Benghazi to Derna, while XXI Panzer advanced across the desert through Msus and through Tengeder and Mechili and from there to Tobruk. The vital British petrol dump at Msus was destroyed, depriving the retreating forces of their manoeuvrability.

7th Australian Division, with some tanks, was sent in by sea to hold Tobruk, which would deprive Rommel of an advance base and threaten his flank. Rommel failed in an ill-coordinated attack on April 10–11 and a larger assault was also thrown back on April 14. Consolidating his position around Tobruk with Italian troops, Rommel then advanced to the Egyptian frontier and attacked through Sollum and the Halfaya Pass to come to a halt on a line from Buq Buq to Sofafi. A major assault to take Tobruk at the very end of April was held by the defenders (map 3).

Above: (1) The Axis and the Allied advance positions at the end of Wavell's offensive in Cyrenaica. Tripoli was the main Axis base. Rommel arrived in North Africa only three days after Allied troops reached El Agheila and within six weeks had launched a counter-offensive.

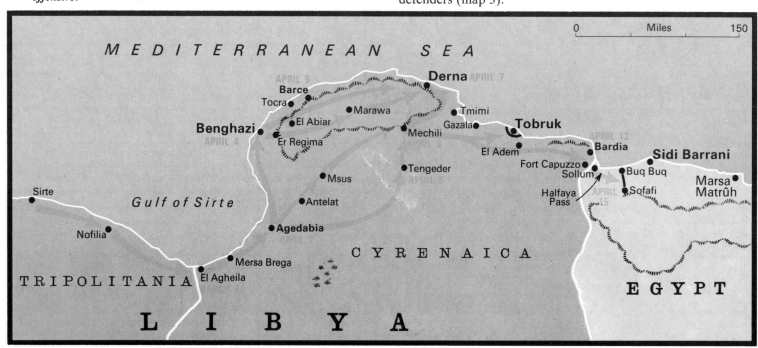

Above: (2) Taking advantage of the depleted state of the Allied forces, Rommel recovered Cyrenaica between the end of March and the second week in April 1941. Only Tobruk remained in Allied hands.

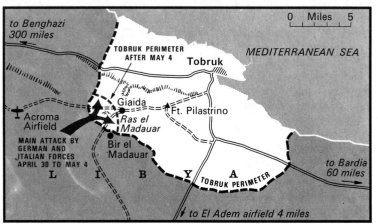

Left: (3) Rommel's first attack on Tobruk was only half-hearted, with troops that were rushed in as soon as they arrived. His first full-scale attack was launched on April 30, during which he achieved a salient at Ras el Madauar. This was contained by the garrison after four days' fighting. Under the command of Major-General Morshead and Major-General Scobie, the defenders put up determined resistance.

Brevity and Battleaxe

Halfaya Pass was strategically important to both sides. When Rommel captured it in his April offensive, Wavell ordered Brigadier Gott to recapture the pass and to advance through Sollum and Fort Capuzzo towards Tobruk. Operation Brevity was a three-pronged attack launched on May 15 (map 1). Halfaya Pass and Fort Capuzzo were both taken but when Rommel counter-attacked, expecting to encounter a major advance, he quickly recaptured Capuzzo and found that 7th Armoured Division had withdrawn on Gott's orders to Halfaya. Rommel's VIII Panzer Regiment outflanked the pass and recaptured it on May 27.

Wavell's long-awaited 'Tiger' convoy arrived on May 12, giving him the necessary armour to support what was to be his last desert offensive, Operation Battleaxe (map 2). Forbidden to advance and hampered by supply problems, Rommel was dug in at Halfaya Pass and on Points 206 and 208. Wavell ordered a frontal attack on Halfaya and a left-flanking attack on Fort Capuzzo and Sollum. The attack on Halfaya Pass began on June 15 but Rommel's entrenched 88-mm anti-aircraft guns turned the assault. At Point 206, Capuzzo and Hafid Ridge, Rommel absorbed the initial attacks and then counter-attacked, bombarding the Allies with artillery. V Light Division was sent to outflank the attack in the direction of Sidi Omar, where 7th Armoured Division suffered heavy losses. V Light Division then swung east towards Halfaya Pass. It was joined by VIII Panzer Regiment and Halfaya Pass was relieved by June 17. The Allies withdrew to their original positions.

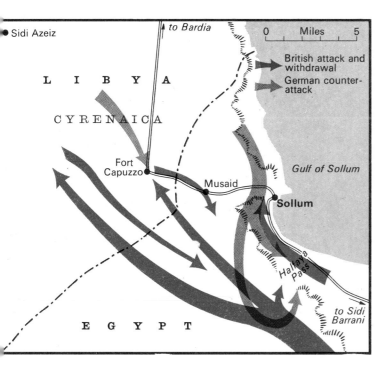

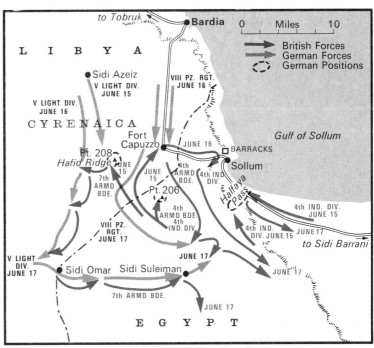

Above left: (1) Operation Brevity, which began with a three-pronged assault on May 15 and achieved some initial successes. Twelve days later, Rommel had recaptured Halfaya Pass and strengthened its fortifications with his 88-mm anti-aircraft guns.

Above right: (2) Operation Battleaxe was Wavell's last attempt to break Rommel's hold in Cyrenaica and to relieve Tobruk. In three days, between June 15 and 17, Rommel's defences absorbed the first attacks and then counter-attacked to drive the Allies back.

Right: The 'Crusader' tanks were brought immediately from the important 'Tiger' convoy into battle. Unfamiliar to their crews and in unfamiliar surroundings, they suffered heavy losses.

Operation Crusader

After the failure of Operation Battleaxe, Auchinleck replaced Wavell and Cunningham was put in command of the newly named 8th Army. Anticipating an all-out attack by Rommel on Tobruk, Operation Crusader opened on November 18, 1941, with 13th Corps advancing on Halfaya Pass and Fort Capuzzo, while 30th Corps advanced through Gabr Saleh towards Tobruk (map 1). 7th Armoured Brigade reached Sidi Rezegh with little difficulty but 22nd Armoured Brigade was halted by the Ariete Division and 4th Armoured Brigade was stopped by XXI Panzer Division.

While Rommel was preoccupied with Tobruk, Cruewell commanded the Afrika Korps counter-attack (map 2), first to Sidi Azeiz, then south (November 20) against 4th and 22nd Armoured Brigades, then north (November 21) against 7th Armoured Brigade at Sidi Rezegh. Meanwhile the New Zea-land Division moved up to Sidi Azeiz. But the Allied spearhead had already been blunted and, on the night of November 22, XV Panzer Division virtually destroyed the 4th Armoured Brigade (map 3). In further confused fighting between Sidi Rezegh and Bir el Gubi on November 23, XV Panzer Division shattered 5th South African Brigade (map 4), its second Allied victim.

On November 24, Rommel made a 'dash for the wire' to relieve the Halfaya garrison and cut off the 8th Army (map 5). The threat posed by the New Zealand advance on Tobruk in his rear forced him to turn back and, despite determined counter-attacks against the recovering 30th Corps, he was finally exhausted. Confronted by the more vigorous action of General Ritchie, who had replaced Cunningham, Rommel withdrew to El Agheila before his forces were cut off in the Benghazi bulge (map 6).

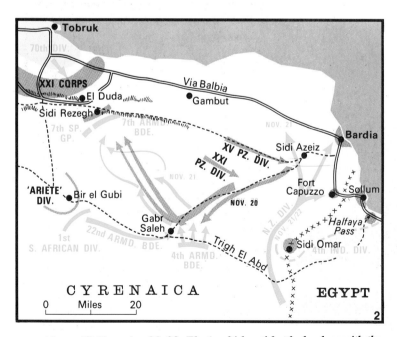

Above: (1) November 18–19. Operation Crusader begins with 13th Corps holding on the right flank while 30th Corps makes a strong advance on the left and in the centre.

Above: (2) November 20–22. The 'multi-layer' battle develops with the counter-attack by Cruewell and the Afrika Korps, turning south and then north again towards Sidi Rezegh.

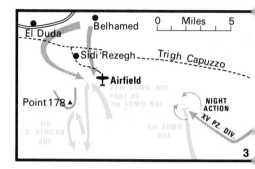

Right: (3) November 22. The British spearhead is blunted and 4th Armoured Brigade is broken by XV Panzer Division.

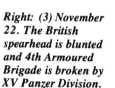

Right: (4) November 23. XV Panzer Division encounters and destroys 5th South African Brigade, which loses two-thirds of its men and equipment.

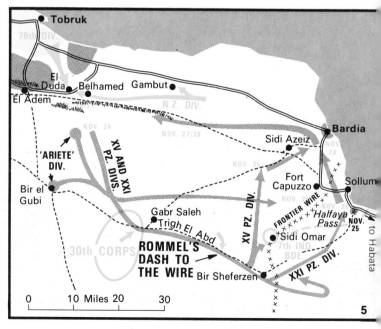

Above: (5) November 24–28. Rommel's 'dash to the wire' is frustrated by renewed Allied determination and the threat in his rear by the New Zealand Division advancing on Tobruk.

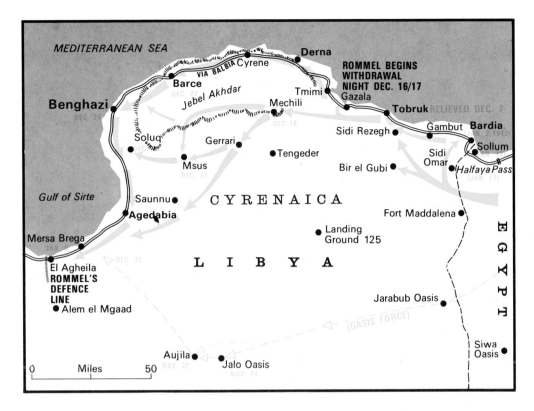

Right: (6) Crusader was not a runaway victory. Both sides were ready for an offensive and there was a hard slogging match before Rommel finally withdrew from the perimeter of Tobruk and retreated to El Agheila. His retreat was a tactical withdrawal, for he did not want to get cut off in the bulge of Benghazi.

Below: Rommel (right) was concentrating his personal attention on the siege of Tobruk when Crusader opened. It was General Cruewell who started the Afrika Korps counter-offensive.

Bottom: A 25-pounder opens up on the German siege lines around Tobruk in the early stages of Operation Crusader.

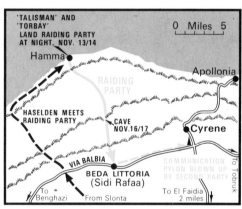

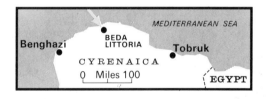

Keyes' Raid

On the night of November 13–14, only a few days before Operation Crusader, a daring and ill-fated commando raid led by Lieutenant-Colonel Geoffrey Keyes was launched behind the enemy lines to seize Rommel and to put his HQ out of action (maps above). Keyes' targets were the Rommelhaus at Beda Littoria and the communications pylon near Cyrene. Early intelligence for the raid obtained by Captain Haselden proved unreliable. Rommel was not at the HQ when the raid took place. Keyes himself was killed and all but two of the raiders were captured. Keyes was awarded a post-humous VC.

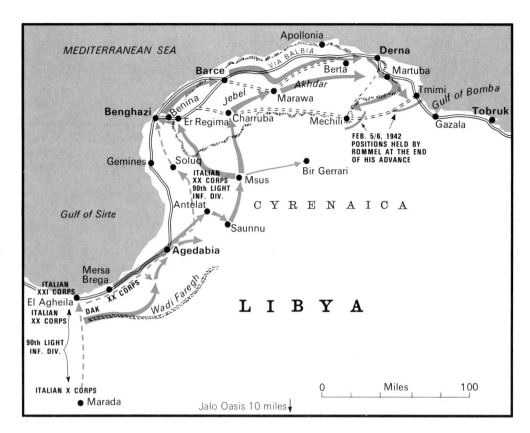

Left: (1) Rommel's second offensive in
Cyrenaica followed much the same lines as
his first offensive in March and April, 1941.
The Allied outposts were quickly disrupted
and, with its lines of supply already
overstretched, 8th Army was driven back to
the Gazala Line within two weeks.

Below: (2) The Gazala Line is turned. The
defensive line of minefields and
interconnected brigade boxes stretched from
Gazala to Bir Hachim, with open desert
beyond, easy to drive round. Ritchie hoped to
use 30th Corps to crush the Panzers against
the rear of the line once Rommel swept north.
But Ritchie left his counterblow too long and
Rommel had leisure to overwhelm 150th
Brigade box and open up his own supply
lines.

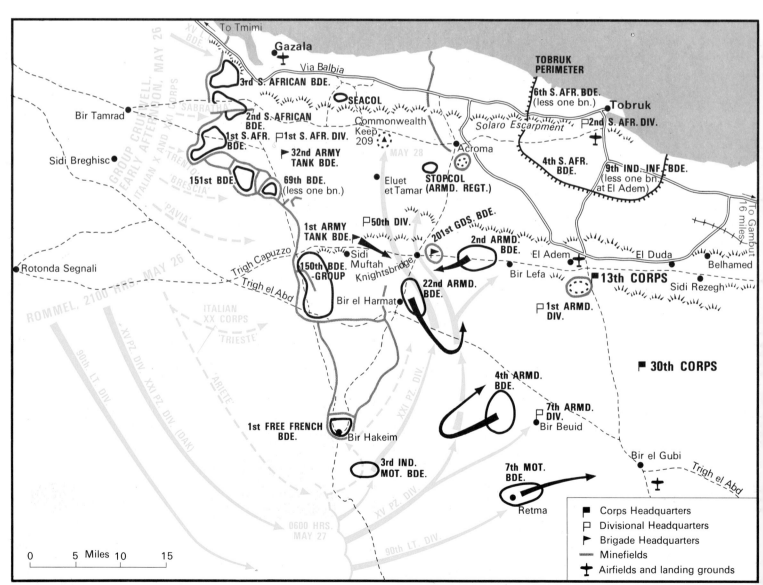

Rommel's Advance to Gazala

Driven back towards his base in Tripolitania, Rommel was able to rebuild his own forces more quickly than could the 8th Army, now far from its own base in Egypt. On January 21, 1942, only a few weeks after falling back on El Agheila, Rommel advanced once again through Agedabia and Benghazi (map 1). On February 5–6 he came up against 8th Army's defensive line between Gazala and Bir Hachim. Both sides rested on this line for nearly four months, gathering their strength.

Rommel took the initiative on May 26, sweeping round Bir Hachim and turning north behind the Allied lines, while Cruewell pinned down the defences in the north (map 2). He hoped to open a supply line through Trigh Capuzzo and Trigh el Abd but failed to identify the 150th Brigade box in the Cauldron. Hard pressed by 30th Corps and Allied aircraft, running low on fuel, Rommel moved into the Cauldron to prepare for the Allied counter-offensive (map 3). Ritchie failed to seize his opportunity to attack and Rommel had time to crush 150th Brigade and to open supply lines through the minefield. The fight for 150th Brigade box (map 4) was particularly severe and lasted for about 72 hours. The box succumbed to Rommel's armour and the Stukas.

Ritchie's counter-attack came too late, on June 5–6, and was easily beaten back (map 5). On June 10–11, the Free French Brigade were driven out of Bir Hachim and on June 11 the Axis forces broke out of the Cauldron, burst through 30th Corps and headed for Tobruk. The Allies fell back hastily before the onslaught and Tobruk was surrounded by June 18. This time, Rommel meant to seize the prize without delay.

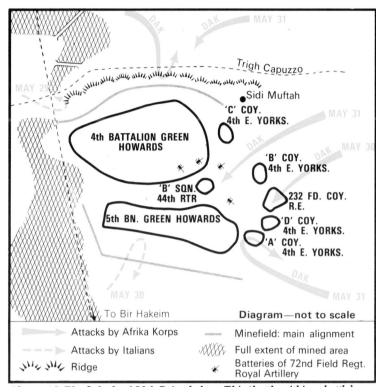

Above: (3) Rommel turns on 150th Brigade box in the area known as the Cauldron, concentrating all his Panzers on this point.

Above: (4) The fight for 150th Brigade box. This 'battle within a battle' was an epic of brave resistance.

Below: (5) Ritchie's belated counterblow on June 5–6 was beaten off and Rommel broke from the Cauldron on June 11, hard on the heels of the Free French Brigade withdrawing from Bir Hachim.

Below: A British tank ablaze and with one track ripped off. Rommel's Panzers were once again on the offensive.

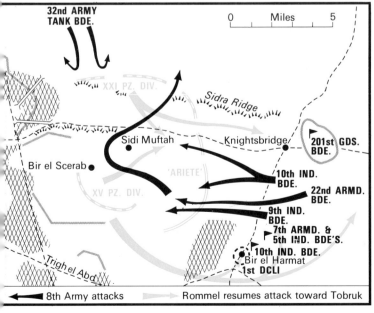

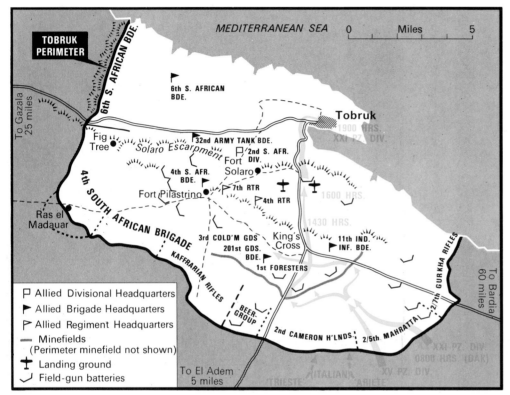

Above: The garrison of Tobruk fought gallantly under the command of Major-General Klopper but they were quickly overrun by Rommel's attack with three armoured divisions.

Left: (1) Rommel's attack on Tobruk, June 1942. Having failed to take Tobruk on his first offensive, this time Rommel chose to attack from the south-east rather than the south-west. The attack was completely successful. The defenders of Tobruk surrendered within four days. Rommel had removed the thorn that had stuck in his side on his previous advance to the Egyptian border.

The Fall of Tobruk and Marsa Matruh

Facing the imminent possibility of defeat after Rommel's breaching of the Gazala Line, 8th Army withdrew along the coast towards the Egyptian frontier, leaving Tobruk to stand alone. Rommel reached the perimeter of the defences on June 18, 1942. On his previous assault he had attacked from the south-west corner and failed to take the port. This time, he followed O'Connor's example during Wavell's offensive and attacked at the south-east corner. Major-General Klopper, newly appointed commander of the 2nd South African Division, was in charge of the defence.

Rommel attacked on June 20 (map 1). Three armoured divisions made a co-ordinated assault and by 1600 hours the Axis were in control of the airfield. Within three hours, XXI Panzer Division had reached the harbour. Klopper resisted with determination, while destroying the precious quantities of fuel, but he was eventually forced to surrender. The last Allied troops laid down their arms on the evening of June 21. They had waited for the promised help from Ritchie in vain. Klopper and 33,000 men were taken prisoner.

Rommel determined to press on, despite his own losses, for 8th Army was weakened by defeat and indecisive leadership and the once powerful 30th Corps was almost shattered. Ritchie withdrew in disorder to a defensive line at Marsa Matruh but at this point Auchinleck relieved him and took over direct command. Realizing that his depleted and demoralized forces would probably be unable to hold the line between Marsa Matruh and Sidi Hamzah, he decided on a strategic withdrawal to the Alam Halfa Ridge, between El Alamein and the Qattara Depression. At the same time, he determined to fight a delaying action at Marsa Matruh.

Rommel began to move his forces forward against the Marsa Matruh line on June 26 (map 2). As at Gazala, he aimed at a flanking attack around the southern end of the line, combined with a parallel attack to the north which would cut the coast road east of Matruh. The advance was rapid. By 1200 hours on June 27, the Axis were threatening 13th Corps, which was forced to withdraw despite attempts at a counter-attack by 10th Corps. Orders were sent from 8th Army HQ that 10th Corps should also withdraw but these orders were not received until the following morning. On June 28, 10th Corps was trapped with its back to the sea. 13th Corps failed to come to the assistance of 10th Corps in time and only small units of 10th Corps managed to break out independently, leaving 7,000 prisoners.

The remains of 8th Army fell back to El Alamein (map 3), only 60 miles west of Alexandria, but by then both sides were completely exhausted and a few tentative probes by Rommel July were easily rebuffed by the entrenched Allies. The stage was set for the preliminary moves in the final confrontation.

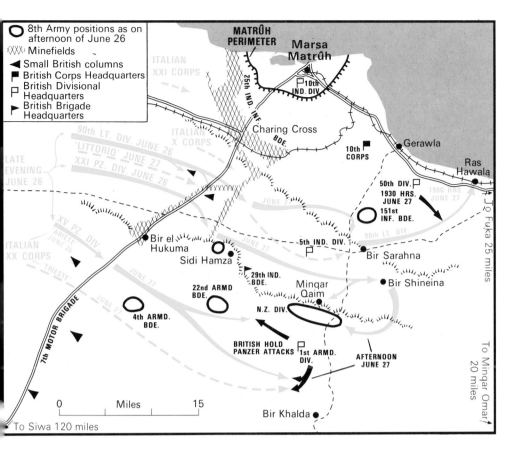

Map Legend

- ⭕ 8th Army positions as on afternoon of June 26
- ⤬⤬⤬ Minefields
- ◀ Small British columns
- ⚑ British Corps Headquarters
- ▢ British Divisional Headquarters
- ▶ British Brigade Headquarters

MATRÛH PERIMETER
Marsa Matrûh

ITALIAN XXI CORPS

10th IND. DIV

25th IND. INF. BDE

Charring Cross BDE

ITALIAN X CORPS

90th LT. DIV. JUNE 26
'LITTORIO' JUNE 27
XXI PZ. DIV. JUNE 26

LATE EVENING JUNE 26

10th CORPS

Gerawla

Ras Hawala

50th DIV.
1930 HRS.
JUNE 27

1900 HRS JUNE 27

151st INF. BDE.

90th LT. DIV.

To Fuka 25 miles

XV PZ. DIV.
ARIETE JUNE 26
ITALIAN XX CORPS

JUNE 27

5th IND. DIV.

Bir el Hukuma

TRIESTE JUNE 27

Sidi Hamza

29th IND. BDE.

22nd ARMD BDE.

4th ARMD. BDE.

Bir Sarahna

Minqar Qaim

N.Z. DIV.

Bir Shineina

BRITISH HOLD PANZER ATTACKS

1st ARMD. DIV.

AFTERNOON JUNE 27

7th MOTOR BRIGADE

To Minqar Omar 20 miles

0   Miles   15

To Siwa 120 miles

Bir Khalda

Left: (2) Churchill was deeply upset by the fall of Tobruk and tried to bully Ritchie into making a stand at Marsa Matruh. But Auchinleck relieved Ritchie of command and decided on a rearguard action and a withdrawal to El Alamein. Rommel merely repeated his tactics from Gazala and swept round the southern end of the defences while simultaneously attacking in the north to cut off 10th Corps. His victory was complete within four days.

MEDITERRANEAN SEA

Barce

Benghazi

Tmimi

Gazala **GAZALA LINE**

Tobruk

Bardia

Sidi Barrani

Nile Delta

CYRENAICA

Bir Hakeim

FIRST PHASE OF ROMMEL'S ADVANCE JAN/FEB

Bir el Sheferzen

Marsa Matrûh

Fuka

Alexandria

Agedabia

SECOND PHASE MAY/JUNE

E G Y P T

El Alamein

0   Miles   100

El Agheila

L I B Y A

Bab el Qattara

Qattara Depression

Cairo

Above: (3) Rommel's two-phase advance through Cyrenaica and into Egypt. This was the pinnacle of his success in North Africa. For a while, however, it seemed to the shattered 8th Army that he could not be stopped from reaching Alexandria and achieving his ultimate objectives.

Left: General Nehring of the victorious Afrika Korps poses beside a captured British 25-pounder on the edge of the desert. Tobruk itself had been well furnished with stores of all kinds and the British suffered tremendous losses when the port fell. The defenders made gallant efforts to destroy the huge supplies of petrol stockpiled in Tobruk and to cause as much damage to the port as possible before they were finally forced to surrender.

The First Battle of El Alamein

Pushed back from Tobruk and Marsa Matruh, Auchinleck was determined to hold El Alamein. It was his last chance to stop Rommel reaching Alexandria, but he had barely time to reassemble his remaining forces (only two operative infantry divisions and a still disorganized armoured division) before Rommel was attacking once again. This time, as Rommel later admitted, Auchinleck proved to be the equal of the 'Desert Fox'. Instead of putting his faith in fixed lines of defence, Auchinleck used a fluid line based on the Ruweisat Ridge and Bab el Qattara. He determined to channel Rommel's attack into prepared paths that he could successfully counter-attack.

Rommel himself believed that he had 8th Army on the run and that he could easily break through the opposition, pass by El Alamein, and continue in triumph towards Alexandria and Cairo. On July 1, 1942, he committed his main Panzer attack to the centre, with a supplementary attack further north (map 1). Between July 2 and 4, Rommel was twice repulsed on the Ruweisat Ridge (map 2) and on July 3 a southward move by the Italians was rebuffed by the New Zealanders. Rommel had to abandon his hopes of a quick victory.

On July 10–11, Auchinleck moved the fresh 9th Australian Division against the Sabratha Division in the north and successfully attacked Tell el Eisa (map 3), forcing Rommel to commit his last reserves. On July 14–15 Auchinleck struck at Ruweisat Ridge (map 4). Rommel retook Point 63 on July 15 but suffered severe losses. Auchinleck launched a second attack on the ridge on July 21–22 (map 5) but it gained no ground. Both sides dug in with minefields and prepared to regroup. Auchinleck had successfully made his stand. Now he, like Wavell before him, was to be replaced.

Below: (1) First Alamein: Rommel strikes in the centre on July 1, while Auchinleck prepares to hold the Panzers and strike back.

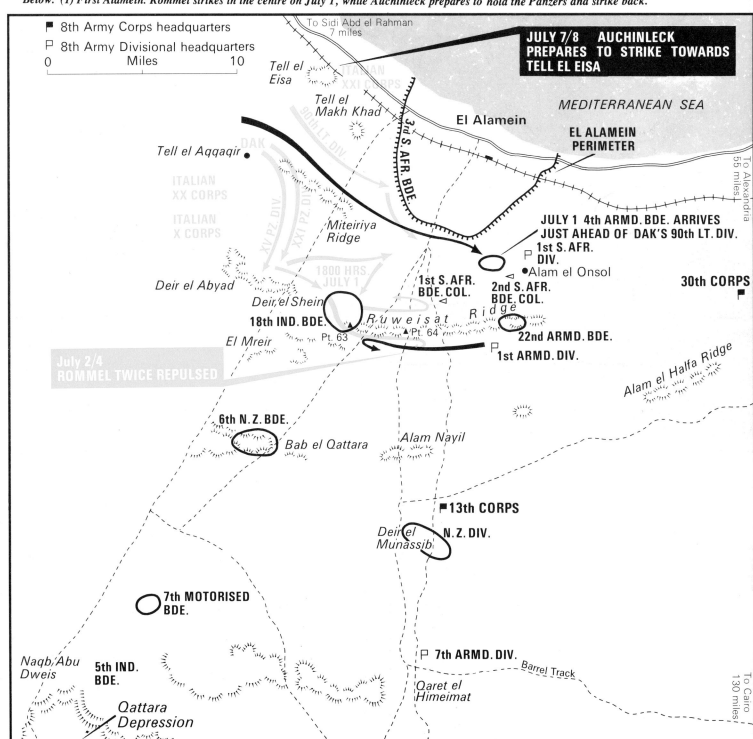

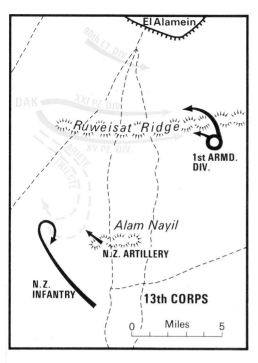

Left: (2) July 3. The Afrika Korps (DAK) are held on Ruweisat Ridge and the Ariete Division are turned back in the south.

Right: (3) July 10–11. While Rommel's extended line fails to make further advances, the Sabratha Division in the north is destroyed. Rommel's counter-attacks on July 13–14 are turned away with heavy losses.

Map 2 labels:
El Alamein
90th LT. DIV.
DAK
XXI PZ. DIV.
XV PZ. DIV.
ARIETE
TRIESTE
Ruweisat Ridge
1st ARMD. DIV.
Alam Nayil
N.Z. ARTILLERY
N.Z. INFANTRY
13th CORPS
0   Miles   5

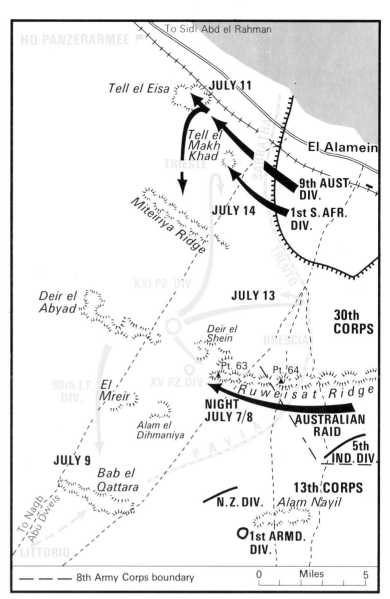

Map 3 labels:
To Sidi Abd el Rahman
HQ PANZERARMEE
Tell el Eisa   JULY 11
El Alamein
Tell el Makh Khad
JULY 14
SABRATHA
TRIESTE
9th AUST. DIV.
1st S. AFR. DIV.
Miteiriya Ridge
XXI PZ. DIV.
JULY 13
30th CORPS
Deir el Abyad
Deir el Shein
BRESCIA
90th LT. DIV.
XV PZ. DIV.
Pt. 63   Pt. 64
El Mreir
Ruweisat Ridge
NIGHT JULY 7/8
AUSTRALIAN RAID
Alam el Dihmaniya
PAVIA
5th IND. DIV.
JULY 9
Bab el Qattara
13th CORPS
N.Z. DIV.   *Alam Nayil*
To Naqb Abu Dweis
1st ARMD. DIV.
LITTORIO
– – – – 8th Army Corps boundary
0   Miles   5

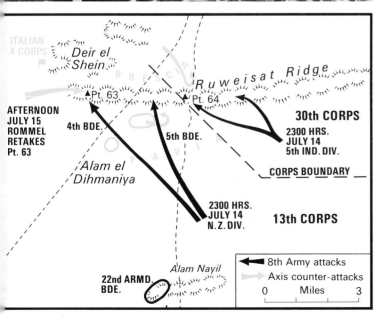

Left: A German sapper lifting a British mine. This dangerous task was to become an important preliminary to all future attacks on both sides. Minefields were a prime form of defence.
Bottom left: (4) July 14–15. Auchinleck's first strike at Ruweisat Ridge achieved most of its objectives, except for Point 63, which was retaken by Rommel on July 15.
Bottom right: (5) July 21–22. Auchinleck's second assault on Ruweisat Ridge and El Mreir. He still failed to take Point 63 and now the position of both fronts was crystallizing.

Map 4 labels:
ITALIAN X CORPS
Deir el Shein
BRESCIA
Ruweisat Ridge
Pt. 63   Pt. 64
AFTERNOON JULY 15 ROMMEL RETAKES Pt. 63
4th BDE.
5th BDE.
30th CORPS
2300 HRS. JULY 14 5th IND. DIV.
CORPS BOUNDARY
Alam el Dihmaniya
PAVIA
2300 HRS. JULY 14 N.Z. DIV.
13th CORPS
Alam Nayil
22nd ARMD. BDE.
← 8th Army attacks
← Axis counter-attacks
0   Miles   3

Map 5 labels:
ITALIAN X CORPS
Deir el Shein
XXI PZ. DIV.
DAK
Pt. 63
5th IND. BDE.
Ruweisat Ridge   Pt. 64
El Mreir
23rd ARMD. BDE.
PROBABLE EXTENT OF ENEMY MINEFIELD
2nd ARMD. BDE.
DAK PZ. REGTS.
XV PZ. DIV.
N.Z. DIV.
First 8th Army objective
Second 8th Army objective
ITALIAN XX CORPS
0   Miles   3

The Malta Convoys

During the fluctuating fortunes of the conflict in North Africa, the island fortress of Malta remained the one Allied stronghold in the central Mediterranean (map 1). The first bombs fell only a few hours after Italy entered the war, on the night of June 10, 1940, and from January 1941, the island was subjected to the much more severe attacks of the *Luftwaffe*. On January 16, 80 Stukas from Sicily attacked the dockyard and the carrier *Illustrious*, which was in the harbour. Further concentrated attacks followed throughout the year. Supply convoys were hit so hard by the Axis that at times they had to be temporarily suspended.

By August 1942, Rommel was at the height of his success in North Africa. The Allies had been pushed back to El Alamein and Malta was at the end of its resources of food and fuel. The loss of Malta at this stage would have been disastrous. On August 3, a convoy of 14 merchantmen, codenamed Operation Pedestal, including the tanker *Ohio* and escorted by two battleships, three carriers, seven cruisers, 32 destroyers and eight submarines, left the Clyde in a desperate bid to save

Malta. Seven days later, the convoy passed through the Straits of Gibraltar and was quickly spotted and shadowed.

At 1323 hours on August 11, a U-boat sank the aircraft carrier *Eagle* (map 2). On the same day came the first air strikes from Sardinia, which were beaten off without damage to the convoy. On August 12, the Axis attacked mercilessly from the air and from the sea. The freighter *Deucalion* was hit and later sank. In the evening, the destroyer *Foresight* was sunk and the carrier *Indomitable* rendered useless. Later that same evening, the cruiser *Cairo* was sunk; so were two more merchant ships, the *Empire Hope* and *Clan Ferguson*. The cruisers *Nigeria* and *Kenya* were damaged; so were the *Brisbane Star* and the *Ohio*. The convoy was thrown into confusion. Five more merchant ships and a cruiser were lost in the night and another merchant ship in the morning. Only three ships reached Malta in convoy: the *Port Chalmers*, *Melbourne Star* and *Rochester Castle*. They were later joined by the *Brisbane Star* and the battered *Ohio*, which was towed into Valletta harbour on August 15. Her vital oil cargo enabled Malta to hold out until December. Two more convoys reached Malta by the end of the year.

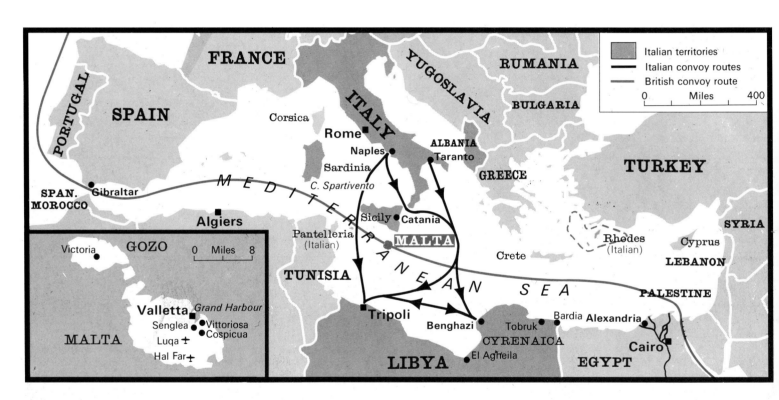

Above: (1) Malta was the vital link in the Allied supply line between Gibraltar and Alexandria; it also bestrode the Axis supply lines between Italy and North Africa.

Below: The carrier **Eagle** *was Pedestal's first casualty. She was torpedoed by U-73 shortly after midday on August 11; she capsized and sank within minutes of the attack.*

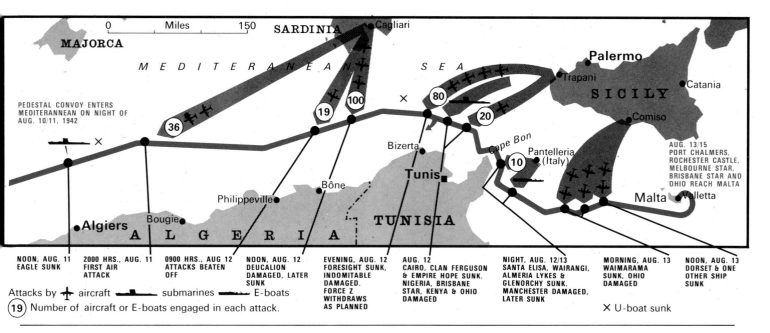

PEDESTAL CONVOY ENTERS
MEDITERANNEAN ON NIGHT OF
AUG. 10/11, 1942

AUG. 13/15
PORT CHALMERS,
ROCHESTER CASTLE,
MELBOURNE STAR,
BRISBANE STAR AND
OHIO REACH MALTA

| NOON, AUG. 11 EAGLE SUNK | 2000 HRS., AUG. 11 FIRST AIR ATTACK | 0900 HRS., AUG 12 ATTACKS BEATEN OFF | NOON, AUG. 12 DEUCALION DAMAGED, LATER SUNK | EVENING, AUG. 12 FORESIGHT SUNK, INDOMITABLE DAMAGED. FORCE Z WITHDRAWS AS PLANNED | AUG. 12 CAIRO, CLAN FERGUSON & EMPIRE HOPE SUNK. NIGERIA, BRISBANE STAR, KENYA & OHIO DAMAGED | NIGHT, AUG. 12/13 SANTA ELISA, WAIRANGI, ALMERIA LYKES & GLENORCHY SUNK. MANCHESTER DAMAGED, LATER SUNK | MORNING, AUG. 13 WAIMARAMA SUNK, OHIO DAMAGED | NOON, AUG. 13 DORSET & ONE OTHER SHIP SUNK |

Attacks by ✈ aircraft ▬ submarines ▬ E-boats

⑲ Number of aircraft or E-boats engaged in each attack.   ✕ U-boat sunk

*Above: (2) The route of the Pedestal convoy, after it entered the
Mediterranean. The concerted attacks of August 12 threw the convoy
into confusion. The heaviest losses were during the evening of August
12 and the night of August 12–13. Only five merchantmen, including
the Ohio, reached Malta, out of the fourteen that had set out from the
Clyde.*

*Below: Pedestal's precious oil tanker, Ohio, lies in the Grand Harbour,
Valletta, after surviving an Italian torpedo hit and two crashing
German dive bombers.*

The Battle of Alam Halfa

Some important changes in the Allied command followed the first battle of El Alamein. Auchinleck felt as much in need of regrouping his exhausted forces as did Rommel and he refused to attack again until the middle of September. Churchill wanted a more immediate attack and a vigorous and determined commander for 8th Army. Auchinleck was withdrawn and so was Ritchie. Overall command was given to Alexander. Churchill's first choice to take over 8th Army, against the advice of many, was General Gott; but Gott was shot down on August 7 on his way to Cairo. Churchill favoured Maitland-Wilson as a successor but he was persuaded to accept Montgomery instead. It may have been a reluctant decision but it was an important one.

Auchinleck relinquished command in the Middle East on August 15, 1942, apparently in disgrace, but it was Rommel himself who redeemed Auchinleck's reputation. He said later that 'Auchinleck was a very good leader . . . At Alamein, Auchinleck took the initiative himself and executed his operations with deliberation and noteworthy courage.'

Alexander and Montgomery took over in principle the existing plan of defence for 8th Army, which was to hold the line between El Alamein and Ruweisat Ridge in strength and to counter-attack from a prepared position on the Alam el Halfa Ridge. On his side, Rommel needed to make a last bid to break through to the Nile before his resources dwindled completely, while Montgomery built up his own resources for the battle of annihilation he planned to fight when the time was ripe. Meanwhile, Montgomery had his work cut out to consolidate his hold on the hearts and minds of his convalescent army and to plan meticulously for Rommel's forthcoming attack.

Montgomery had to face that attack within little more than two weeks of his new command. For once, 8th Army had resources and weapons to match the Afrika Korps and the Italians. Rommel's plan was similar to that which had proved so successful in earlier battles: a holding attack in the north and a southern sweep round the end of the defensive line to attack the Alam Halfa Ridge from the south-east (see map). He attacked on the night of August 30–31. Initially he made a break through the Allied lines but then he ran into 7th Armoured Division and was compelled to turn north earlier than he wished. It was 22nd Armoured Brigade, at the western end of the Alam Halfa Ridge, who subsequently received the brunt of Rommel's attack. Although XV Panzer Division succeeded in working round the flank of 22nd Armoured Brigade to stop a link up between 22nd and 8th Armoured Brigades, it was finally stopped by the tanks on Alam Halfa Ridge and by a lack of fuel.

Insufficient supplies of fuel were Rommel's undoing at Alam Halfa. On September 2, Rommel was forced to withdraw to the line between El Taqa and Bab el Qattara, constantly harassed by Allied air attacks. The New Zealand Division, in the centre, attempted a counter-attack on September 3–4 but was withdrawn and Montgomery risked no further counter-attacks. Once again, the opposing fronts settled down and Rommel himself dug in to a defensive line in depth.

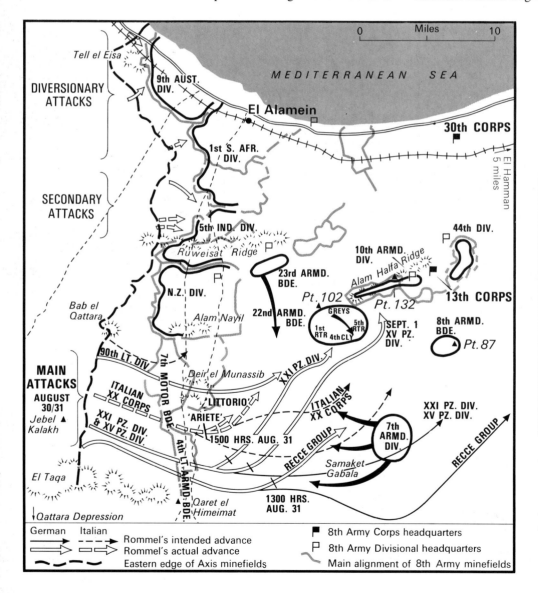

Above: Axis infantry finding it hard work in soft, windswept sand. They made only a few attacks. Once again, the main assault was undertaken by Rommel's armour.
Left: Rommel repeated his successful tactics from Gazala: a diversionary attack in the north and a southern flank attack. This time, he was stopped.

Allied armour awaiting attack.

Inset: Long-range desert raiders, sent out in September 1942 against Tobruk, Benghazi and Barce, were a costly failure, but reminded Rommel that his enemy could be daring as well.

The Battle of El Alamein

Montgomery was determined not to launch his own attack on Rommel until he had absolute superiority, especially in armour and in the air. In the seven weeks between Alam Halfa and El Alamein, 8th Army was well-rested, carefully trained and supplied with weapons and equipment superior both in quantity and quality to those of the Axis. Moreover, the Allied troops knew from experience now that the enemy was not invincible.

On the eve of El Alamein, the Allies had 195,000 men against 50,000 Germans and 54,000 Italians; they had 1,029 tanks against 489 German and Italian tanks; they had 2,311 guns against 1,219 Axis guns; they had 750 aircraft (530 serviceable) against 675 Axis aircraft (350 serviceable). The Axis had been carefully led to expect an attack in the south from 13th Corps and the DAK was split, with XV Panzer Division in the north and XXI Panzer Division in the south. Rommel himself was in hospital in Germany when the battle opened and General Stumme was in command. Stumme died of a heart attack on the opening day and was replaced by Thoma. Rommel did not return until October 25, the second day of the battle.

Montgomery launched his direct attack on the night of October 23–24, 1942, preceded by a 1,000-gun artillery barrage (map 1). Twenty minutes later, 30th Corps advanced to push two corridors through the minefields into the enemy lines to the north, while 13th Corps began a diversionary attack to the south. By dawn on October 24, most of the units of 30th Corps had reached their destinations on the Oxalic Line and the armoured divisions of 10th Corps were advancing down the two corridors (map 2). The Italians resisted stubbornly and XV Panzer Division mounted a counter-attack. The advance along both corridors was held up.

Montgomery switched his attack to the extreme north on October 26, sending 9th Australian Division to cut the coast-road behind the enemy lines (map 3). This forced Rommel to concentrate his reserves in the north. The continuous tank battle that raged in this area for almost a week took a heavy toll of the Axis forces. Meanwhile, Montgomery withdrew front-line units to create a reserve with which he intended to make his final push. His first plan had been to use 10th Corps to break through in the north but he decided against this when German reinforcements advanced along the coast-road. Instead, he chose to attack by Kidney Hill.

Operation Supercharge was launched on November 2 (map 4), with two infantry brigades followed by 9th Armoured Brigade, which suffered heavy casualties, and 1st Armoured Division. By that evening Rommel had decided to retreat but was forbidden to do so by Hitler. He finally withdrew on the night of November 3–4, with heavy losses, leaving the Italians to crumble before the Allied attack. The tables had turned at last but Montgomery failed to follow up his victory with a swift annihilation, as many believed that he should have done.

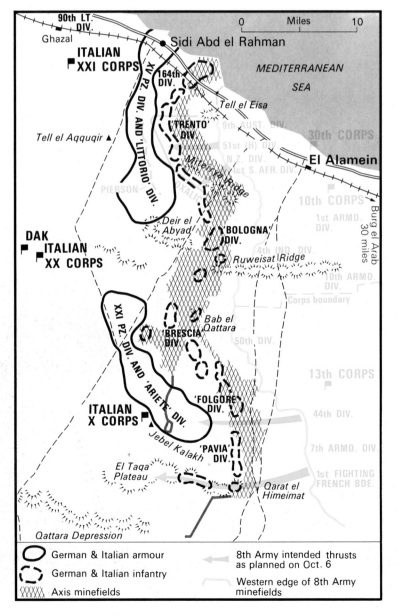

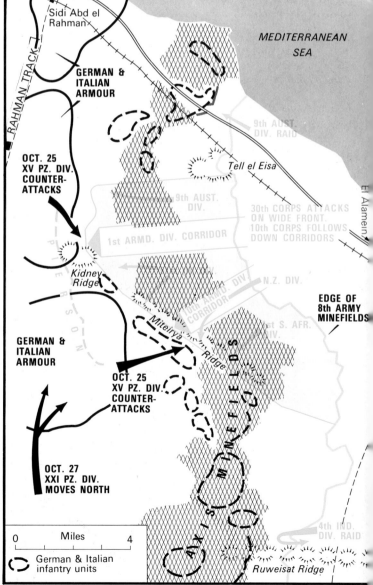

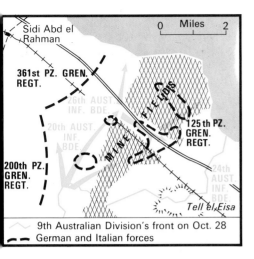

Sidi Abd el Rahman

361st PZ. GREN. REGT.

125 th PZ. GREN. REGT.

200th PZ. GREN. REGT.

MINE FIELDS

Tell el Eisa

Miles 0 2

〰 9th Australian Division's front on Oct. 28
- - - German and Italian forces

Opposite page, left: (1) October 23–24. 13th Corps makes a diversionary attack in the south, while 30th Corps opens up two corridors through the enemy minefields in the north, to reach the Oxalic Line. Pierson had been the original objective for the armour of 10th Corps advancing through the corridors.

Opposite page, right: (2) The two armoured divisions of 10th Corps were held by determined Italian resistance as well as a counter-attack by German and Italian armour. Despite this, Montgomery continued to attempt to push through the southern of the two corridors.

Above: (3) The thrust in the extreme north by 9th Australian Division, which attempted to reach the sea and forced Rommel to commit his reserves in the north.

Right: (4) Operation Supercharge was Montgomery's breakthrough attack, which began in the early hours of November 2 and by November 4 was assured of success.

Below: During the savage fighting in 30th Corps sector, the crew of one of Rommel's precious Panzers surrenders to a British infantryman.

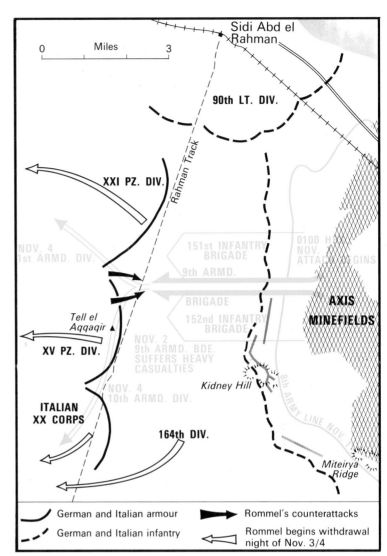

Sidi Abd el Rahman

90th LT. DIV.

XXI PZ. DIV.

NOV. 4
1st ARMD. DIV.

Rahman Track

151st INFANTRY BRIGADE

9th ARMD.

0100 H
NOV.
ATTACK BEGINS

Tell el Aqqaqir

BRIGADE

152nd INFANTRY BRIGADE

AXIS MINEFIELDS

XV PZ. DIV.

NOV. 2
9th ARMD. BDE. SUFFERS HEAVY CASUALTIES

Kidney Hill

8th ARMY LINE NOV.

NOV. 4
10th ARMD. DIV.

ITALIAN XX CORPS

164th DIV.

Miteirya Ridge

Miles 0 3

⌒ German and Italian armour   ► Rommel's counterattacks
- - - German and Italian infantry   ⇦ Rommel begins withdrawal night of Nov. 3/4

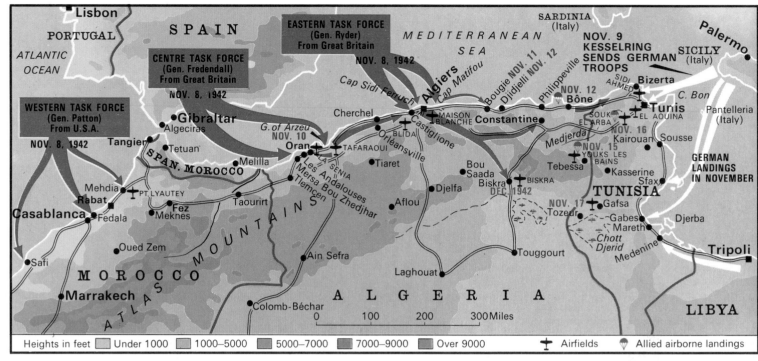

Heights in feet ▢ Under 1000 ▢ 1000–5000 ▢ 5000–7000 ▢ 7000–9000 ▢ Over 9000 ✈ Airfields ⛳ Allied airborne landings

Above: (1) Operation Torch, November 8, 1942. The three-pronged Allied landings had hardly established themselves before the Germans responded by landing their own troops from Sicily to form a strong bridgehead in Tunisia.

Operation Torch

Four days after Montgomery's victory at El Alamein, a co-ordinated attack was launched by American and British forces in French North Africa. There had been several political problems before the plan was perfected. The Americans had pressed for an early landing in France and it had taken determined British arguments to promote landings in North Africa that would eventually enable them to invade the 'soft underbelly' of Europe. Secondly, it was not known how the French themselves in North Africa would react, fearing perhaps to antagonize the Germans in case the invasion failed, yet wishing to offer help to the Allies to speed their own liberation. The majority of the invasion force was American, since it was decided that the Americans would be more welcome to the French than the British.

This was the largest amphibious landing of the war thus far and involved long preliminary sea voyages. The Western Task Force (35,000 men in 39 vessels sailing directly from America)

landed at Casablanca under Patton. The Central Task Force (39,000 men in 47 vessels) was also American but had sailed from Great Britain to Oran. The Eastern Task Force (33,000 men in 34 vessels) contained British elements and landed at Algiers. The landings were perfectly co-ordinated for the morning of November 8, 1942 (map 1). All three met varying degrees of resistance but on November 9 Admiral Darlan of the French forces ordered a cease-fire, after being taken into protective custody. Although this was countermanded by the Vichy Government, most of the French forces obeyed.

The Germans reacted to the invasion with surprising speed. Kesselring sent troops from Sicily on November 9 to hold Tunisia (map 2), which was vital to Rommel's retreat. Despite Allied parachute drops ahead of the advancing army under General Anderson, the Germans were able to establish a strong bridgehead. Anderson's 1st Army had hoped to link up quickly with 8th Army heading west in pursuit of Rommel, but Anderson was too slow and his attacks were piecemeal.

A race developed to seize the major airfields. With attacks and counter-attacks on both sides, a front line was established by December that ran from Bou Arada in the south through Medjez el Bab and Sidi Nsir and past Sedjenane. By this time, 1st Army had outrun its supply lines and lacked impetus.

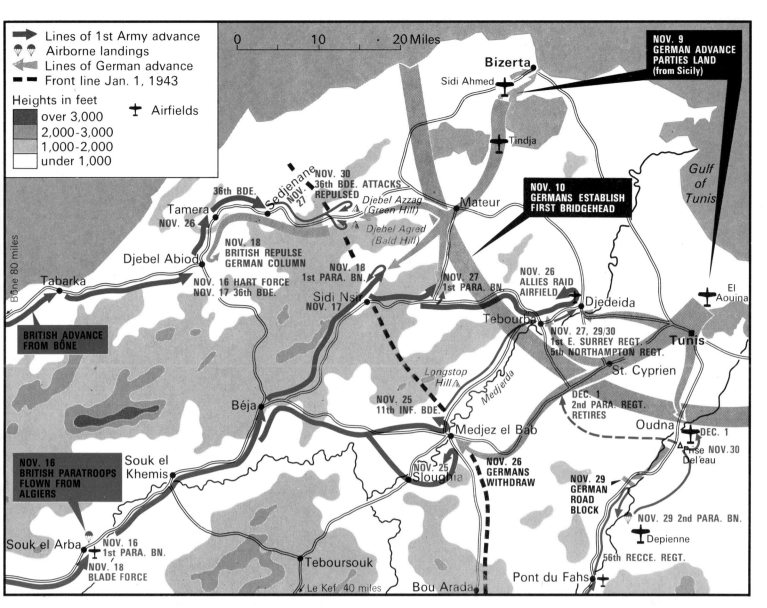

Legend:
- → Lines of 1st Army advance
- ⌄⌄ Airborne landings
- ← Lines of German advance
- - - Front line Jan. 1, 1943

Heights in feet
- over 3,000
- 2,000-3,000
- 1,000-2,000
- under 1,000

✝ Airfields

0   10   20 Miles

NOV. 9 GERMAN ADVANCE PARTIES LAND (from Sicily)

Bizerta
Sidi Ahmed
Tindja
Mateur

NOV. 10 GERMANS ESTABLISH FIRST BRIDGEHEAD

Gulf of Tunis

El Aouina

Bône 80 miles

36th BDE.
Tamera
NOV. 26
Sedjenane NOV. 27
NOV. 30 36th BDE. ATTACKS REPULSED
Djebel Azzag (Green Hill)
Djebel Agred (Bald Hill)

NOV. 18 BRITISH REPULSE GERMAN COLUMN

Djebel Abiod
NOV. 18 1st PARA. BN.

Tabarka
NOV. 16 HART FORCE
NOV. 17 36th BDE.

Sidi Nsir
NOV. 17

NOV. 26 ALLIES RAID AIRFIELD
Djedeida

NOV. 27 1st PARA. BN.

Tebourba

BRITISH ADVANCE FROM BÔNE

Tunis

NOV. 27, 29/30 1st E. SURREY REGT. 5th NORTHAMPTON REGT.

St. Cyprien

Longstop Hill

Medjerda

DEC. 1 2nd PARA. REGT. RETIRES

Béja
NOV. 25 11th INF. BDE.

Medjez el Bab

Oudna   DEC. 1
Prise NOV. 30
Del'eau

NOV. 16 BRITISH PARATROOPS FLOWN FROM ALGIERS

Souk el Khemis

NOV. 25
Sloughia
NOV. 26 GERMANS WITHDRAW

NOV. 29 GERMAN ROAD BLOCK

NOV. 29 2nd PARA. BN.
Depienne

Souk el Arba
NOV. 16 1st PARA. BN.
NOV. 18 BLADE FORCE

Teboursouk

56th RECCE. REGT.

Le Kef 40 miles   Bou Arada   Pont du Fahs

Above: (2) German reaction to Operation Torch was faster than any of the Allied planners had anticipated. Allied parachute drops required back-up from Anderson's 1st Army if they were to succeed but 1st Army strength did not arrive in time. After initial successes, the Allies were held back by the Germans and a stalemate had been reached by the end of the month. The hoped-for link with 8th Army was delayed by several months.

Below: Allied forces move out from the coast into Algeria after French resistance came to an end following Admiral Darlan's call to lay down arms. The Admiral had been caught unexpectedly on a private visit to Algiers. His controversial co-operation with the Allies brought the condemnation of the Vichy Government and resulted in his own assassination on December 24, 1942, but it helped to smooth the Allied landings.

Above: Axis artillery in Tunisia, December 1942. The Allies were surprised by the swift build up of heavy equipment.

Above: A German tank knocked out during the thrust for Medjez el Bab at the end of November 1942.

The Battle of Kasserine

While Operation Torch had been landing the Allies in French North Africa, Rommel had been withdrawing west in front of the advancing 8th Army. Once safely behind the Mareth Line, to the south of the Gulf of Gabès, Rommel needed to remove the threat from the 1st Army in his rear before having to face Montgomery on the Mareth Line itself (see next page). His immediate plan was to cut through the 1st Army to reach the sea at Bône (map 1). In turn, Anderson's 1st Army needed to break through to the Gulf of Gabès to split Rommel's Afrika Korps from von Arnim's V Army farther north.

There were clashes on December 6 and December 22–25, 1942, towards the north at Longstop Hill (map 2) and farther south in the second half of January. The Axis gained control of the major passes through the Eastern Dorsal preparatory to their planned attack in the south once Rommel was clear of

Below: Crusaders of 17–21st Lancers near Kzar Mezouar. The Allies found manoeuvring difficult in the hilly countryside.

Mareth. This attack began early on February 14, 1943, with a double blow by von Arnim to take Sidi Bou Zid (map 3). US 1st Armoured Division counter-attacked on February 15, but failed to retake Sidi Bou Zid. On the same day, Rommel struck Gafsa and headed north to Feriana. By February 18, both Kasserine and Sbeitla were in Axis hands. Allied counter-attacks were only piecemeal.

On February 19, Rommel advanced towards Le Kef, expecting support from von Arnim which did not come. Rommel probed north to Sbiba, Thala and Tebessa against increasing Allied resistance, while von Arnim withdrew to a defensive position farther north. At this point, Alexander assumed control of the Allied forces and forbade any further retreat from the Western Dorsal. He moved units of 6th Armoured Division south to hold the line, just in time to thwart a breakthrough. By February 22, Rommel had decided to retire to his Mareth position. On February 25, the Allies recaptured Kasserine and Sidi Bou Zid. Rommel had been beaten back but the Allies had been badly shaken.

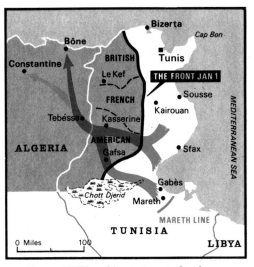

Above: (1) *The ultimate targets for the offensive by Rommel and von Arnim in the third week of February 1943.*

Right: (3) *The Battle of Kasserine, which rattled the Allies and showed that Rommel retained some of his old skills.*

Below: (2) *The Axis captured Longstop Hill in December 1942 and pinned the Allies down with a series of attacks in January.*

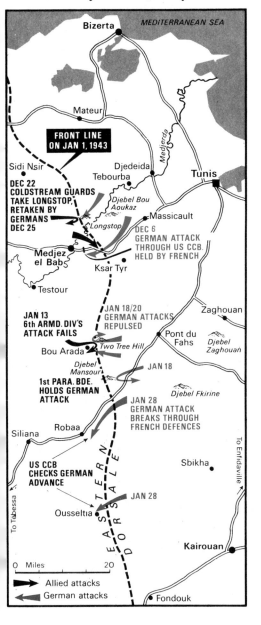

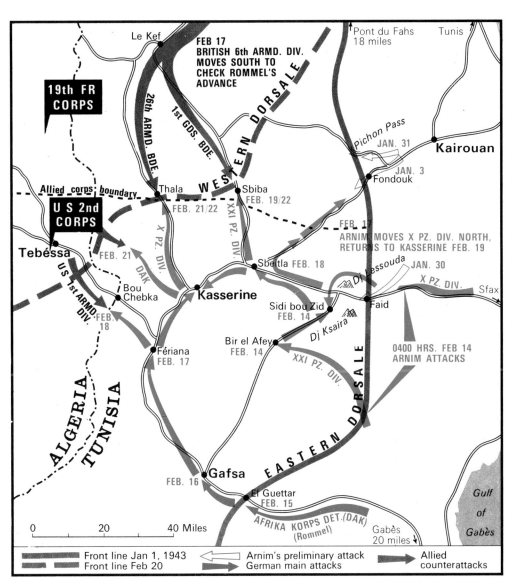

Below: *A Valentine tank captured and used by the Axis, then recovered by the Allies at Thala.*

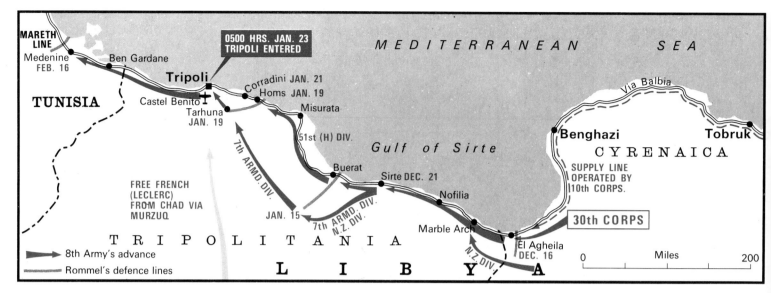

Breaking the Mareth Line

The steady pace of Montgomery's advance from El Alamein to Medenine had been frustrating for those who hoped to destroy Rommel's Afrika Korps before it reached Tunisia (map 1) but Montgomery was taking no chances. He forced Rommel to withdraw from El Agheila on December 16, 1942, by a long desert flanking attack and a similar flanking movement flushed Rommel out of Buerat on January 15, 1943. The advance guard of 8th Army entered Tripoli in the early morning of January 23.

Allied troops crossed into Tunisia on February 4 and reached Medenine by February 16. Rommel then turned his attention from 1st Army to 8th Army and on March 6 watched for the last time as his Afrika Korps went into action against Montgomery's prepared positions (map 2). Launching his main

attack in the centre, he sent X Panzer Division to attack farther south but he was twice repulsed with the loss of one-third of his tanks.

After his failure at Medenine, Rommel relinquished command of the Afrika Korps and returned to Germany, a sick man. The Mareth Front was taken over by General Messe. Meanwhile Alexander kept von Arnim guessing as to where the next blow would fall, from east or west. On March 17, US 2nd Corps opened an offensive on Gafsa and took the town. On March 20, Montgomery opened his own offensive on the Mareth Line.

Montgomery launched his main attack on the Mareth Line itself, while the New Zealand Corps made a long-range flanking attack on the Tebaga Gap (map 3). As planned, 50th Division achieved a bridgehead across the Wadi Zigzaou on March 20 but by March 22 the division had been badly savaged by a counter-attack by XV Panzer Division (map 4). Meanwhile the New Zealand Corps was being held by XXI Panzer Division and 164 Light Division at Tebaga.

At this point, Montgomery decided to change the direction of his main attack from the Mareth Line to Tebaga Gap. On March 23, 1st Armoured Division began to arrive at Tebaga Gap, while 4th Indian Division prepared for a short hook through the Matmata Hills. On the night of March 26, the Allies breached Tebaga Gap in the wake of a barrage of fire from both ground and air. Outflanked, the Axis managed to hold the Allies long enough in the El Hamma Plain to escape and to pull their forces back to the Wadi Akarit. Skill and brute force had won the day but not for the first time the battle had proved to be inconclusive.

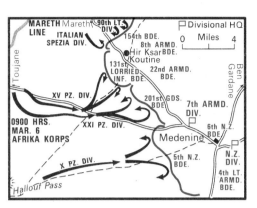

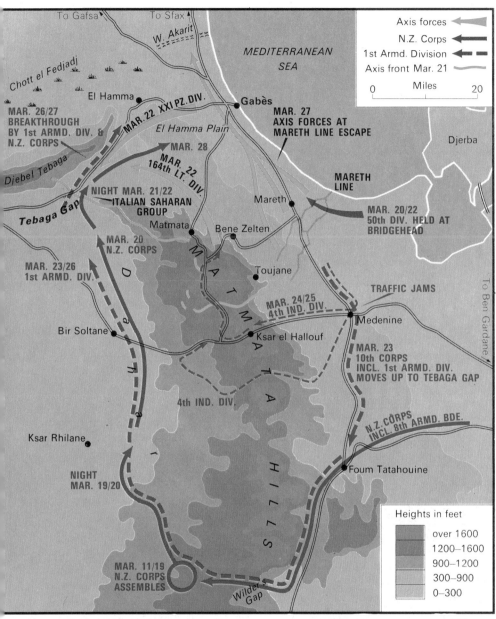

Above: (3) The Mareth Line ran from the sea to the foothills of the Matmata Hills. Montgomery sent the New Zealand Corps on a long detour through Wilder's Gap into the desert to make a diversionary attack through Tebaga Gap, which eventually became the main focus of the assault.

Top right: (2) Rommel spread his forces too widely for his attack on Medenine and ran straight into the Allied artillery barrage.

Centre right: (4) The Wadi Zigzaou formed a natural barrier on which were based the main defences of the Mareth Line. 50th Division forced a bridgehead after bitter fighting but were nearly destroyed by XV Panzer Division.

Bottom right: Men of 8th Army move slowly forward during an action against Rommel's retreating army.

Victory in Africa

With the breaking of the Mareth Line, the scene was set for the final confrontation in North Africa. On April 5–6 the Axis defences on the Wadi Akarit were breached by 4th Indian Division (map 1) but through hesitation on the part of 8th Army HQ the Axis forces slipped away once again.

To the north, 1st Army was recovering from the battle for the Kasserine Pass and preparing for a breakout into the Tunisian Plain. There was fierce fighting for important vantage points at several places along the line. On February 26, Axis forces in the centre thrust along the Sidi Nsir valley towards Beja (map 2) and over-ran Allied units at Sidi Nsir after bitter fighting. They reached Hunt's Gap on February 27 but were repulsed during the next two days and finally withdrew on March 2. On March 27, the Allies replied with an attack on Fondouk Pass by US 34th Infantry Division but this attack faded out under heavy artillery fire. On April 7, 9th Corps began a major attack on the pass (map 3) and broke through to take the town of Kairouan but no great advance was made.

On April 19–20, 8th Army launched an attack on Enfidaville but made little progress. Once again, the emphasis swung north. On April 20–21, an Axis spoiling attack on 1st Army positions between Goubellat and Medjez el Bab was repulsed with heavy losses. Then 1st Army built up the pressure (map 4). British 5th Corps advanced to capture the hills around Longstop and Peter's Corner and moved on Tunis through Massicault. US 2nd Corps attacked towards Mateur through Hill 609 and The Mousetrap. British 9th Corps attacked towards the Goubellat Plain. Encountering stiff resistance, Alexander then moved 7th Armoured and 4th Indian Divisions from 8th Army to 9th Corps to prepare for the final breakthrough.

US 2nd Corps successfully broke through in the north to threaten Mateur, while farther south, fighting with renewed vigour, the Allies captured Djebel Bou Aoukaz on May 5. Supported by heavy bombing, 6th and 7th Armoured Divisions advanced on Tunis, which fell on May 7 (map 4). US 2nd Corps took Bizerta the same day. 6th Armoured Division then made a decisive drive from Hammam Lif on May 8 to Hammamet, at the heart of the Axis final defences. Axis resistance had virtually ceased by May 11 and on May 13 Messe surrendered. More than 250,000 prisoners were taken.

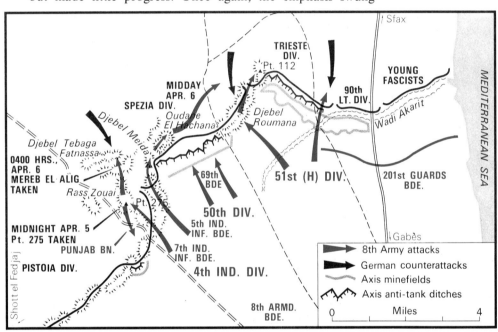

Above: (1) Wadi Akarit, also known as the Battle of Gabès, April 5–6, 1943. The successful advance made by 4th Indian Division and the advance of 51st Highland Division offered a chance to eliminate the southernmost of the Axis armies defending Tunis. Once again the potential advantage was not followed through and many of those involved felt a deep sense of frustration.

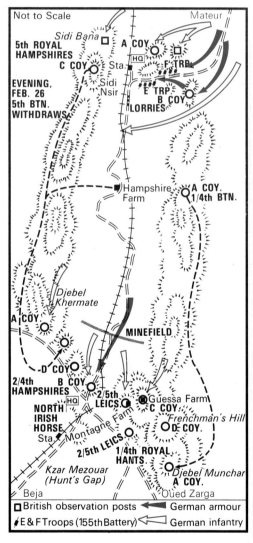

Above: (2) Axis thrusts towards Sidi Nsir and Hunt's Gap at the end of February and in the first days of March 1943.

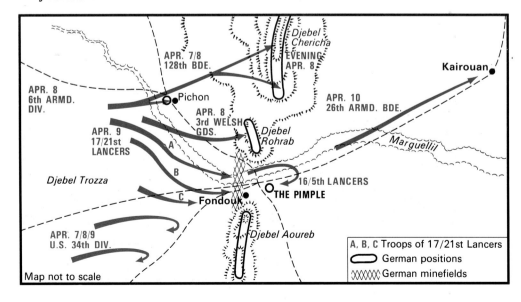

Left: (3) The Allied attack on Fondouk, which took the town of Kairouan in early April 1943.

Above: Sherman tank of 1st Army, immaculately turned out, in contrast to the Shermans of 8th Army, whose camouflage and casual appearance betrayed their hard slog through Libya.

Below: (4) The last few days of April saw a major offensive by the Allies against Axis strongpoints that barred their way. They were halted by determined resistance until help came from 8th Army units sent north by agreement between Montgomery and Alexander.

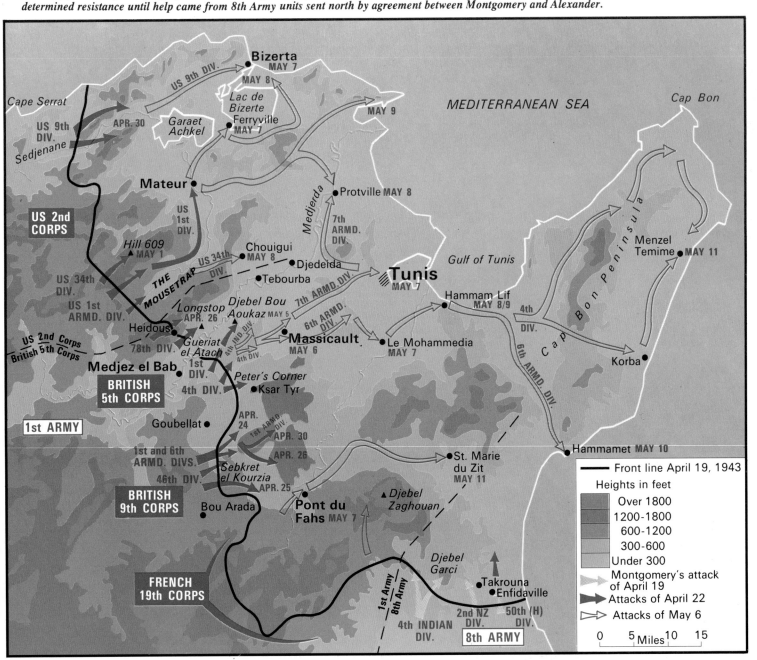

Cape Serrat

US 9th DIV.

Bizerta MAY 7

MAY 8

MAY 9

Lac de Bizerte

US 9th DIV. Sedjenane

APR. 30

Garaet Achkel

Ferryville MAY 7

MEDITERRANEAN SEA

Cap Bon

Mateur

Medjerda

Protville MAY 8

7th ARMD. DIV.

US 1st DIV.

US 2nd CORPS

Hill 609 MAY 1

THE MOUSETRAP

US 34th DIV.

Chouigui MAY 8

Djedeida

Tebourba

7th ARMD. DIV.

Tunis MAY 7

Gulf of Tunis

Menzel Temime MAY 11

US 34th DIV.

US 1st ARMD. DIV.

Longstop APR. 26

Heidous

Djebel Bou Aoukaz MAY 5

6th ARMD. DIV.

Hammam Lif MAY 8/9

4th DIV.

US 2nd Corps / British 5th Corps

78th DIV.

Gueriat el Atach

4th IND DIV

Massicault MAY 6

4th DIV.

Le Mohammedia MAY 7

6th ARMD. DIV.

Korba

Medjez el Bab

1st DIV.

BRITISH 5th CORPS

4th DIV.

Peter's Corner Ksar Tyr

1st ARMY

Goubellat

APR. 24

1st ARMD DIV

APR. 30

APR. 26

St. Marie du Zit MAY 11

Hammamet MAY 10

1st and 6th ARMD. DIVS.

46th DIV.

Sebkret el Kourzia

APR. 25

BRITISH 9th CORPS

Bou Arada

Pont du Fahs MAY 7

Djebel Zaghouan

FRENCH 19th CORPS

Djebel Garci

Takrouna Enfidaville

1st Army / 8th Army

2nd NZ DIV.

50th (H) DIV.

4th INDIAN DIV.

8th ARMY

— Front line April 19, 1943

Heights in feet

Over 1800

1200-1800

600-1200

300-600

Under 300

Montgomery's attack of April 19

Attacks of April 22

Attacks of May 6

0   5 Miles 10   15

63

The War in Italy

American strategy preferred to concentrate on an assault on the coast of France but since this was not possible in 1943 the Americans were persuaded by the British to attack from North Africa through Sicily to Italy. The Axis had been deceived into expecting only a feint at Sicily with a major attack in Sardinia, from which they believed the Allies would attack northern Italy from the Gulf of Genoa.

The landings on Sicily began on July 10, 1943, and, thanks mainly to the poor state of Italian morale, went largely unopposed. The Italian Badoglio Government made overtures to the Allies on July 28 but these were at first ill-received because of the American determination to enforce unconditional surrender. The chaos that eventually resulted from the Italian surrender enabled the Germans to take control of the situation and strongly resist the Allies in Italy.

Despite criticisms of the Italian campaign, it served several purposes and for a time was the largest Allied campaign being waged in Europe. It tied down many German divisions and thereby deprived Hitler's Russian front of vital reinforcements. It also enabled the Allies to encourage partisan movements in the Balkans and Yugoslavia. Unfortunately, the campaign was hindered by having to take second place to preparations for the Normandy landings in 1944.

The Landings in Sicily and Southern Italy

This great amphibious operation (8 divisions compared to 5 in Normandy) was preceded by aerial bombardment of Pantelleria, Sicily, Sardinia and southern Italy. Operation Husky began on July 10, 1944 (map 1). US 7th Army under Patton landed in the Gulf of Gela while Montgomery's 8th Army landed in the Gulf of Syracuse. The Italians were largely taken by surprise but German divisions counter-attacked on July 11–12. Patton worked his way round the western end of Sicily, while Montgomery worked up the east coast. It was Patton who won the race to Messina, on August 17, but by then more than 100,000 Axis soldiers had escaped to the mainland, with most of their equipment and weapons.

The Allies planned three assaults on the mainland (map 2). *Baytown* carried the main weight of 8th Army across the Straits of Messina on September 3, the same day on which the Armistice with Italy was signed (map 4). *Slapstick* bore further 8th Army units to Taranto on September 9. On the same day, *Avalanche* landed General Mark Clark's US 5th Army at Salerno (map 3). But here the Germans were ready and heavy counter-attacks almost dislodged the Americans. It was not until September 18 that they managed to consolidate their beach-head. The Germans withdrew towards the Gustav Line.

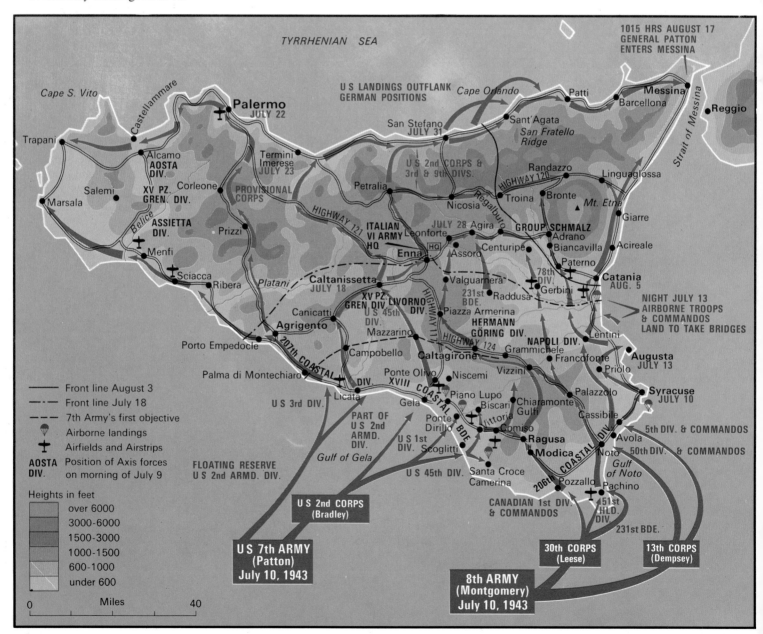

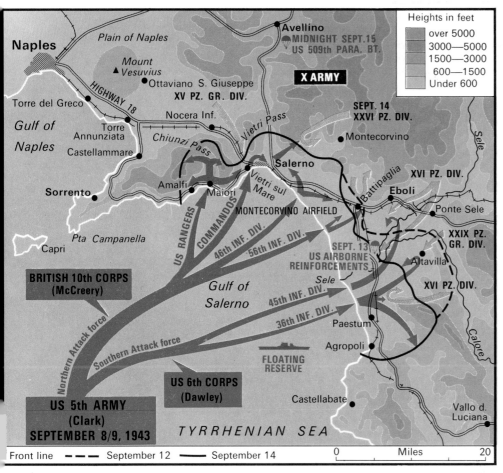

Naples

Plain of Naples

Avellino

MIDNIGHT SEPT.15
US 509th PARA. BT.

Mount Vesuvius

Ottaviano S. Giuseppe

X ARMY

XV PZ. GR. DIV.

Torre del Greco

Nocera Inf.

SEPT. 14
XXVI PZ. DIV.

Gulf of Naples

Torre Annunziata

Chiunzi Pass

Montecorvino

Castellammare

Vietri Pass

Heights in feet
over 5000
3000—5000
1500—3000
600—1500
Under 600

Salerno

Amalfi

Sorrento

Vietri sul Mare

Maiori

Battipaglia

XVI PZ. DIV.

Eboli

MONTECORVINO AIRFIELD

Ponte Sele

Pta Campanella

Capri

SEPT. 13
US AIRBORNE REINFORCEMENTS

Sele

Altavilla

XXIX PZ. GR. DIV.

BRITISH 10th CORPS
(McCreery)

Gulf of Salerno

46th INF. DIV.

56th INF. DIV.

45th INF. DIV.

36th INF. DIV.

XVI PZ. DIV.

Paestum

Calore

Agropoli

FLOATING RESERVE

US 6th CORPS
(Dawley)

Castellabate

Vallo d. Luciana

US 5th ARMY
(Clark)
SEPTEMBER 8/9, 1943

TYRRHENIAN SEA

Front line — – – September 12 —— September 14

0 Miles 20

YUGOSLAVIA

ITALY

Corsica (French)

ADRIATIC SEA

Rome

Bari

Naples

Salerno

Brindisi

Sardinia

TYRRHENIAN SEA

Taranto

From Oran

Palermo

Reggio

Bizerta

Sicily

AVALANCHE
US 5th ARMY

BAYTOWN
8th ARMY

Tunis

SLAPSTICK
8th ARMY

TUNISIA

Malta

MEDITERRANEAN SEA

0 Miles 100

LIBYA Tripoli

Above: (2) The plan for the three-pronged thrust at the Italian mainland. Baytown and Slapstick met little resistance but Kesselring was ready for Avalanche.

Left: (3) The near-disastrous landings at Salerno on September 9. Mark Clark's US 5th Army had not reckoned on Kesselring's lightning redeployment of his troops and the stubborn German resistance.

Above: Montgomery and Patton, in command of British 8th Army and US 7th Army respectively in the assault on Sicily. They became unofficial rivals in the race to seize Messina in the north-east corner of the island.

Left: (1) Operation Husky, the invasion of Sicily, July 10, 1943. It was originally intended that 8th Army should be the 'sword' to cut through to Messina while 7th Army warded off German attacks. But Montgomery ran into much greater opposition than he had expected and it was Patton who achieved a classic armoured thrust across the island and reached Messina first on August 17.

Right: (4) Kesselring was eventually forced to withdraw from Salerno in the face of reinforcements for Clark's beleaguered army and the threat posed by 8th Army to the south and east.

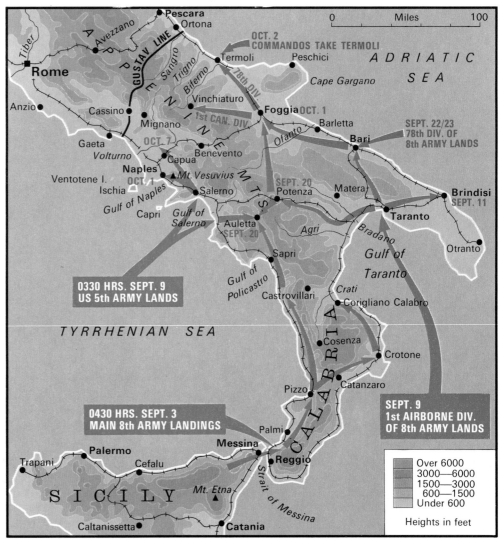

0 Miles 100

Pescara

Ortona

Tiber

Avezzano

GUSTAV LINE

Sango

Trigno

OCT. 2
COMMANDOS TAKE TERMOLI

Termoli

Peschici

ADRIATIC SEA

Rome

Cassino

Biferno

Vinchiaturo

78th DIV.

Cape Gargano

Anzio

Mignano

1st CAN. DIV.

Foggia OCT. 1

SEPT. 22/23
78th DIV. OF 8th ARMY LANDS

Gaeta

OCT. 7

Volturno

Capua

Benevento

Ofanto

Barletta

Bari

Brindisi
SEPT. 11

Ventotene I.

Naples
OCT. 1

Mt. Vesuvius

SEPT. 20

Potenza

Matera

Ischia

Salerno

Gulf of Naples

Capri

Gulf of Salerno

Auletta
SEPT. 20

Agri

Taranto

Bradano

SEPT. 20

Sapri

Gulf of Taranto

Otranto

Castrovillari

Crati

Corigliano Calabro

0330 HRS. SEPT. 9
US 5th ARMY LANDS

Gulf of Policastro

TYRRHENIAN SEA

Cosenza

Crotone

Trapani

Palermo

Cefalu

Pizzo

Catanzaro

0430 HRS. SEPT. 3
MAIN 8th ARMY LANDINGS

Palmi

Messina

Reggio

SEPT. 9
1st AIRBORNE DIV.
OF 8th ARMY LANDS

Strait of Messina

S I C I L Y

Mt. Etna

Over 6000
3000—6000
1500—3000
600—1500
Under 600

Caltanissetta

Catania

Heights in feet

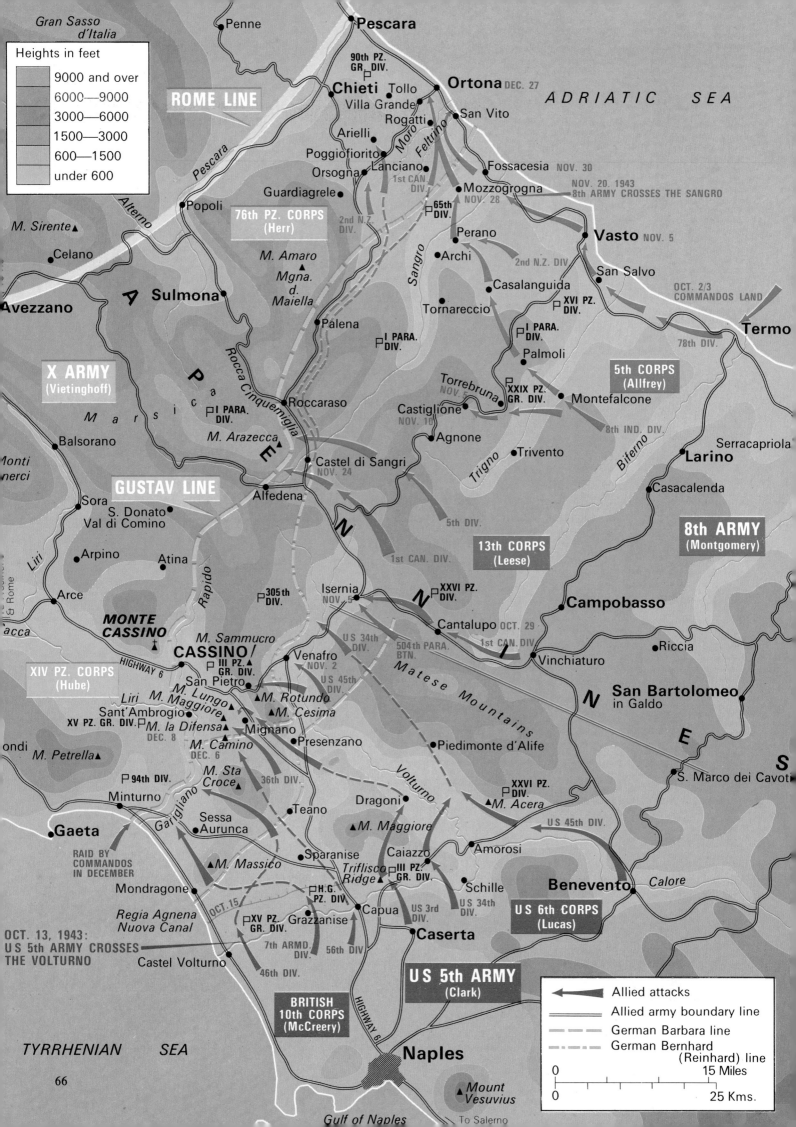

Gran Sasso
d'Italia

Heights in feet

	9000 and over
	6000—9000
	3000—6000
	1500—3000
	600—1500
	under 600

Penne
Pescara

ROME LINE

90th PZ.
GR. DIV.
Chieti   Tollo
Villa Grande
Rogatti
Arielli
Poggiofiorito
Orsogna   Lanciano
Guardiagrele
Popoli

76th PZ. CORPS
(Herr)

2nd N.Z.
DIV.

M. Amaro

Mgna.
d.
Maiella

Palena

I PARA.
DIV.

M. Sirente
Celano

Sulmona
Avezzano

M. Amaro

ADRIATIC SEA

Ortona   DEC. 27

San Vito

Moro   Feltrino

1st CAN.
DIV.

Fossacesia   NOV. 30
NOV. 20, 1943
8th ARMY CROSSES THE SANGRO
Mozzogrogna
NOV. 28

65th
DIV.

Perano
Archi

Sangro

Casalanguida

2nd N.Z. DIV.

Vasto   NOV. 5
San Salvo

XVI PZ.
DIV.

OCT. 2/3
COMMANDOS LAND

Termo

I PARA.
DIV.

Palmoli

5th CORPS
(Allfrey)

Montefalcone

78th DIV.

Tornareccio

Torrebruna
NOV. 5

XXIX PZ.
GR. DIV.

8th IND. DIV.

X ARMY
(Vietinghoff)

Balsorano

Sora
S. Donato
Val di Comino
Arpino
Atina
Arce

Rocca Cinquemiglia

Roccaraso

I PARA.
DIV.

M. Arazecca

GUSTAV LINE

Castel di Sangri
NOV. 24
Alfedena

Castiglione
NOV. 10

Agnone

Trivento

Biferno

Serracapriola

Larino

Casacalenda

8th ARMY
(Montgomery)

13th CORPS
(Leese)

5th DIV.

1st CAN. DIV.

Isernia
NOV. 5

XXVI PZ.
DIV.

Cantalupo   OCT. 29
1st CAN. DIV.

Campobasso

Riccia

Vinchiaturo

San Bartolomeo
in Galdo

S. Marco dei Cavoti

305th
DIV.

MONTE
CASSINO

M. Sammucro
HIGHWAY 6   CASSINO
III PZ.
GR. DIV.
San Pietro
Liri   M. Lungo
M. Maggiore
Sant'Ambrogio
XV PZ. GR. DIV.   M. la Difensa
DEC. 8
M. Camino
DEC. 6

M. Petrella

94th DIV.

Minturno

Gaeta

RAID BY
COMMANDOS
IN DECEMBER

XIV PZ. CORPS
(Hube)

Rapido

US 34th
DIV.
Venafro
NOV. 2
US 45th
DIV.

M. Rotundo
M. Cesima
Mignano
Presenzano

504th PARA.
BTN.

Matese Mountains

Piedimonte d'Alife

Volturno

Dragoni

M. Sta
Croce   36th DIV.

M. Maggiore

Teano
Sessa
Aurunca

M. Massico

Sparanise

Caiazzo

Amorosi

Triflisco
Ridge   III PZ.
GR. DIV.

Schille

XXVI PZ.
DIV.
M. Acera

US 45th DIV.

Benevento   Calore

US 6th CORPS
(Lucas)

Mondragone

OCT. 15

H.G.
PZ. DIV.

XV PZ.
GR. DIV.   Grazzanise

Capua

US 3rd
DIV.

US 34th
DIV.

Caserta

OCT. 13, 1943:
US 5th ARMY CROSSES
THE VOLTURNO

Castel Volturno

7th ARMD.
DIV.   56th DIV.

46th DIV.

BRITISH
10th CORPS
(McCreery)

HIGHWAY 6

Naples

US 5th ARMY
(Clark)

TYRRHENIAN   SEA

66

Regia Agnena
Nuova Canal

Mount
Vesuvius

Gulf of Naples

To Salerno

◄━━	Allied attacks
	Allied army boundary line
– – –	German Barbara line
–·–·–	German Bernhard (Reinhard) line

0   15 Miles
0   25 Kms.

Kesselring Stands at the Gustav Line

Hitler originally favoured Rommel's plan, to make a stand in the northern Apennines with Army Group B (map 1) but in late November, 1943, Rommel was moved to France and Kesselring took command of the whole Italian theatre. His brilliantly flexible tactics forced the Allied advance to a miserable crawl.

Having reached Naples on October 2, the Allies halted on the Volturna-Termoli line. Mark Clark's 5th Army advanced on October 12 and the next day started the painful crossing of the Volturna, swollen by autumn rains, its bridges destroyed by the retreating Germans (map 2). Progress beyond the river was no faster, in the roadless, rain-sodden mountains. To the east, Montgomery's 8th Army advanced on October 22 and forced the Trigno. Meanwhile Kesselring was strengthening the Gustav Line (10 miles wide in places), which ran behind the Garigliano and Rapido in the west and behind the Sangro in the east. This line was held by Vietinghoff's X Army. On November 15, Alexander halted the Allied advance to rest and regroup.

Clark's 5th Army faced the strongest part of the line, the mountains and Monte Cassino. He resumed his offensive on November 20 but ran into stiff resistance, snow, ice and tough terrain. By the end of the year, he was still five miles south of the Rapido. In the east, Montgomery forced a crossing of the Sangro, broke through the Gustav Line and reached Ortona on December 27. He was replaced by Leese and sent to join Eisenhower to prepare for the offensive in the west.

Above: (1) Kesselring and Rommel disagreed on where to make a stand.

Left: Sherman of British 7th Armoured Division reaches the north bank of the River Volturna.

Opposite: (2) Autumn 1943, the Allied advance to the Gustav Line.

Below left: The German X Army stopped the Allies again and again.

Below: Kesselring performed a brilliant defence.

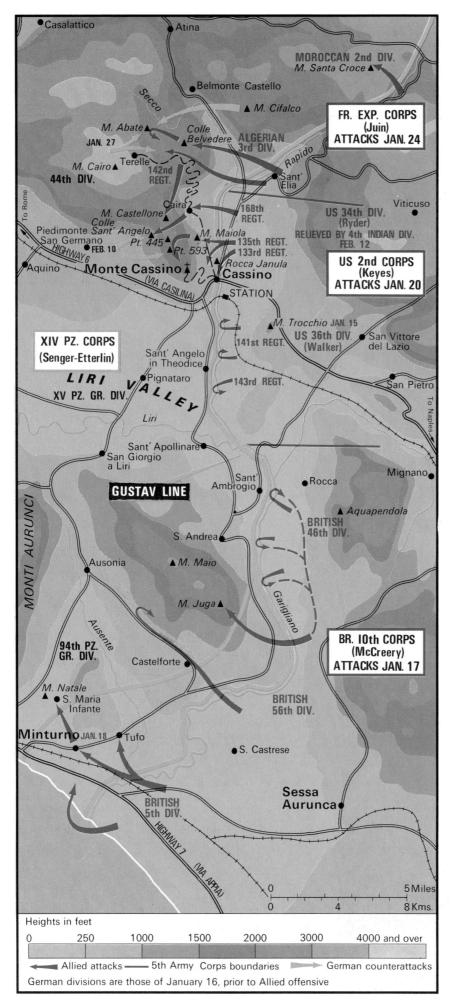

Casalattico
Atina
MOROCCAN 2nd DIV.
M. Santa Croce ▲

Belmonte Castello
▲ M. Cifalco

Secco
M. Abate ▲   Colle
JAN. 27   Belvedere   ALGERIAN
                             3rd DIV.
M. Cairo ▲ Terelle   Rapido
44th DIV.   142nd   Sant'
            REGT.   Elia

FR. EXP. CORPS
(Juin)
ATTACKS JAN. 24

Caira   168th   Viticuso
M. Castellone ▲   REGT.
Colle   US 34th DIV.
Piedimonte Sant' Angelo ▲   (Ryder)
San Germano Pt. 445 M. Maiola   RELIEVED BY 4th INDIAN DIV.
HIGHWAY 6   FEB. 10 ▲ Pt. 593   135th REGT.   FEB. 12
Aquino   133rd REGT.

US 2nd CORPS
(Keyes)
ATTACKS JAN. 20

Monte Cassino ✝   Rocca Janula
(VIA CASILINA)   Cassino
                        STATION

XIV PZ. CORPS
(Senger-Etterlin)

M. Trocchio JAN. 15
141st REGT.   US 36th DIV.   San Vittore
              (Walker)   del Lazio

Sant' Angelo
in Theodice
Pignataro   143rd REGT.

L I R I *V A L L E Y*
XV PZ. GR. DIV.
                                          San Pietro
Liri

Sant' Apollinare
San Giorgio
a Liri   Sant'   Rocca   Mignano
                         Ambrogio
GUSTAV LINE
                                         ▲ Aquapendola
                         S. Andrea   **BRITISH**
                                         46th DIV.

MONTI AURUNCI
                ▲ M. Maio
Ausonia

                M. Juga ▲

Ausente   Garigliano
94th PZ.
GR. DIV.
                                  BR. 10th CORPS
M. Natale   Castelforte **(McCreery)**
S. Maria   **ATTACKS JAN. 17**
Infante
                                  BRITISH
Minturno JAN. 18 Tufo   **56th DIV.**

                    S. Castrese

                              Sessa
                              Aurunca
BRITISH
5th DIV.
            HIGHWAY 7 (VIA APPIA)

0   5 Miles
0   4   8 Kms.

Heights in feet

0   250   1000   1500   2000   3000   4000 and over

◄── Allied attacks ── ── 5th Army Corps boundaries ──► German counterattacks

German divisions are those of January 16, prior to Allied offensive

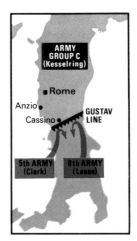

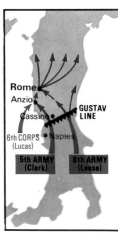

ARMY
GROUP C
(Kesselring)
■ Rome
Anzio
Cassino   GUSTAV
                 LINE
5th ARMY   8th ARMY
(Clark)   (Leese)

■ Rome
Anzio
Cassino   GUSTAV
                 LINE
6th CORPS   ● Naples
(Lucas)
5th ARMY   8th ARMY
(Clark)   (Leese)

Above left: (1) By the end of December 1943, the Allies were halted in front of the Gustav Line.

Above right: (2) In January 1944, Clark and Alexander prepared for a frontal assault on the Cassino sector in combination with a seaborne hook to sever the German rear. Anzio was intended to be a short cut to Rome.

Left: (3) The assault on the Gustav Line and Monte Cassino began in mid-January. Initial advances made by the French to the east and the British to the west were brought to a halt, while US 2nd Corps came to a disastrous stop against the German defences in the centre.

Below: French Goums under Juin crossed the Rapido and struck into the mountains north of Cassino at the opening of the January offensive.

Right: US 5th Army bombardment smashes the heights above the fast-disappearing town of Cassino but fails to dislodge the stubborn defenders. The heights controlled the avenues of attack.

Below: (4) March 15, 1944. The attack on Monte Cassino by 2nd New Zealand Division and 4th Indian Division was also halted.

Bottom: The frontal assaults on Cassino at first made only slow and bitter progress against determined German opposition.

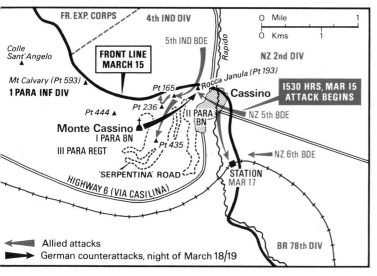

FR. EXP. CORPS
4th IND DIV
Colle Sant'Angelo
5th IND BDE
FRONT LINE MARCH 15
NZ 2nd DIV
Mt Calvary (Pt 593)
1 PARA INF DIV
Rocca Janula (Pt 193)
Pt 165
1530 HRS, MAR 15 ATTACK BEGINS
Cassino
Pt 236
Pt 444
Monte Cassino
I PARA BN
III PARA REGT
II PARA BN
NZ 5th BDE
Pt 435
NZ 6th BDE
'SERPENTINA' ROAD
STATION MAR 17
HIGHWAY 6 (VIA CASILINA)
BR 78th DIV
0 Mile 1
0 Kms 1

◄ Allied attacks
► German counterattacks, night of March 18/19

Stalemate at Monte Cassino

After their successful landings in southern Italy in September 1943, the Allies (and, in particular, Winston Churchill) had hoped to be in Rome by Christmas, but they were still behind the Gustav Line at the beginning of January 1944 (map 1). Alexander planned to break the western end of the Gustav Line by launching a frontal attack across the Rapido and Garigliano. At the same time he sought to distract German attention by an amphibious assault at Anzio (see page 72), to cut off German lines of communication and to prise the Germans loose from their defensive line (map 2). Had he been equipped with more landing craft (which were being assembled for the landings in France), he might have concentrated his main blow at Anzio. As it was, he seemed indecisive, and the Allies were blocked on both fronts.

The land battle for the Gustav Line began on January 17 (map 3). On the right, the French Expeditionary Corps crossed the Rapido and swung south to outflank Cassino. On the left, British 10th Corps secured a bridgehead across the Garigliano. But in the centre, US 2nd Corps came to a stop before the defences of Monte Cassino itself and the whole emphasis of the battle shifted to this point. Stalemate quickly developed (as it was doing at the Anzio beach-head). Ignoring German assurances that they were not using the Benedictine monastery of Monte Cassino as a fortress vantage point, the Allies bombed it into rubble, making an even better fortress of it. The bombing was followed by an unsuccessful attack by the New Zealand Corps between February 15 and 18.

On March 15, after another heavy barrage, yet another frontal assault was made by 2nd New Zealand Division and 4th Indian Division (map 4). This achieved some small success but was eventually frustrated in its attempts to encircle Cassino. By March 22, Alexander had at last decided to halt the frontal attacks on the German defences and began to look for other ways to break the stalemate.

The Fall of Monte Cassino

Alexander halted his unavailing frontal assaults and regrouped his forces after the failure of the attack in late March by the New Zealand and Indian Divisions. He opened his final offensive against Monte Cassino and the Gustav Line on May 11, 1944 (see map). This was launched on a 20-mile front from the sea to a point east of Monte Cassino, with US 2nd Corps on the left, the French to their right, the Canadians in the centre and the British and Poles on the right of the line ready to outflank the monastery.

The French Expeditionary Corps took Monte Faito on May 12 but the Poles were held at Colle Sant'Angelo in the Heights above Cassino. On May 13, the French advanced to Monte Maio and Castelforte and prepared to strike across the Monti Aurunci and to head for Rome. US 2nd Corps was held up at Santa Maria Infante but took the village on May 13. At the same time, the British widened their bridgehead across the Rapido.

By May 17, Kesselring realized that his position was already hopeless and he ordered a withdrawal. It fell to the Poles to seize the honour of capturing the shattered ruins of Monte Cassino on May 18. Shortly afterwards, Canadian 1st Corps reached Pontecorvo on the Adolf Hitler Line. The breakthrough was complete after five months of frustrating loggerhead.

Recently reinforced from the sea, 6th Corps broke out of its beach-head at Anzio on May 23. Two days later, the first units of US 2nd Corps made contact with 6th Corps and together they turned their attention towards Rome. It was paradoxical that the Cassino front had eventually come to the relief of the Anzio beach-head, since Alexander's original intention had been that it was the Anzio beach-head that should have relieved the pressure on the Cassino front. The Allies had paid a heavy price for their obsession with Monte Cassino. It was hardly surprising that now they wanted the propaganda victory of taking Rome.

Above: Throughout the battle for Cassino, the Allies came up against unexpectedly strong German resistance, even in the bombed-out ruins of the town.

Left: German propaganda in the form of leaflets dropped to Allied troops held up before Cassino. the mountains and valleys of 'Sunny Italy' wait to gobble up luckless British and American soldiers. The mountains took a heavy toll of Frenchmen, Canadians, Gurkhas and New Zealanders.

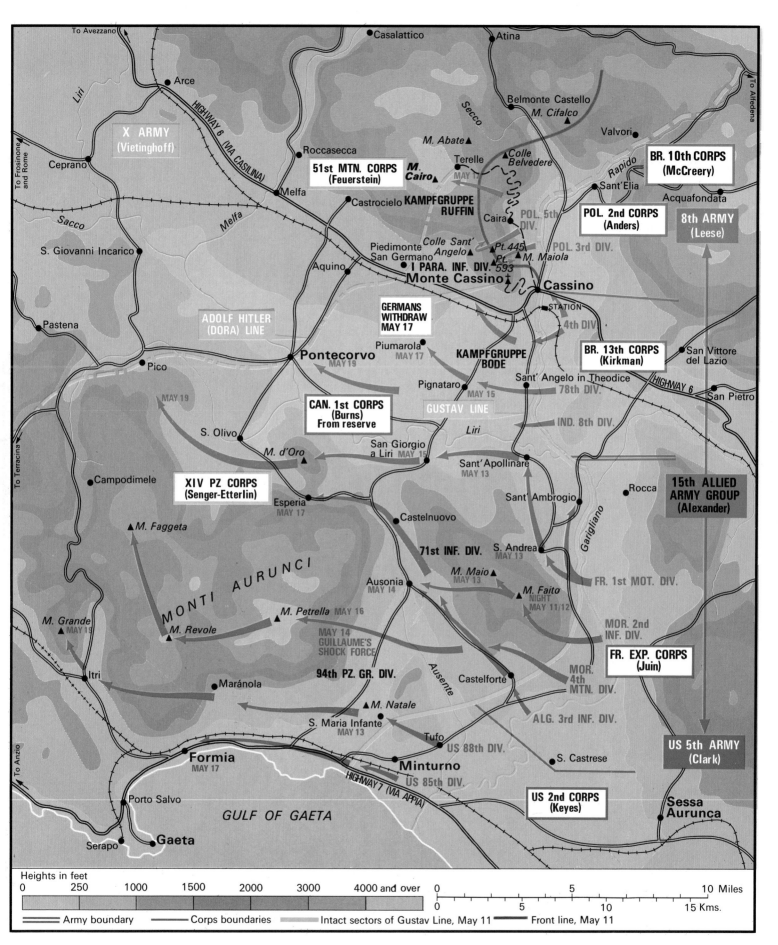

Map labels:

To Avezzano
Casalattico
Atina
Arce
Liri
Belmonte Castello
M. Cifalco
Secco
X ARMY (Vietinghoff)
Roccasecca
HIGHWAY 6 (VIA CASILINA)
M. Abate ▲
Valvori
Terelle
Colle Belvedere
BR. 10th CORPS (McCreery)
Ceprano
To Frosinone and Rome
M. Cairo ▲
MAY 17
Rapido
Sant'Elia
Melfa
51st MTN. CORPS (Feuerstein)
Castrocielo
KAMPFGRUPPE RUFFIN
Caira
POL. 5th DIV.
Acquafondata
POL. 2nd CORPS (Anders)
8th ARMY (Leese)
Sacco
Melfa
S. Giovanni Incarico
Piedimonte
Colle Sant' Angelo ▲
Pt. 445
POL. 3rd DIV.
San Germano
Aquino
I PARA. INF. DIV.
Pt. 593
M. Maiola ▲
Pastena
Monte Cassino ┼
Cassino
ADOLF HITLER (DORA) LINE
STATION
GERMANS WITHDRAW MAY 17
Piumarola MAY 17
4th DIV.
Pontecorvo MAY 19
KAMPFGRUPPE BODE
BR. 13th CORPS (Kirkman)
San Vittore del Lazio
Pico
Pignataro
Sant' Angelo in Theodice
78th DIV.
HIGHWAY 6
MAY 19
CAN. 1st CORPS (Burns) From reserve
MAY 15
San Pietro
GUSTAV LINE
Liri
IND. 8th DIV.
MAY 19
S. Olivo
San Giorgio a Liri MAY 15
Sant'Apollinare MAY 13
M. d'Oro ▲
Campodimele
XIV PZ CORPS (Senger-Etterlin)
Sant' Ambrogio
Rocca
15th ALLIED ARMY GROUP (Alexander)
Esperia MAY 17
Castelnuovo
Garigliano
M. Faggeta ▲
71st INF. DIV.
S. Andrea MAY 13
M. Maio ▲ MAY 13
FR. 1st MOT. DIV.
Ausonia MAY 14
M. Petrella MAY 16
M. Faito NIGHT MAY 11/12
M. Grande ▲ MAY 19
M. Revole ▲
MONTI AURUNCI
MAY 14 GUILLAUME'S SHOCK FORCE
MOR. 2nd INF. DIV.
Itri
94th PZ. GR. DIV.
Ausente
Castelforte
MOR. 4th MTN. DIV.
FR. EXP. CORPS (Juin)
Maránola
M. Natale ▲
ALG. 3rd INF. DIV.
S. Maria Infante MAY 13
Tufo
US 88th DIV.
S. Castrese
US 5th ARMY (Clark)
To Anzio
Formia MAY 17
Minturno
US 85th DIV.
Porto Salvo
HIGHWAY 7 (VIA APPIA)
US 2nd CORPS (Keyes)
Sessa Aurunca
GULF OF GAETA
Serapo
Gaeta

Heights in feet
0   250   1000   1500   2000   3000   4000 and over
0   5   10 Miles
0   5   10   15 Kms.

Army boundary   Corps boundaries   Intact sectors of Gustav Line, May 11   Front line, May 11

Above: There was a lull of more than six weeks, after the failure in March to take Monte Cassino by storm, before the Allies were once more ready to launch an offensive. The attack on May 11 opened up along the whole 20-mile front. Although at first it made slow progress on both flanks, there was a decisive breakthrough by the French in the *centre. By May 17, they had advanced 25 miles behind the German forward positions and threatened to cut off the German lines of communication. It was at this point that Kesselring was forced to order a retreat and the following day the Poles captured Monte Cassino.*

The Anzio Beach-head

The Anzio landings were meant to be part of the double attack that would break the Gustav Line in January 1944. They failed dismally. 'I had hoped that we would be hurling a wildcat ashore,' complained Churchill, 'but all we got was a stranded whale.'

Operation Shingle began on January 22 with every appearance of success (see map). US 6th Corps under Major-General Lucas began landing without opposition. Most troops were ashore within the next two days and a beach-head seven miles deep had been achieved, preparatory to an advance into the Alban Hills to cut German communications between Rome and Cassino. Then Lucas failed to move. Remembering the failure to establish a beach-head properly at Salerno, he dug in to wait for his tanks and heavy artillery. General Clark, in command of 5th Army, agreed with Lucas's decision.

Kesselring immediately improvised XIV Army under Mackensen, which quickly pinned 6th Corps to its beach-head. The Germans launched their counter-attack on February 16 and, although they were halted within a few days, they drove in the outlying units. Lucas was replaced by Truscott on February 23 and both sides settled down to a siege that lasted three grim months, during which the narrow beach-head was under continuous fire. Heavy casualties were suffered before reinforcements arrived in May and 6th Corps was able to break out to link with US 2nd Corps.

Below: German propaganda leaflet which capitalized on the Anzio setback.

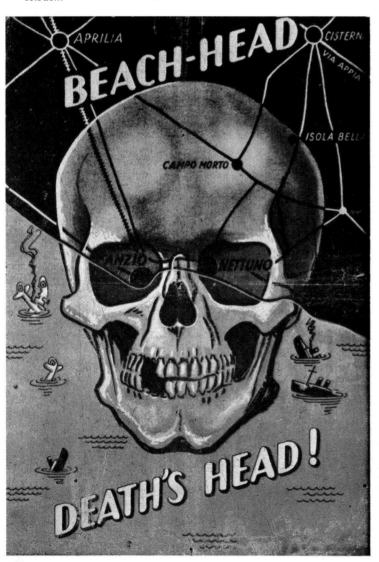

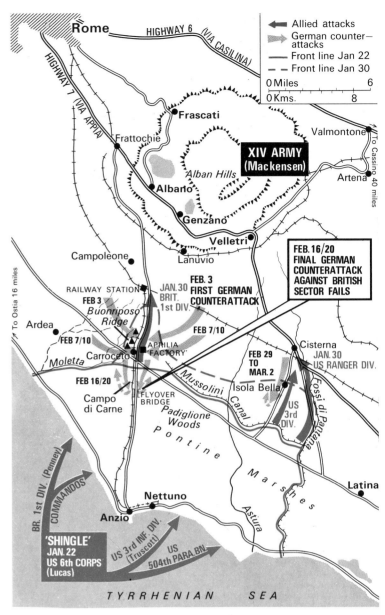

Above: Operation Shingle and the German counter-attack, January—February 1944.

Right: German remote-controlled Goliath demolition charge, used without great success against the Anzio beach-head.

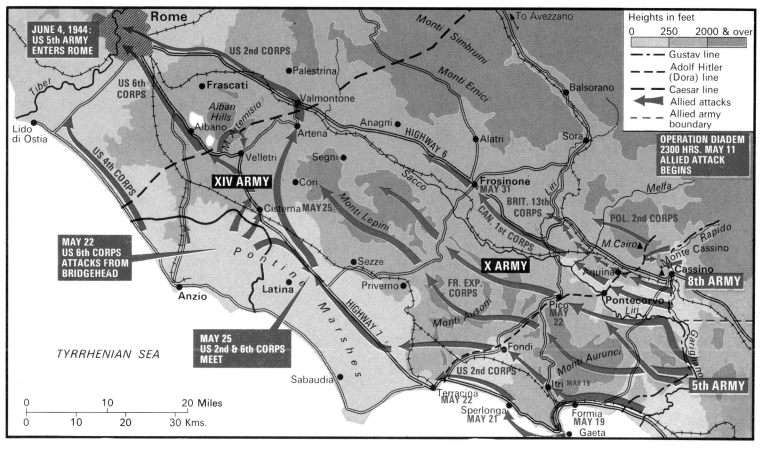

As 5th and 8th Armies advance beyond the Gustav Line, Clark ignores the opportunity to encircle the German X Army and turns north to reach Rome as quickly as possible. He entered the Italian capital 12 days after the breakout from Anzio.

The Race to Rome

After breaking out of the Anzio beach-head and finally breaching the Gustav Line, Mark Clark's US 5th Army could possibly have cut off the German X Army, commanded by Vietinghoff, if Clark had immediately swung eastwards. He did not do so, because he was more interested in the apparent glory of reaching Rome than in destroying the German army. Rome had little strategic value but, in the eyes of Clark and many others, enormous propaganda value. It was, after all, one of the Axis capitals and a symbol of what the Allies were fighting against, even if the Italians were no longer active.

The break-out from Anzio on May 23 took US 6th Corps to Cisterna on May 25 and on the same day elements of the US 6th and 2nd Corps met farther south on Highway 7 (see map). It was four months later than they were originally meant to have met. Having reached Cisterna, Clark then swung north towards Rome. Moving with their customary speed, the Germans were able to stall his advance and to dig in around Valmonte on the Caesar Line. It was not until the bulk of 5th and 8th Armies caught up that the Allies were able to break through the defences at Valmonte on May 30–31.

The delay had given Kesselring time to extricate X and XIV Armies intact from their perilous situation. Three days later he received Hitler's authorization to withdraw from Rome. The first Allied troops entered Rome on June 4, fulfilling Clark's ambition just two days before the Normandy landings. 'We had won the race to Rome by only two days,' said Clark later. 'Even while I stood there, Ike's army was embarking for Normandy.' It was a costly piece of propaganda, for Kesselring was now able to continue his delaying tactics on the Gothic Line, to which he carefully withdrew. On the other hand, the fall of the first Axis capital just before the Normandy landings did have great value for morale and the Allied spring offensive in Italy had undoubtedly succeeded in tying down German formations that might otherwise have been used on the Russian and western fronts.

Below: US armour passes the Colosseum as the first Axis capital falls to the Allies, June 4, 1944.

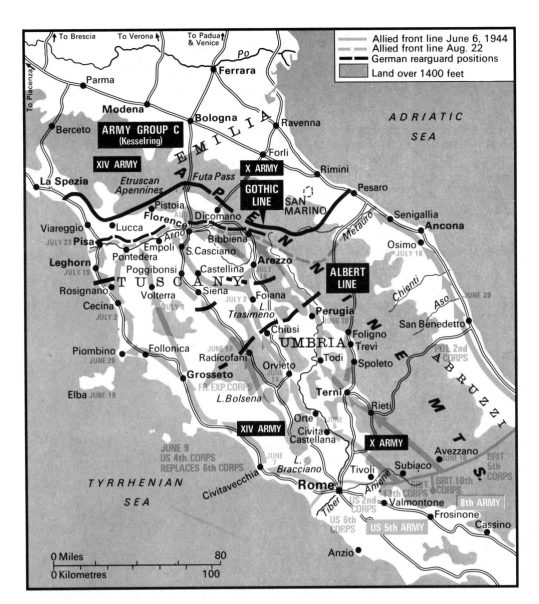

Map legend:
- Allied front line June 6, 1944
- Allied front line Aug. 22
- German rearguard positions
- Land over 1400 feet

Left: (1) The Germans fought an imaginative withdrawal from Rome to the Gothic Line, capitalizing on the limitations of the rigid advance on a broad front by the Allied armour. The hard slog up the Italian Peninsula was more difficult than many critics have imagined and, with the interest now in the Allied Front in France, 5th and 8th Armies inevitably felt less enthusiasm than a year before. It took two months of soul-destroying fighting against a determined enemy to work their way up to the River Arno and the Gothic Line.

Breaking the Gothic Line

Having forfeited one chance to destroy the German forces before entering Rome on June 4, US 5th Army forfeited a second chance by not immediately following on the heels of XIV Army, which was virtually in flight after the fall of Rome. Although Clark paused only briefly to set up defensive positions north and north-east of Rome, it was time enough to let the Germans slip away again to regroup.

The Allies showed a remarkable inability to take advantage of sudden opportunities. They seemed to prefer to stick to fixed plans and to rely on sheer force and a massive superiority in armour. Unfortunately, the awkward Italian terrain demanded greater flexibility and more imaginative use of infantry. The Germans were repeatedly able to hold the Allies with cleverly planned defensive lines. One other aspect hampered the Allies: although they enjoyed air superiority, their troops and the landing craft necessary for amphibious assaults along the coast were whittled down to mount the invasion of southern France (Operation Anvil, see page 126), while at the same time the Germans were bolstered by reinforcements from northern Europe, Germany and the Balkans.

During June and July, the Allies slogged their way up the Peninsula, penetrating the Albert Line and reaching the Arno at the end of July and beginning of August 1944 (map 1). Pisa was reached on July 23. Florence was entered on August 4. Meanwhile the Germans had managed to withdraw behind the Gothic Line without suffering one serious defeat, although their losses had been considerable both in men and materials.

On August 25–26, 5th Army crossed the Arno to attack the Gothic Line but the key to the German defences was seen to be on the right flank, where 8th Army under Leese prepared to attack inland from the coast with the intention of seizing the commanding positions, beyond the Gothic Line, of the Gemmano and Coriano Ridges. The attack was led by 5th Corps on August 30, with Canadian 1st Corps on its right (map 2). The Gothic Line itself proved less of an obstacle than was expected but beyond it the Germans resisted savagely to stop Leese's armour getting through to the plains. Alongside the withering fire poured down by the Germans, the rains began on September 6, and it was not until September 14, when Croce was taken, that the Germans were forced slowly to retire. They did so without giving the Allies any chance to gather momentum. It was another week before Rimini fell, on September 21.

To the west, US 5th Army had battled through the Gustav Line and, in the first three weeks of October, made a last bid to break through to Bologna before all efforts were thwarted by winter weather. The unsuccessful advance was halted on October 20 and the only further advance made that winter was by the British, who pushed their line to the Senio on the right. Alexander was now succeeded by Clark as commander of 15th Army Group. Truscott took over 5th Army and McCreery took over 8th Army from Leese. Alexander became Supreme Allied Commander in the Mediterranean.

Top: A British self-propelled gun climbs one of the interminable hills on the road to the Gothic Line.

Top right: Mortar fire on attacking Allied forces by German troops of X Army in one of their many defensive positions.

Above: The wreckage of a German Mark IV tank which had been backed into a house to provide a makeshift strongpoint. The Germans relied on a flexible and imaginative defence.

Above right: South Africans use a Bofors 40-mm anti-aircraft gun to provide ground support for an infantry assault.

Right: (2) The battle for the coastal gate, through which it was intended that the Allied armour should reach Rimini. Although the Gothic Line was breached with relative ease, the real battle took place over control of the Gemmano and Coriano Ridges, where the Allies were held up for nearly two weeks. This area saw some of the most savage fighting of the Italian campaign.

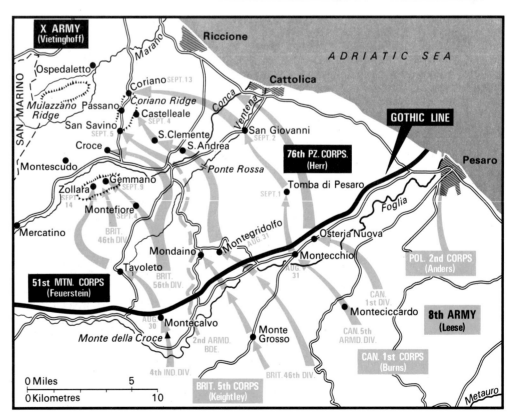

X ARMY (Vietinghoff)

Riccione

ADRIATIC SEA

Ospedaletto

Marano

Coriano SEPT.13

Cattolica

SAN MARINO

Mulazzano Ridge

Passano

Coriano Ridge

Castelleale

SEPT.5

Conca

Ventena

San Savino

SEPT.5

S.Clemente

San Giovanni

SEPT.2

76th PZ. CORPS. (Herr)

GOTHIC LINE

Croce

S.Andrea

Montescudo

Ponte Rossa

Pesaro

Zollara

Gemmano SEPT.9

SEPT.14

Montefiore

SEPT.1

Tomba di Pesaro

Foglia

Mercatino

BRIT. 46th DIV.

Montegridolfo

AUG.31

Osteria Nuova

POL. 2nd CORPS (Anders)

Mondaino

Montecchio

AUG.31

Tavoleto

BRIT. 56th DIV.

CAN. 5th ARMD. DIV.

51st MTN. CORPS (Feuerstein)

AUG.30

Montecalvo

Monte Grosso

Monteciccardo

8th ARMY (Leese)

CAN. 5th ARMD. DIV.

CAN. 1st CORPS (Burns)

Monte della Croce

2nd ARMD. BDE.

4th IND. DIV.

BRIT. 5th CORPS (Keightley)

BRIT. 46th DIV.

Metauro

0 Miles 5

0 Kilometres 10

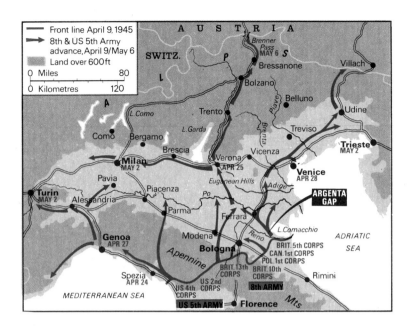

Front line April 9, 1945
8th & US 5th Army
advance, April 9/May 6
Land over 600ft
0 Miles 80
0 Kilometres 120

Above: (1) The Allied advance to the Alps in April, and the first week of May, 1945. This was the last offensive of the protracted and exhausting campaign, which concluded with the first well-planned and well-executed Allied attack.

Victory in Italy

After their failure to break through to Bologna at the end of 1944, the Allies began to retrain and re-equip themselves in preparation for a more carefully planned offensive in the spring of 1945. Kesselring was moved to the western front and Vietinghoff took over command of Army Group C. Hitler having refused him permission to withdraw behind the Po, he was busily occupied in strengthening the defences along his front.

With Alexander's support, Clark proposed a powerful double blow at the Axis defences (maps 1 and 2). McCreery's 8th Army would move forward first on the right and make its way through the Argenta Gap towards Ferrara. A few days later, Truscott's 5th Army would make their strike on the left against Bologna. This brief time-lapse between the two attacks would enable the overwhelming Allied air superiority to be used to best advantage, first in full support of the right and then in full support of the left.

On April 9, 1945, 8th Army began its assault, accompanied by heavy air and artillery strikes (map 2). It seemed that German X Army, commanded by Herr, was going to hold this attack, until X Army was disrupted by an amphibious assault across Lake Comacchio that threatened to envelop its left flank. Herr was forced to pull back and 8th Army moved forward through the Argenta Gap, south-east of Ferrara, and into the valley of the Po.

On April 14, again preceded by heavy air and artillery bombardment, 5th Army began their advance on the Allied left (map 2). Breaking into the Po valley by April 20, 5th Army occupied Bologna on April 21. Vietinghoff threw in his last reserves in an attempt to hold 5th Army but failed to do so. He was forced to make a hasty withdrawal. Although most of his forces managed to cross the Po safely, they had to abandon almost all their heavy equipment, weapons and armour. On the left, US 10th Mountain Division reached the Po on April 22 and, on the right, 8th Indian Division reached the river on April 23.

Without delay this time, both 5th and 8th Armies continued their advance north and west, towards Austria and France (map 1). Behind the retreating German lines, partisans captured Mussolini, who was trying to escape to Germany. They killed

Above: General Mark Clark in Rome, June 1944. The city was not of strategic value. There were still ten more months of weary fighting before the Germans were finally defeated in Italy.

Above: A GI of US 88th Division in the attack on Vicenza. The Allies fanned out after crossing the Po, expecting a last ditch stand by the Germans in the mountains.

Above: British troops pick their way through the ruins of Argenta. Once through the Argenta Gap, the Allies moved on to the Po valley and Ferrara.

him on April 28 but by that time his death was a matter of little importance to the outcome of the war. The following day, Vietinghoff agreed to unconditional surrender of the German troops in Italy. The surrender came into force on May 2. In that same first week of May, the Allies moved up into the Brenner Pass and made contact with units of 7th Army advancing from the north-west. At the same time, contact was made in the west with French troops. The victory in Italy was complete. Both Hitler and the Allies believed that the campaign had been an important drain on the other's resources. Whatever the merits of the case, it was clear that Mussolini's involvement in the war had been a disaster for his country.

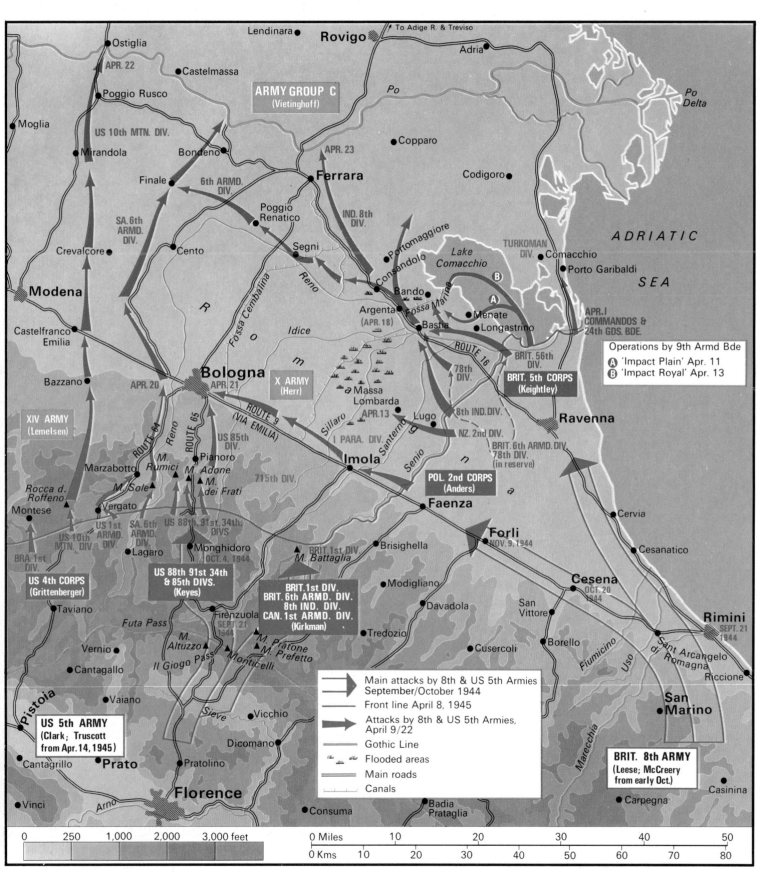

Above: (2) There was stalemate in the winter of 1944–45 but by spring 1945 the Allies were ready for their final offensive. The keys to their advance were the Argenta Gap and Bologna.

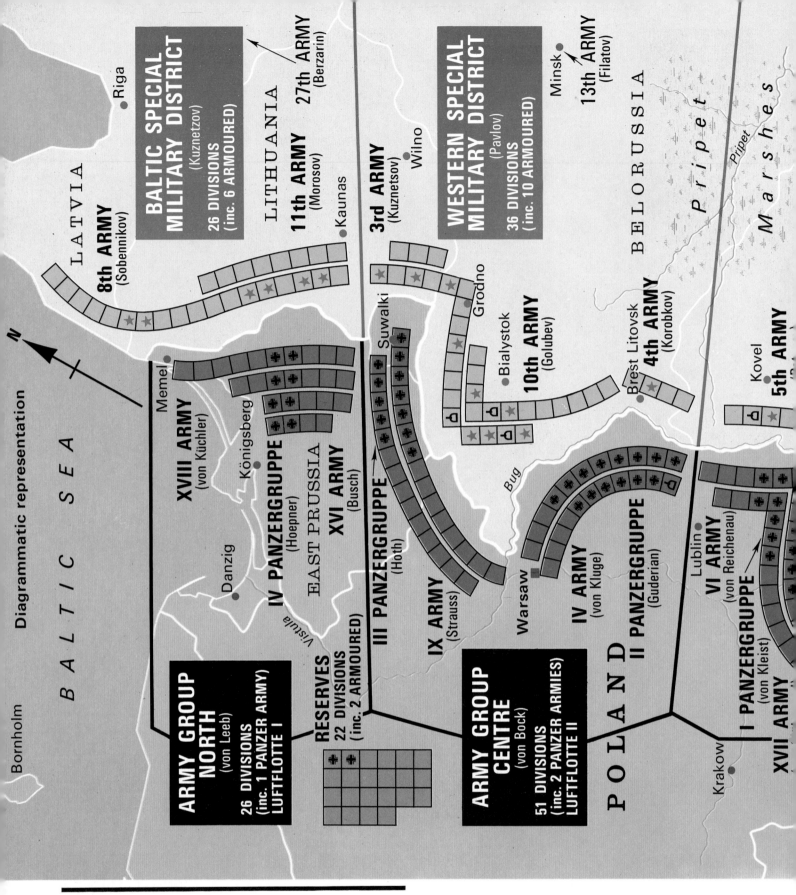

The Russian Front

Hitler's real ambitions for *Lebensraum* lay to the east, across the Carpathians, in the black soil of eastern Europe and southern Russia. He had been planning for the move since the late summer of 1940 and by the summer of 1941 he had amassed nearly three million men on Russia's western borders in preparation for the launching of Operation Barbarossa.

Stalin, too, had nearly three million at the front, with at least another million in immediate reserve and untold millions to

draw on as the war progressed. Right from the beginning, Hitler miscalculated the greatest Russian strength of all, sheer manpower, just as he ignored the lessons of history that should have taught him not to get caught by a Russian winter. But the Russians were weak at the outset of the war. Their forces were too far forward and too spread out to withstand a *Blitzkrieg* attack. Their equipment was not yet comparable in quality to that of the Germans. Their morale was low after Stalin's purges of the Soviet Officer Corps in 1937 and after their poor showing

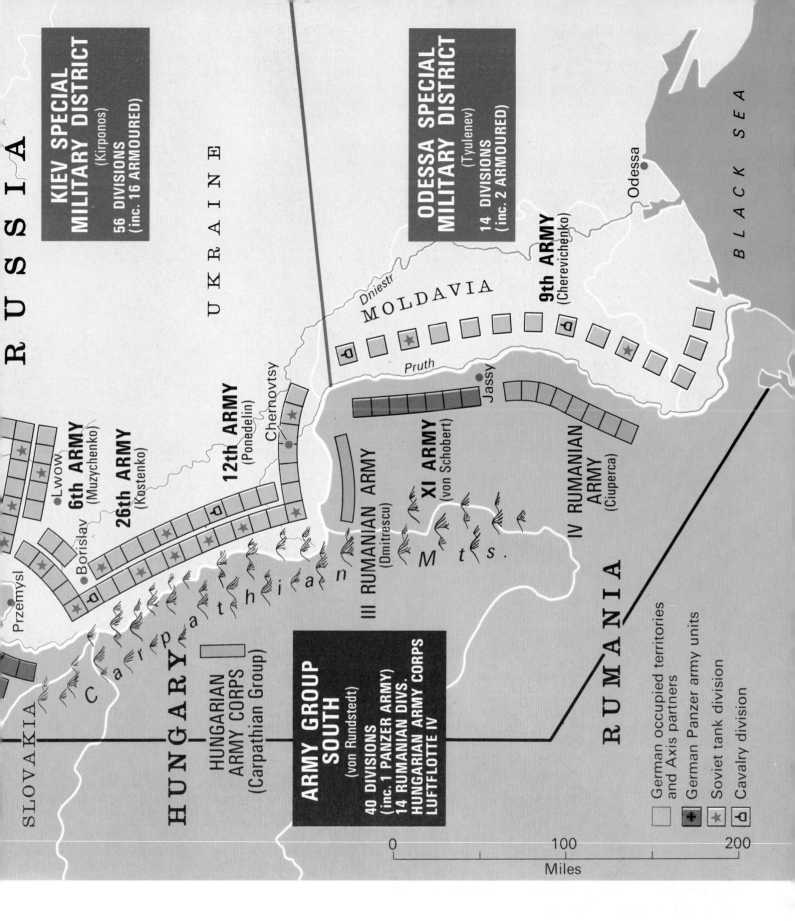

RUSSIA

KIEV SPECIAL MILITARY DISTRICT
(Kirponos)
56 DIVISIONS
(inc. 16 ARMOURED)

ODESSA SPECIAL MILITARY DISTRICT
(Tyulenev)
14 DIVISIONS
(inc. 2 ARMOURED)

BLACK SEA

Odessa

UKRAINE

Dniestr

MOLDAVIA

9th ARMY
(Cherevichenko)

Pruth

Jassy

Chernovtsy

6th ARMY
(Muzychenko)

Lwow

26th ARMY
(Kostenko)

Borislav

12th ARMY
(Ponedelin)

III RUMANIAN ARMY
(Dmitrescu)

XI ARMY
(von Schobert)

IV RUMANIAN ARMY
(Ciuperca)

M t s .

Przemysl

C a r p a t h i a n

RUMANIA

SLOVAKIA

HUNGARY

HUNGARIAN ARMY CORPS
(Carpathian Group)

ARMY GROUP SOUTH
(von Rundstedt)
40 DIVISIONS
(inc. 1 PANZER ARMY)
14 RUMANIAN DIVS.
HUNGARIAN ARMY CORPS
LUFTFLOTTE IV

German occupied territories
and Axis partners

German Panzer army units

Soviet tank division

Cavalry division

0   100   200
Miles

in the winter campaign against Finland of 1939–40.

Hitler's plan for Barbarossa was to make the major strikes against Leningrad and Moscow, north of the Pripet Marshes. A third strike, south of the marshes, was to reach Kiev through the Ukraine. Von Leeb commanded Army Group North and Leningrad was his target. Although his Panzer strength was less than that of the other two Army Groups, the enemy were badly placed to withstand the shock of his *Blitzkrieg* attack. Von Bock had the greatest number of Panzer formations and

responsibility for capturing Smolensk and opening the road to Moscow. He was provided with a perfect opportunity for a pincer movement with his Army Group Centre against the Soviet Bialystock salient in Belorussia. Von Rundstedt's Army Group South was to act in co-operation with the southern wing of Army Group Centre as required but also to make the approach to Kiev. The scene was set, from the Baltic to the Black Sea. Hitler was ready to march in the footsteps of Napoleon.

Barbarossa: Centre and South

Hitler invaded Russia on June 22, 1941, the 129th anniversary of Napoleon's crossing of the Niemen on a similar campaign. It was also the first anniversary of the signature of the French Armistice in the Forest of Compiègne. The attack achieved complete tactical surprise and the Chief of Army General Staff, Halder, believed that the Russian campaign would be finished within eight or ten weeks. Hitler had earlier suggested four months.

All three Army Groups attacked simultaneously along a 2,000 mile front. The advance in the north and centre was at once rapid but in the south, after an initial breakthrough, I Panzergroup encountered a determined counter-attack before reaching the outskirts of Kiev. Bock's Army Group Centre successfully pinched the Bialystok salient and sealed off the Soviet forces into containable pockets by the end of June (map 4). II and III Panzergroups met to the west of Minsk on June 29 and by July 9 had put an end to Soviet resistance in the Minsk pocket, taking nearly 300,000 prisoners, 2,500 tanks and 1,400 guns. They moved on immediately towards Smolensk (map 5). Panzers had crossed the Dniepr on July 10–11 and had broken through to Smolensk by July 16 but Soviet counter-attacks kept the trap from being completely shut.

In the south, despite fierce resistance from the directions of Korosten and Kazatin, Rundstedt had advanced to within 10 miles of Kiev by July 11 (map 6). As he prepared a pincer movement to cut off the Uman pocket and as Guderian prepared to complete the destruction of the Soviet forces at Smolensk, Hitler suddenly stepped in with a change of plan that in the long term proved fatal. Anxious to secure control of the raw materials and agricultural produce of the Ukraine and to reach the Crimea, Hitler disregarded Guderian's objections and stopped the eastward drive towards Moscow, ordering that the weaker flanks of the long front should be supported before the advance in the centre continued. II Panzergroup and II Army were ordered to turn south to support Rundstedt.

Guderian struck first at Roslavl, on August 3, to break up concentrations of the Soviet forces (map 7). By August 7, Soviet resistance in the Smolensk pocket had ended and on the same day Rumanian forces began the 73-day siege of Odessa (map 6). Two days earlier Rundstedt had completed his pincer grip on Uman by bringing together his forces at Pervomaisk (map 6). Russian resistance in the Uman pocket ended on August 8. On August 23, Guderian moved south through Gomel and Starodub (map 7), brushing aside belated Russian counter-attacks. Rundstedt crossed the Dniepr at the end of August and began moving north from Kremenchug and Cherkassy on September 12. The German forces met at Lokhvitsa on September 15, closing the trap on four Soviet armies in the Kiev pocket. Kiev itself fell on September 19 and Budenny's Southwest Group seemed shattered.

Evolution of the plan to conquer Soviet Russia.
Above left: (1) The Marcks Plan, August 5, 1940. The main drives were to be in the north through Belorussia and in the south towards Kiev. Flanking attacks along the Baltic and Black Sea were seen as subsidiary.

Above right: (2) The Halder Variant, December 5, 1940, added a third major thrust, to Leningrad. The Moscow drive was strengthened at the expense of the southern drive to Kiev. The 'final line' was to reach from Archangel to the Volga.

Left: (3) Hitler's Variant (Barbarossa), December 18, 1940. The emphasis shifted north. Leningrad became the prime target, with Moscow to follow. The southern operation was at first intended only to occupy the western Ukraine. It was important to all three variants that the Soviet forces should be destroyed along the front before they could withdraw into the interior.

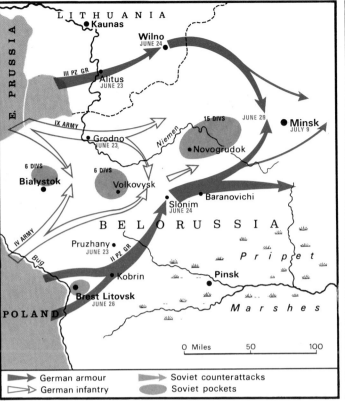

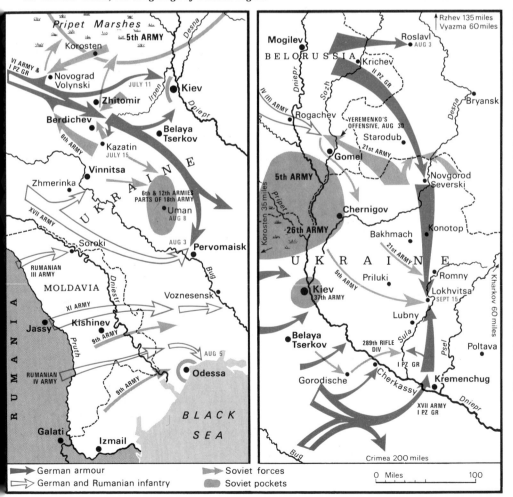

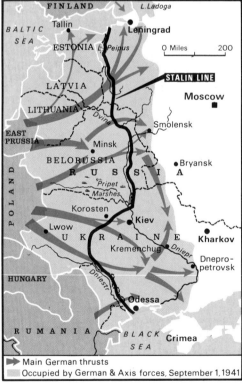

Above: (4) Army Group Centre devours the Bialystock salient, clears Belorussia, and quickly encompasses the Minsk pocket.

Above: (5) Army Group Centre moved on swiftly from Minsk towards Smolensk but was then ordered by Hitler to stop until the ring had been completely closed on Smolensk.

Below: (6) Army Group South met stiff resistance before reaching Zhitomir but then moved on towards Kiev and to surround Uman. In the extreme south, the long siege of Odessa began.

Below centre: (7) Ordered to move south, Guderian joined up with Rundstedt's Army Group South at Lokhvitsa, completely surrounding the Kiev Pocket.

Above: (8) The eastern front by the end of September 1941, well to the east of the Stalin defence line. In the north, the Germans had begun bombarding Leningrad and Barbarossa seemed on the way to triumph. But the Soviets were not yet eliminated and winter was setting in.

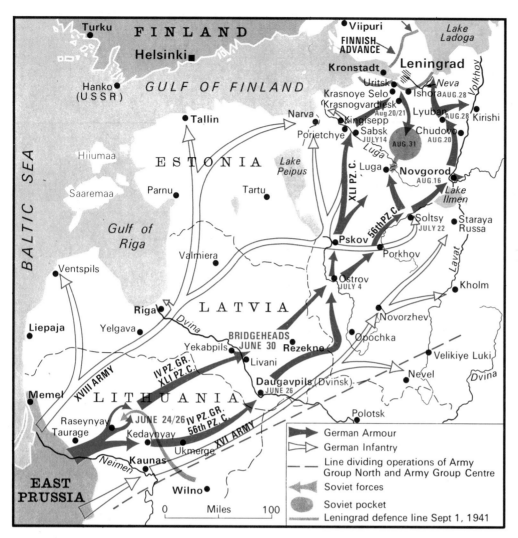

Above: Field Marshal von Leeb, commander of Army Group North during the Barbarossa offensive of 1941.

Below: (2) Having set his heart on the capture of Leningrad, Hitler decided to leave it encircled by Army Group North, to be starved into submission, while his main forces were concentrated farther south. He never imagined (nor did anyone else) that the besieged city would hold out for 900 days until finally relieved.

Above: (1) Barbarossa and Army Group North, from June to September 1941. Army Group North achieved a remarkable advance over great distances in a short time, only to be slowed down when almost within reach of its objective and finally brought to a halt outside the walls of Leningrad.

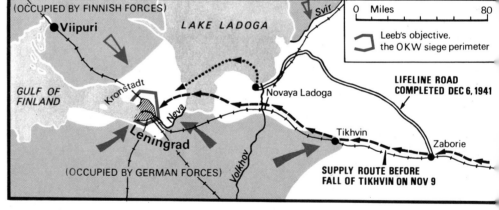

Barbarossa in the North

Leeb's Army Group North advanced farther than the two other army groups in a shorter time and with less armour. The assault began simultaneously on June 22 and Army Group North had crossed the Dvina by the end of the month (map 1). Ostrov was reached by July 4 and the Luga River by July 14. By July 20, the commander of XLI Panzer Corps felt ready for the final thrust towards Leningrad but at this stage the advance was slowed down. There was a sense of caution among the army commanders and a feeling of exhaustion among the troops. Soviet resistance was hardening and the emphasis was being switched to the right flank to assist the thrust of Army Group Centre. Novgorod was finally reached on August 16 and the Volkhov River was crossed. Having destroyed the Soviet forces caught in the Luga pocket in the first two weeks of September, Army Group North then completed the encirclement of Leningrad.

The Germans decided not to assault the city but to besiege it and starve it into surrender. Their bombardment began on September 1. Since there was only enough food in the city to last for about a month, thousands of people had already died by the end of November. The supply route from Tikhvin was cut off when the Germans took the town on November 9 (map 2) and it was not until December 6 that a new lifeline was completed farther north. The final stage for provisions going into Leningrad was by barge or across the 'ice road'.

On December 9, the Russians recaptured Tikhvin during their great winter offensive. They pushed the Germans back behind the Volkhov but could not relieve the city. The provisions that got through were insufficient. On Christmas Day, 1941, it was estimated that 3,700 people died of starvation in Leningrad. Those who survived endured a siege of 900 days in one of the most tragic episodes of Russian history.

Above: General Dietl (left) commander of the crack German ski troops, confers with Finland's Marshal Mannerheim. The Germans failed in their main objective, which was Murmansk. Mannerheim achieved what he wanted, which was to regain his pre-1939 frontiers, but failed to live up to the expectations of the Germans, who had looked on him as an integral part of the Russian offensive.

Right: The Soviet-Finnish battle front, June to December, 1941. Had the Finns been prepared to go beyond their original frontiers, Germany might have had greater success in the north and might have reasonably expected to capture Leningrad. Yet the Soviet defence was much stronger in places than had been anticipated and Hitler was already turning his attention again to Moscow and the south; to the Ukraine, where he saw richer economic rewards.

Finland Recovers Lost Ground

Hitler had one ready ally in Finland, which had suffered defeat at the hands of the Russians in the winter of 1939–40. A co-ordinated effort between Dietl's German troops in northern Norway, Mannerheim's Finnish Army and Leeb's Army Group North was an integral part of the Barbarossa plan.

Dietl's force advanced on Murmansk on June 29, 1941, but was halted on the Litsa river (see map). The German–Finnish advance in the centre also ground to a halt. Farther south, Mannerheim's Karelian Army, which had inflicted severe losses on the Soviets in the 1939–40 campaign, invaded Russia on July 10. The Finns reached the northern shores of Lake Ladoga on July 16 but the Russians managed to withdraw their threatened forces by water and the Finnish advance stopped near the 1939 border on September 1, 1941.

In the first week in August, Mannerheim prepared to recover the Karelian isthmus. He reached Vuosalmi a week later but failed to cut off the Russian forces as they withdrew from Viipuri. By September, the Finns had again reached

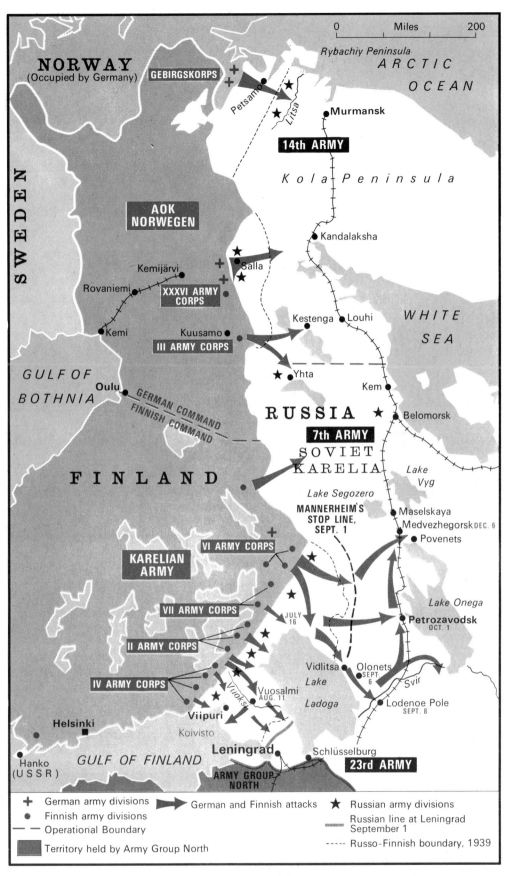

the pre-1939 frontier defences of Leningrad. Just when it seemed that Leningrad was going to be caught tightly between the Finns and Army Group North, Mannerheim showed reluctance to be drawn beyond his original borders or to become further involved in the invasion of Russian territory.

Mannerheim did capture Petroza-

vodsk, north of Lake Ladoga, before Russian resistance became too stiff and the southern front stabilized by the end of October. Once Medvezhegorsk had been taken on December 6, Mannerheim went on the defensive. His reluctance to move beyond his own frontiers gave Leningrad the breathing space it needed to survive.

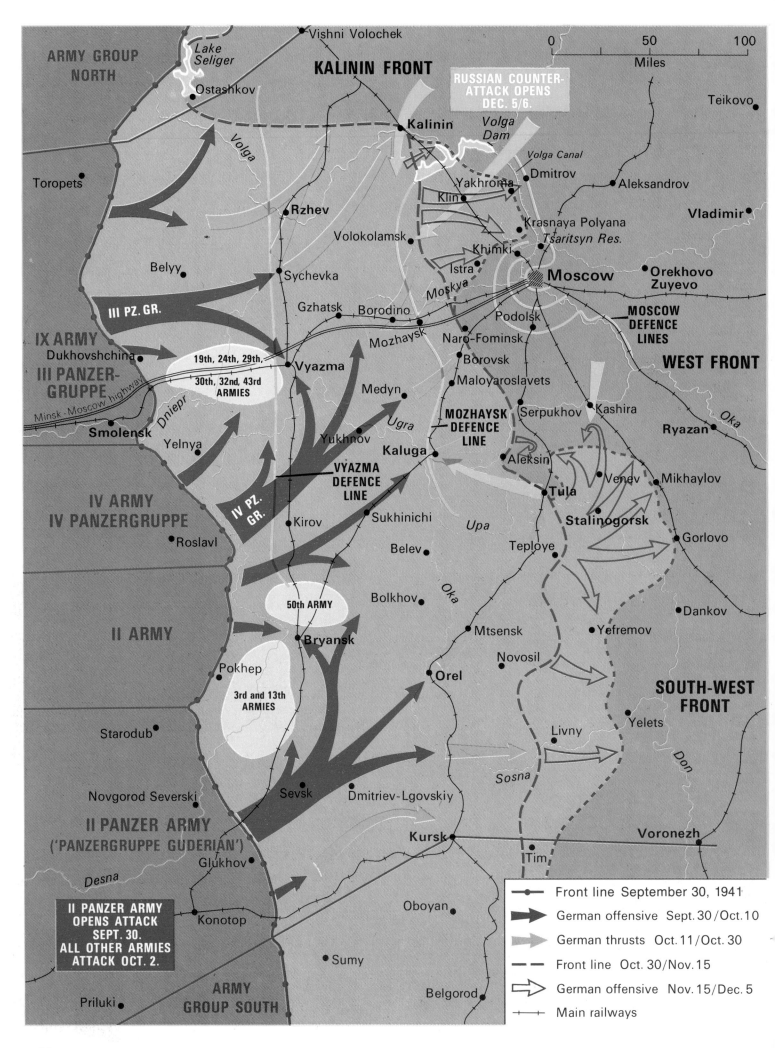

ARMY GROUP NORTH

Lake Seliger

Ostashkov

Vishni Volochek

KALININ FRONT

RUSSIAN COUNTER-ATTACK OPENS DEC. 5/6.

0   50   100
Miles

Teikovo

Toropets

Volga

Kalinin

Volga Dam

Volga Canal

Dmitrov

Aleksandrov

Yakhroma

Klin

Vladimir

Rzhev

Krasnaya Polyana

Tsaritsyn Res.

Belyy

Sychevka

Volokolamsk

Khimki

III PZ. GR.

Gzhatsk   Borodino

Istra

Moscow

Orekhovo
Zuyevo

IX ARMY

Dukhovshchina

III PANZER-GRUPPE

19th, 24th, 29th,
30th, 32nd, 43rd
ARMIES

Vyazma

Mozhaysk

Moskva

Naro-Fominsk

Podolsk

MOSCOW
DEFENCE
LINES

WEST FRONT

Minsk - Moscow highway

Dniepr

Medyn

Borovsk

Maloyaroslavets

MOZHAYSK
DEFENCE
LINE

Smolensk

Yelnya

Ugra

Yukhnov

Serpukhov

Kashira

Oka

Ryazan

IV ARMY
IV PANZERGRUPPE

VYAZMA
DEFENCE
LINE

Kaluga

Aleksin

Venev

Mikhaylov

IV PZ.
GR.

Roslavl

Kirov

Sukhinichi

Upa

Tula

Stalinogorsk

Gorlovo

II ARMY

Belev

Oka

Teploye

Bolkhov

Dankov

50th ARMY

Bryansk

Oka

Mtsensk

Novosil

Yefremov

Pokhep

3rd and 13th
ARMIES

Orel

SOUTH-WEST
FRONT

Starodub

Livny

Yelets

II PANZER ARMY
('PANZERGRUPPE GUDERIAN')

Novgorod Severski

Sevsk

Dmitriev-Lgovskiy

Sosna

Don

Glukhov

Desna

Kursk

Voronezh

II PANZER ARMY
OPENS ATTACK
SEPT. 30.
ALL OTHER ARMIES
ATTACK OCT. 2.

Konotop

Tim

Sumy

Oboyan

Priluki

ARMY
GROUP SOUTH

Belgorod

●—●—●	Front line September 30, 1941
➤	German offensive Sept. 30/Oct. 10
➤	German thrusts Oct. 11/Oct. 30
– – –	Front line Oct. 30/Nov. 15
⟹	German offensive Nov. 15/Dec. 5
+–+–+	Main railways

The Battle for Moscow

In late September 1941, Hitler turned his attention to Moscow once again. His resources were now more thinly stretched and his troops were ill-equipped for approaching winter. It was necessary to capture Moscow quickly. Guderian's Panzergroup advanced on September 30 towards Orel. The attacks farther north began two days later. Soviet pockets west of Vyazma and Bryansk were sealed off by October 7 but the next day the heavy autumn rains began and the mobile German units in the van were steadily strangled. Resistance ended in the Vyazma pocket on October 14 and in the Bryansk pocket on October 20.

The problems of mud and overstretched supply lines and increasing Soviet resistance halted the offensive at the end of October some way short of Moscow. Snow and ice followed the rain and the hardened roads gave the chance for a final offensive on November 15. Marshal Zhukov was now in command of the central Soviet forces barring the way to Moscow. By November 27, units of III Panzergroup had fought through to the Volga canal, within 19 miles of the northern outskirts of the city, and German patrols had even reached the suburbs. On November 25, units of II Panzer Army reached Kashira.

Both advances were then halted by the Russians. Unable to receive support or to make further headway, both forces were withdrawn on December 5, with Hitler's unwilling agreement and only after obstinate argument. The Germans prepared to retreat upon safer defensive positions for the winter. The following day, the Soviet counter-offensive began.

Opposite page: Operation Typhoon, the German advance on the Soviet capital. The offensive opened with the encirclement of nearly three-quarters of a million men in the Vyazma and Bryansk pockets but, by the time the Germans approached Moscow, Zhukov had prepared his defences and had shrewdly assessed the Wehrmacht's limitations.

Right: A group of Soviet soldiers is trapped in the open by a German patrol.

Below: Fresh troops parade in Red Square in late November 1941, preparing for the defence of Moscow.

The Moscow Counterblow

The Soviet Army suffered losses that ran into millions of men, as well as 15–20,000 tanks and 20–30,000 guns, during the German offensive up to the end of November 1941. By most estimates, the Soviet war machine should have been shattered beyond recovery but, by an enormous drive of energy and determination, more troops were brought forward, more arms and equipment were made ready and, on December 6, the day after the Germans began to pull back to defensive positions for the winter, the Soviet Army counter-attacked. They took the Germans by surprise, not only in their timing but also in their apparently inexhaustible supply of men and arms.

The main thrusts of the counterblow were to cut off the German salients at Klin, north of Moscow, and at Stalinogorsk, south of Moscow (map 2). Kalinin was retaken on December 15 and Kaluga shortly afterwards. German resistance was courageous but the troops were weary and shocked by the scale of the attacks. By January 1, 1942, the northern salient had been straightened out and the southern salient reversed.

Encouraged by this success, Stalin decided to expand his offensive, against the advice of Zhukov and other commanders who maintained that if the objectives were widened then the central counter-offensive would be weakened. They also pointed out that the strain on Soviet resources was already immense. Stalin would not listen to them. On December 17–18 an assault had already begun against Army Group North. On January 5, 1942, he decided on an all-out offensive along the entire front (map 1).

One of the main objectives of this wider thrust was to try to pinch out the Germans in the centre. As 4th Shock Army in the north headed south towards Vitebsk and Smolensk, to cut off the German supply lines, so the Bryansk Front forced its way west to cut off IV Army. There was fierce fighting within the German salient between Rzhev and Vyazma. The Soviet offensive slowed down and Russian energy was dissipated. Despite further small advances during the early months of 1942, the Soviet forces could not thrust their way any further through stiffening German resistance. The offensive was finished by the end of March. By early April both sides had once again become bogged down in the mud, as the spring thaw began.

Above: A serious heart-attack enabled von Brauchitsch to resign as Commander-in-Chief on the grounds of ill-health on December 7, when the success of the Soviet offensive became clear. Within the next three weeks, 35 army, corps and divisional generals had joined their commander-in-chief in disgrace.

Above: Exhausted German soldiers. These men at least have camouflage capes. But they also have the steel-shod jackboots that caused so many cases of frostbite in the ranks of the Wehrmacht.

Below: Soviet soldiers advance under cover of their tanks. Stalin's insistence on a wide front meant that Russian tanks had to be spread more thinly than they should have been to guarantee success.

Above: (1) The Russian Front, from December 1941 to April 1942, showing the achievements of the Soviet counter-offensive. Stalin extended the initial thrust in the centre to an offensive along the whole front, from the Crimea and Rostov in the south to Leningrad in the north. Both sides were stretched to their limits by the bitter winter campaign.

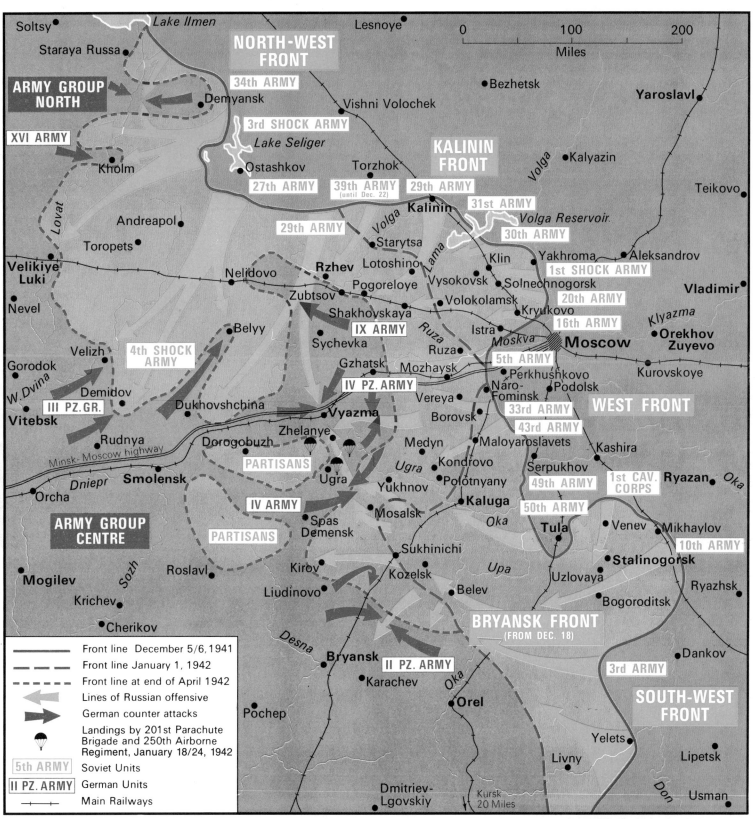

Soltsy

Lake Ilmen

Lesnoye

0   100   200

Miles

Bezhetsk

Yaroslavl

Staraya Russa

NORTH-WEST FRONT

34th ARMY

Vishni Volochek

ARMY GROUP NORTH

Demyansk

3rd SHOCK ARMY

Lake Seliger

KALININ FRONT

Kalyazin

XVI ARMY

Kholm

Ostashkov

27th ARMY

Torzhok

39th ARMY
(until Dec. 22)

29th ARMY

Volga

Teikovo

Andreapol

29th ARMY

Volga

Starytsa

Kalinin

31st ARMY

Volga Reservoir

Aleksandrov

Toropets

30th ARMY

Velikiye Luki

Nelidovo

Rzhev

Lotoshino

Klin

Yakhroma

1st SHOCK ARMY

Nevel

Zubtsov

Pogoreloye

Lama

Vysokovsk

Solnechnogorsk

Vladimir

4th SHOCK ARMY

Belyy

Shakhovskaya

IX ARMY

Volokolamsk

Kryukovo

20th ARMY

Klyazma

Orekhov Zuyevo

Velizh

Sychevka

Ruza

Istra

16th ARMY

Gorodok

Demidov

Gzhatsk

Ruza

Moskva

Moscow

Kurovskoye

W. Dvina

III PZ.GR.

Dukhovshchina

Mozhaysk

5th ARMY

Perkhushkovo

Vitebsk

Rudnya

Dorogobuzh

Zhelanye

Vyazma

IV PZ. ARMY

Vereya

Naro-Fominsk

Podolsk

WEST FRONT

Minsk-Moscow highway

PARTISANS

Borovsk

33rd ARMY

Kashira

Ugra

Medyn

Maloyaroslavets

43rd ARMY

Dniepr

Smolensk

Ugra

Yukhnov

Ugra

Kondrovo

Serpukhov

1st CAV. CORPS

Ryazan

Oka

Orcha

IV ARMY

Polotnyany

49th ARMY

ARMY GROUP CENTRE

PARTISANS

Spas Demensk

Mosalsk

Kaluga

Oka

50th ARMY

Tula

Venev

Mikhaylov

Sozh

Roslavl

Kirov

Sukhinichi

Upa

10th ARMY

Mogilev

Kozelsk

Oka

Uzlovaya

Stalinogorsk

Krichev

Liudinovo

Belev

Uzlovaya

Bogoroditsk

Ryazhsk

Cherikov

Desna

BRYANSK FRONT
(FROM DEC. 18)

Dankov

Bryansk

II PZ. ARMY

3rd ARMY

Karachev

Oka

SOUTH-WEST FRONT

Pochep

Orel

Yelets

Livny

Lipetsk

Dmitriev-Lgovskiy

Kursk
20 Miles

Don

Usman

———	Front line December 5/6, 1941
– – –	Front line January 1, 1942
- - -	Front line at end of April 1942
➡	Lines of Russian offensive
➡	German counter attacks
🪂	Landings by 201st Parachute Brigade and 250th Airborne Regiment, January 18/24, 1942
5th ARMY	Soviet Units
II PZ. ARMY	German Units
+—+—+	Main Railways

Above: (2) The Soviet offensive, from the Kalinin to the Bryansk Fronts. The Russians were over-stretched by their initial success and the Germans eventually managed to hold on to the pocket between Rzhev and Vyazma, despite the threat of being cut off from their supply routes to the west, by the pincer movement of 4th Shock Army in the north, and the Bryansk Front in the south.

Right: Stalin with Voroshilov, the Soviet Commissar for War. Stalin held the supreme power and exerted his will over the arguments of his marshals, just as Hitler did.

The Kharkov Offensives

After Rundstedt's victory at Kiev in September 1941 (see page 80), Army Group South took Kharkov in late October without a major battle (map 1). Despite increasing resistance and bad weather, III Panzer Corps took Rostov on November 21 but held it for only eight days. Soviet 37th Army launched a counter-offensive on the night of November 27–28 and the Germans abandoned the city on November 29. When Hitler refused to allow Runstedt to fall back on the defensible Mius River line, Rundstedt promptly resigned.

The Russians now planned to recross the Donets south of Kharkov and to trap the German troops in Taganrog and Artemovsk (map 2). The offensive began on January 18, 1942 (map 3). The Russians reached the Orel river and cut the Kharkov–Lozovaya railway but German reinforcements brought a stop to the advance by early March. Units of 57th Army, turning south towards Krasnoarmeyskoye, were countered by the Mackensen Group.

Stalin ordered a second offensive in May but the Germans were already preparing to eliminate the Soviet salient south of Kharkov (map 4). The Soviet pincer movement on Kharkov began on May 12 but the Germans contained the attack and launched their counterblow on May 17. They had cut off the Barvenkovo salient by May 23 and had driven back the Soviet advance at Volchansk. The Soviet attempt to retake Kharkov was temporarily halted.

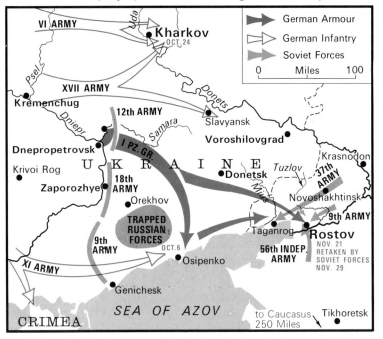

Left: (1) Army Group South reaches Kharkov and heads for its first defeat by the Soviet forces at Rostov, which it held for only eight days.

Right: (2) The plan for the Soviet offensive south of Kharkov, in January 1942. It was successful at first.

Below: (3) The first stage of the Soviet offensive, in January, which was stopped in the south by the Mackensen Group.

Below: (4) The second stage of the Soviet offensive, in May, which was immediately countered by a German offensive that regained the ground lost in January.

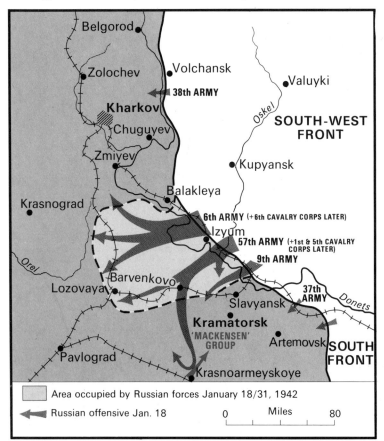

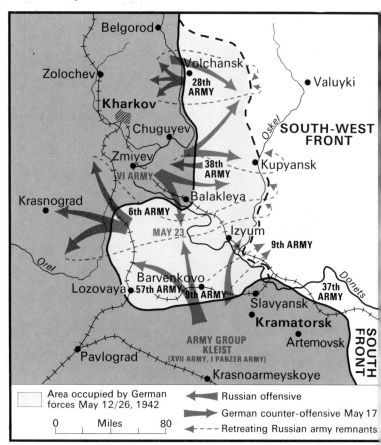

The Siege of Sebastopol

While the Kharkov offensives were in progress, there was hard fighting on the Kerch Peninsula in the Crimea (map 1). Manstein's XI Army won the peninsula by the middle of May 1942. More than 86,000 Soviet soldiers were evacuated with great difficulty across the strait to the Taman Peninsula but Soviet casualties were almost double this number and many of their captured guns were subsequently used against Sebastopol.

The Germans sealed off the city from the sea and preceded their attack by a five-day artillery and air bombardment. Fighting at their best in the confines of the city, the Russians prolonged the siege for 24 days. German LIV Corps attacked the Belbeck–Kamyshly sector on June 7, while XXX Corps attacked along the Yalta highway. Despite initial penetration of the defences, the Germans were then held by fanatical Russian resistance. It was not until the arrival of reinforcements from XVII Army that the Germans broke through to North Bay on June 18.

By June 23, their ammunition almost exhausted, the Russians withdrew to the south side of the bay. The Germans established a bridgehead on the southern side of the bay on the night of June 28–29 and broke into Sebastopol itself on June 30. The remaining Soviet forces were evacuated after further heavy losses in desperate defence of their city.

Above: Women snipers joined the defenders of Sebastopol.

Left: (1) The siege of Sebastopol. The inset map shows the campaign to clear the Crimea and the Kerch Peninsula.

Below: (2) The Anglo-Soviet invasion of Persia, Aug–Sept 1941.

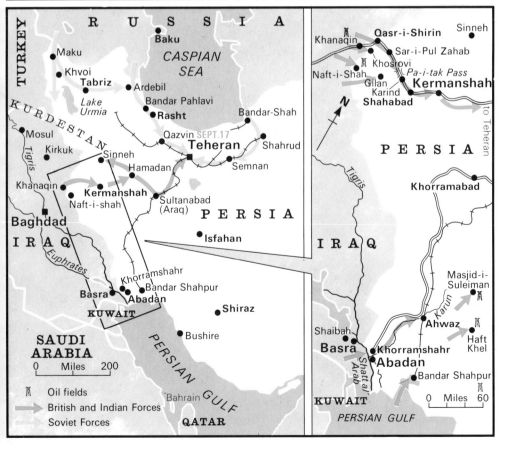

The Anglo-Soviet Invasion of Persia

It was the fear of a German advance in the south-east, through Rostov and the Crimea, that had led to the invasion of Persia in August 1941 by Russia and the western Allies (map 2). Syria, Iraq and Persia were the vital keys to the oil-fields of the Middle East. By June 1941, the Axis had been forestalled in Iraq and the Allies were invading Vichy Syria (see page 34) but when Barbarossa began on June 22, Persia was still highly vulnerable to Axis infiltration, even though Reza Shah had declared his neutrality.

On August 24–25, Soviet and Allied forces advanced from north and south to secure the oil-fields near Kermanshah and Abadan. Token resistance of Persian troops ended on August 28 and the Shah abdicated in favour of his son. Soviet and Allied troops entered Teheran on September 17.

The Arctic Convoys

By the end of the first year of the German offensive in the east, Russia had increasing need of the essential supplies and equipment which had been arriving from Britain by way of the Arctic convoys since August 1941 (map 1). In the summer, the convoys headed north of Jan Mayen and Bear Islands to reach Archangel, keeping at the extreme range of *Luftwaffe* attacks but still vulnerable to U-boats. In the winter, there was less threat from U-boats but the southern limit of the ice edge forced the convoys nearer the *Luftwaffe* bases; the White Sea was sealed off by ice and the ships had to use the more

vulnerable port of Murmansk. German capital ships based in Norwegian fjords also threatened the convoys. Across the length of the Barents Sea, the convoys were out of reach of Allied and Russian land-based air-patrols. The weather was the worst in the world.

The Germans were slow to snatch at such inviting victims, largely because of their lack of air reconnaissance. By the end of 1941, 53 loaded ships had made the voyage in seven convoys without loss, delivering some 750 tanks, 800 fighters, 1,400 vehicles and more than 100,000 tons of stores from hard-pressed Britain. More supplies became available in December, when America joined the war, but by then the ice had closed in on Archangel for the winter and Hitler was taking greater interest in the Norwegian theatre. The *Tirpitz* and *Scheer* were moved north to Trondheim. The last convoy to reach Murmansk unscathed was PQ-12, in early March 1942. From then on, the size and urgency of the convoys increased; so did the German attacks. But Britain had to convince Stalin that it was providing all the support it could. Despite premonitions of disaster, PQ-17 was despatched on June 27.

Left: A German photograph of an early Murmansk convoy. In the foreground, one of the destroyer escort steams at full speed, while a burning merchantman (centre) drops out of the convoy. Below: (1) The summer and winter Arctic convoy routes from Britain to Archangel and Murmansk, showing the dangerous passage around German-controlled Norway.

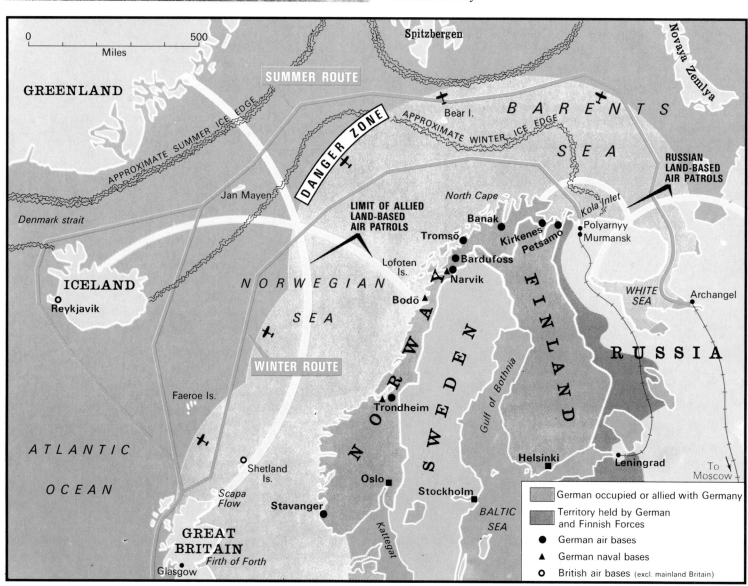

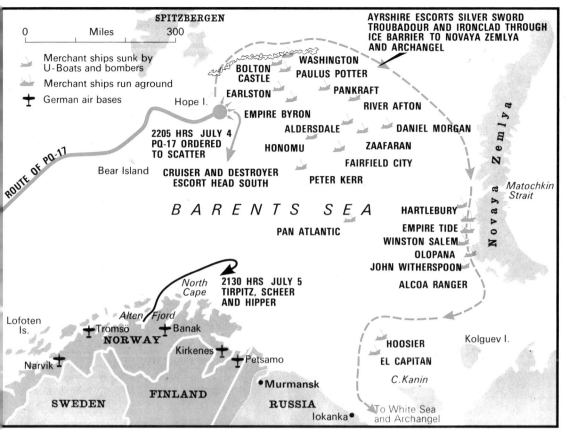

SPITZBERGEN

0   Miles   300

AYRSHIRE ESCORTS SILVER SWORD
TROUBADOUR AND IRONCLAD THROUGH
ICE BARRIER TO NOVAYA ZEMLYA
AND ARCHANGEL

🚢 Merchant ships sunk by
     U-Boats and bombers

🚢 Merchant ships run aground

✠ German air bases

BOLTON
CASTLE
EARLSTON

WASHINGTON
PAULUS POTTER
PANKRAFT
RIVER AFTON

Hope I.

EMPIRE BYRON
ALDERSDALE   DANIEL MORGAN
HONOMU   ZAAFARAN
FAIRFIELD CITY

2205 HRS JULY 4
PQ-17 ORDERED
TO SCATTER

Bear Island   CRUISER AND DESTROYER
ESCORT HEAD SOUTH

PETER KERR

B A R E N T S   S E A

PAN ATLANTIC

HARTLEBURY
EMPIRE TIDE
WINSTON SALEM
OLOPANA
JOHN WITHERSPOON
ALCOA RANGER

N
o
v
a
y
a

Z
e
m
l
y
a

Matochkin
Strait

ROUTE OF PQ-17

North
Cape

2130 HRS JULY 5
TIRPITZ, SCHEER
AND HIPPER

Lofoten
Is.

Alten Fjord
✠ Tromsö   ✠ Banak
NORWAY

Kirkenes ✠
✠ Petsamo

HOOSIER
EL CAPITAN

Kolguev I.

C. Kanin

Narvik ✠

•Murmansk

SWEDEN   FINLAND   RUSSIA

Iokanka •

To White Sea
and Archangel

Left: (2) The threat of the German capital ships haunted Convoy PQ-17 and distracted the attention of the covering force and close escort, though the German surface ships never became involved in the action. Once the convoy scattered, the merchantmen were easy prey for the U-boats and dive-bombers. Tirpitz, Scheer *and* Hipper *turned back to port after the first 24 hours of the massacre. Three merchantmen were saved by the armed trawler* Ayrshire, *which escorted them north through the ice, where they waited for two days until the way was safe to proceed to Novaya Zemlya. Though there was undoubtedly confusion and some error in the way in which the convoy was directed, the Germans did have an overwhelmingly strong hand to play.*

Below: Soviet destroyers move out into the White Sea to escort the remnants of PQ-17 into Archangel.

Convoy PQ-17

In June 1942, the Admiralty learnt that the Germans planned an all-out attack on the next Arctic convoy to Russia. Despite this, Convoy PQ-17 set sail for Archangel from Reykjavik on June 27, with 33 merchant ships, a close escort of destroyers, AA ships, corvettes, minesweepers, trawlers and submarines, and a cruiser and battleship covering force.

On July 1, German scout planes sighted the convoy and U-boats began to trail it. The first limited attacks were beaten off but on July 4 the convoy was attacked by dive and torpedo bombers (map 2). Two merchantmen were sunk. The covering force had already turned home but, aware that the German capital ships *Tirpitz*, *Scheer* and *Hipper* might be moving out to join the attack, the First Sea Lord, Admiral Pound, ordered the covering force to return to the convoy. Some confusion between the covering force and the close escort, moving to counter the threat of the German surface ships, led to the convoy being left defenceless. Pound ordered the convoy to scatter, the better to avoid the German raiders.

Tirpitz, *Scheer* and *Hipper* had no need to attack. When the U-boats and bombers pressed home their advantage on July 5, 12 merchantmen were sunk in the first 24 hours of the massacre. Two ships reached Archangel on July 10; eight more were recovered in the next few days. Twenty-three ships were lost, with 430 tanks, 210 planes, 3,350 vehicles and nearly 100,000 tons of supplies.

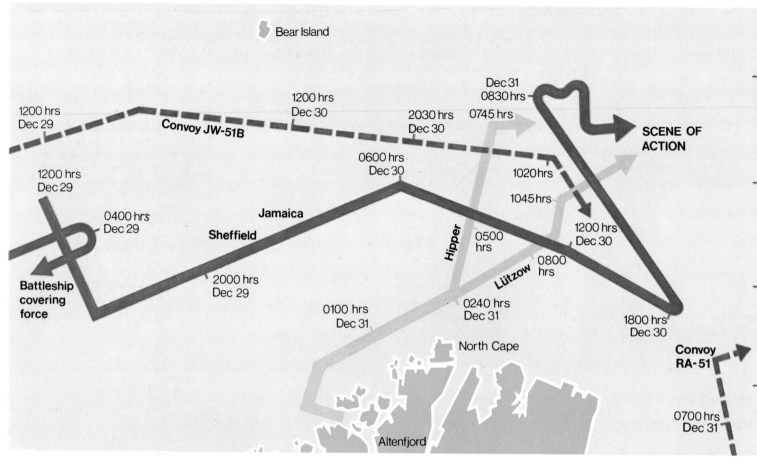

Above: (1) The plan of attack by the Hipper *and* Lutzow *on Convoy JW-51B, December 1942. The attack failed through indecisive action by both ships and their accompanying destroyers.*

Below: The Kriegsmarine *surface fleet in northern waters. The failure to destroy Convoy JW-51B so infuriated Hitler that he ordered it to be scrapped. His decision was reversed.*

The Battles in the Barents Sea

While the Soviets were fighting to relieve Stalingrad, the struggle for supplies continued in the Arctic. Following the disaster of PQ-17 in July 1942, PQ-18 lost 13 out of 40 ships in September. After a lull, the convoys recommenced in December but were split in half. JW-51A, with 15 ships, sailed on December 18 and reached Murmansk safely. The covering cruisers, *Sheffield* and *Jamaica*, under Rear-Admiral Burnett, then turned back to meet JW-51B, which had sailed from Scotland on December 22 with 14 merchantmen escorted by six destroyers under Captain Sherbrooke (map 1).

Driven south by a severe gale, JW-51B was sighted by a U-boat on December 30. Admiral Kummetz was ordered to take out the pocket-battleship *Lutzow* and the heavy cruiser *Hipper*, with six destroyers. *Hipper* was to attack the escort while *Lutzow* attacked the convoy. Kummetz was unaware of Burnett's returning cruiser force. At 0915 hours the German destroyers engaged the British destroyers, which laid a smoke screen between the convoy and the *Hipper*. In a succession of frustrated attacks by the *Hipper*, Sherbrooke's *Onslow* was crippled and the *Achates* was sunk. Meanwhile the *Lutzow* had approached the convoy warily and did not immediately attack.

At 1133 hours, the *Sheffield* and *Jamaica* appeared and fired on the *Hipper*. One German destroyer was sunk and Kummetz broke off the action. Hitler was furious and Admiral Raeder had to dissuade him from scrapping the entire fleet. Raeder resigned as commander-in-chief and was replaced by Doenitz.

Doenitz enjoyed no better luck in the Barents Sea. Almost exactly a year later, in December 1943, Convoy JW-55B was heading east, protected by Burnett's cruisers and covered by Fraser's battleship *Duke of York*. On December 25, the battlecruiser *Scharnhorst*, notorious for her dash through the Channel with *Gneisenau* and *Prince Eugen* in February 1942, left Altenfjord with five destroyers to intercept the convoy (map 2). At 0700 hours on December 26, the destroyers fanned out to search for the convoy and the *Scharnhorst* lost touch with them. Turning north, *Scharnhorst* abruptly encountered Burnett's cruisers, which attempted to keep between the German ship and the convoy. At 1617 hours, the *Scharnhorst* was located by the *Duke of York*. Sandwiched between the cruisers and the battleship, the *Scharnhorst* was smashed at long range by the *Duke of York*'s 14-inch shells. She was eventually sunk at 1945 hours by destroyer torpedoes. Convoy JW-55B reached Murmansk safely the following day, December 27, 1943.

Right: (2) The Scharnhorst's *attempt to attack Convoy JW-55B in December 1943, ended in disaster. The German battle-cruiser was pinched between the British cruisers and the* Duke of York. *Below: The 11-inch main armament of the* Scharnhorst *was no match for the 14-inch guns of the British battleship.*

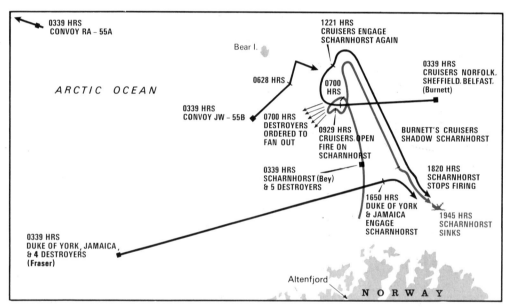

Below: A broadside from the Duke of York, *the battleship that sealed the fate of the* Scharnhorst. *Admiral Fraser had been keen to force an action in the Barents Sea.*

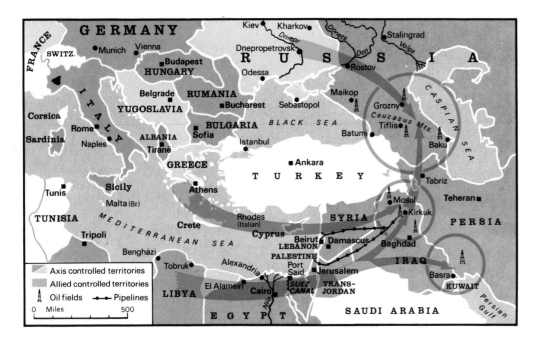

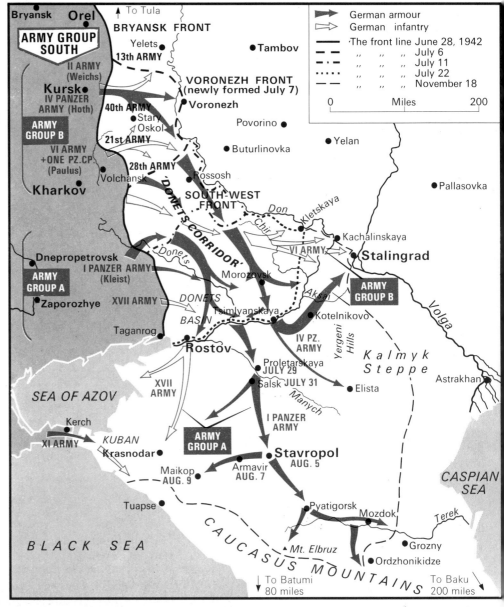

Left: (1) The Axis grand strategic plan for 1942. Hitler envisaged a vast pincer movement from the Caucasus, from Egypt and from the Balkans that would grasp the oil-fields of the Middle East and provide him with much-needed fuel to keep up the momentum of his Panzer divisions. In the summer of 1942, the position of the Allies looked bleak, particularly in North Africa, but by the autumn and early winter the tide had begun to turn. Rommel was pushed back from El Alamein and Paulus faced disaster at Stalingrad.

Above: (2) Directive 41. Hitler's original and more limited plan for summer 1942.

Below: (3) Directive 45. Hitler's extended plan for 1942, with IV Panzer Army switching from north to south to north again.

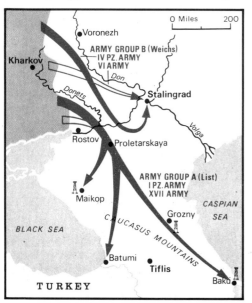

Above: (4) The German offensive in the summer of 1942 began well but ran into trouble: partly because of the enormous ambition of the plan; partly because Hitler changed his objectives more than once in mid-stream. Deprived of IV Panzer Army, Paulus could not press on to Stalingrad as fast as he needed, but when IV Panzer Army was moved north again to help Paulus, Army Group A found itself too thinly stretched to make any further progress on the southern front.

The Attack on Stalingrad

Hitler's strategic plan became increasingly ambitious (map 1). By the summer of 1942, he was aiming at the northern Caucasus and a defensive line along the Don from Voronezh to Stalingrad (map 2). He then extended his objectives to the southern oil-fields, on a line from Baku to Batumi, and to Stalingrad itself (map 3). But his own forces were already overstretched and the Russians were rapidly remanning and re-equipping their armies.

The summer offensive began on June 28, 1942 (map 4). Army Group B advanced towards Voronezh and down the Donets Corridor towards Stalingrad, while Army Group A headed towards the Don crossings between Rostov and Tsimlyanskaya. Hitler then diverted IV Panzer Army to support Army Group A in the south. Progress was rapid and, by early August, Kleist was in the Caucasian foothills. But without IV Panzer Army in the north, Paulus's VI Army had been slowed down and Hitler once again ordered IV Panzer Army to change direction and to support a renewed drive on Stalingrad, where the Russians were already preparing defences.

The Germans reached the Volga north of the city on August 23. Paulus squeezed the defenders into the perimeter of Stalingrad by the end of the month but then, instead of cutting the Soviet supply lines, chose mistakenly to batter his way through the defences on a broad front (map 5). He managed to reach the Volga to north and south in a number of places in October and November and to reduce the city to rubble by a concerted artillery bombardment but the Russians continued to hold substantial pockets on the west bank, supported by their own artillery on the east bank. Both Hitler and Stalin were obsessed by the battle for Stalingrad. By November, Hitler was still short of the ultimate objectives of his summer campaign.

Above: Tanks and infantry of Kleist's Army Group B, who advanced at a tremendous pace towards the Caucasus once they had crossed the Don.

Above right: (5) Paulus's VI Army tried to eliminate Soviet resistance in Stalingrad, but did not set about it in the right way, and underestimated Stalin's determination to save the city.

Right: Soviet Katyushas firing from the east bank of the Volga in support of Russian troops fighting on the west bank.

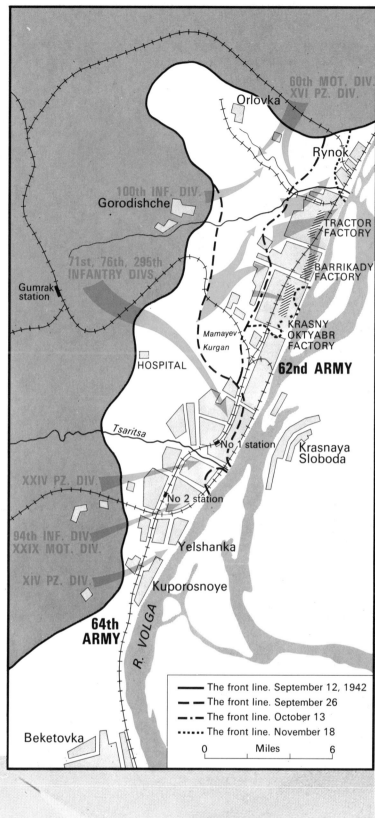

Orlovka

60th MOT. DIV.
XVI PZ. DIV.

Rynok

100th INF. DIV.

Gorodishche

TRACTOR FACTORY

BARRIKADY FACTORY

71st, 76th, 295th
INFANTRY DIVS

Gumrak
station

KRASNY
OKTYABR
FACTORY

*Mamayev
Kurgan*

62nd ARMY

HOSPITAL

Tsaritsa

No 1 station

Krasnaya
Sloboda

XXIV PZ. DIV.

No 2 station

94th INF. DIV.
XXIX MOT. DIV.

Yelshanka

XIV PZ. DIV.

Kuporosnoye

64th
ARMY

R. VOLGA

——— The front line. September 12, 1942

– – – The front line. September 26

–·–·– The front line. October 13

········· The front line. November 18

Beketovka

0   Miles   6

Left: German troops in the Stalingrad front line, mid-November 1942. Paulus's VI Army was already jaded by the time it began the onslaught on Stalingrad and, even as it battled to take the town, the Russians were preparing their carefully conceived counter-attack.

Below: (1) The Soviet counter-attack, which began in the north on November 19 and in the south on November 20. For once, the Russians achieved their objective perfectly and snapped shut the trap on the German VI Army.

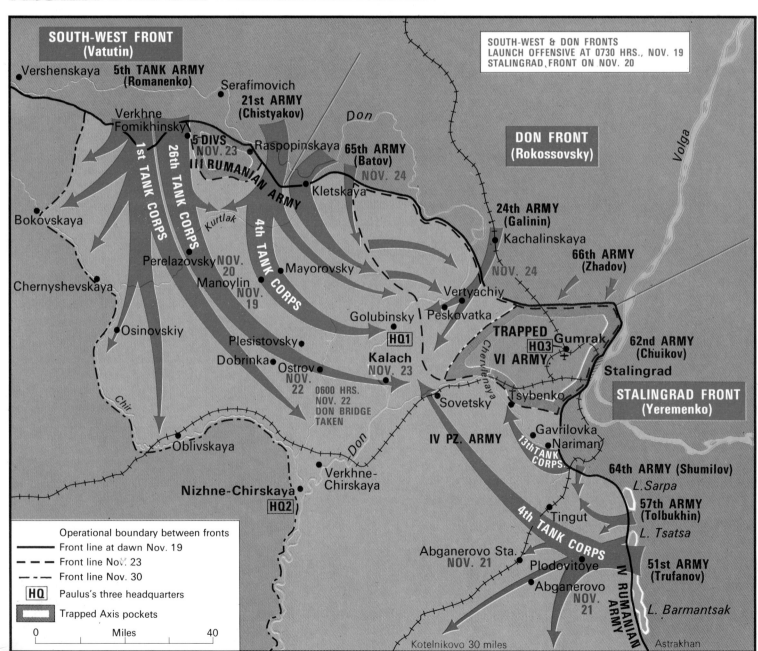

SOUTH-WEST FRONT (Vatutin)

Vershenskaya

5th TANK ARMY (Romanenko)

Serafimovich

21st ARMY (Chistyakov)

Verkhne Fomikhinsky

5 DIVS NOV. 23

III RUMANIAN ARMY

Raspopinskaya

Don

65th ARMY (Batov) NOV. 24

Kletskaya

SOUTH-WEST & DON FRONTS LAUNCH OFFENSIVE AT 0730 HRS., NOV. 19 STALINGRAD FRONT ON NOV. 20

DON FRONT (Rokossovsky)

Volga

1st TANK CORPS

26th TANK CORPS

4th TANK CORPS

Kurtlak

24th ARMY (Galinin)

Kachalinskaya

NOV. 24

66th ARMY (Zhadov)

Bokovskaya

Perelazovsky NOV. 20

Mayorovsky

Manoylin NOV. 19

Vertyachiy

Chernyshevskaya

Golubinsky

Peskovatka

TRAPPED

Gumrak

62nd ARMY (Chuikov)

HQ3

VI ARMY

Osinovskiy

Plesistovsky

HQ1

Stalingrad

Dobrinka

Ostrov NOV. 22

Kalach NOV. 23

Chervlenaya

STALINGRAD FRONT (Yeremenko)

Chir

0600 HRS. NOV. 22 DON BRIDGE TAKEN

Tsybenko

Sovetsky

IV PZ. ARMY

Gavrilovka

Nariman

Don

13th TANK CORPS

Oblivskaya

Verkhne-Chirskaya

64th ARMY (Shumilov)

L. Sarpa

Nizhne-Chirskaya

HQ2

57th ARMY (Tolbukhin)

Tingut

L. Tsatsa

4th TANK CORPS

Abganerovo Sta. NOV. 21

Plodovitoye

51st ARMY (Trufanov)

Abganerovo NOV. 21

IV RUMANIAN ARMY

Operational boundary between fronts

Front line at dawn Nov. 19

Front line Nov. 23

Front line Nov. 30

HQ Paulus's three headquarters

Trapped Axis pockets

0   Miles   40

Kotelnikovo 30 miles

L. Barmantsak

Astrakhan

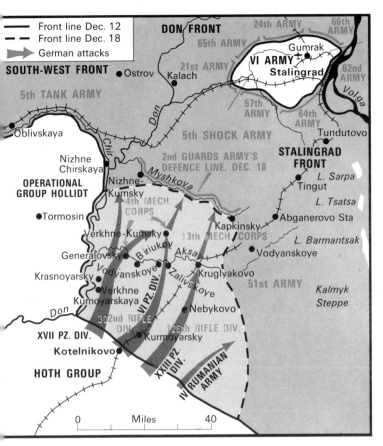

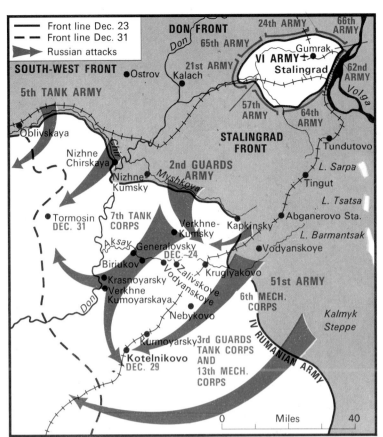

Above left: (2) December 12, 1942. The Hoth Group leads the last desperate attempt to rescue VI Army.

Above right: (3) December 24, 1942. The Soviet counter-attack that successfully pushed the Hoth Group away from Stalingrad.

Right: (4) The final assault on Stalingrad lasted three weeks, from January 10 to February 2.

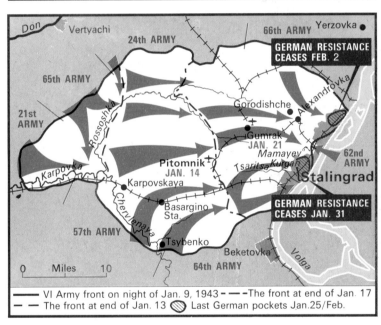

The Relief of Stalingrad

Zhukov opposed Paulus with the minimum force necessary to hold Stalingrad, massing his main force against the weaker Rumanian armies on either flank of VI Army. He intended to cut off the Germans in Stalingrad and deployed his own forces to this end.

Vatutin's South West Front and Rokossovsky's Don Front began their offensive on November 19, 1942 (map 1). On November 20, Yeremenko's Stalingrad Front launched the second wave. By November 21, Paulus had withdrawn his HQ from Golubinsky (HQ1) to Nizhne-Chirskaya (HQ2). Hitler immediately ordered him to advance it again to Gumrak (HQ3). When the two main Soviet forces met on November 23, VI Army and part of IV Panzer Army were trapped (22 German divisions, a total of 330,000 men). On the same day, five divisions of the Rumanian Army surrendered in the north. Weichs' Army Group B escaped, while Hitler stepped in to assume direct command of VI Army and ordered Paulus to stand fast, backed by Goering's promise that the *Luftwaffe* would fly in all the necessary supplies.

As the Soviet hold tightened on VI Army, Manstein's Army Group Don prepared for Operation Winter Storm, to relieve the trapped army (map 2). The Hoth Group struck south of Stalingrad on December 12. It encountered resistance from 5th Shock Army. The Russians reinforced their defences along the Myshkova river. Hoth was halted within 25–30 miles of Stalingrad and on December 24 the Soviet forces counter-attacked (map 3). Army Group Don fell back.

During the first week in January, the Soviet forces prepared for their final offensive, while VI Army suffered frostbite, battle-fatigue and lack of supplies. On January 8, 1943, Rokossovsky proposed to Paulus that he capitulate as he was surrounded by seven Russian armies. Paulus refused. The final assault began on January 10, after a massive artillery bombardment (map 4).

The Russians advanced remorselessly towards the river, pressing VI Army into two small pockets. On January 31, Paulus was forced to surrender the southern pocket. Two days later, Schreck surrendered the northern pocket. Nearly 100,000 Germans died at Stalingrad; almost as many surrendered; some had been evacuated by air. The loss of *matériel* and men was bitter to the Germans, the loss of prestige was shattering. The world watched as the battle for Stalingrad swung first in favour of the Germans and then against them.

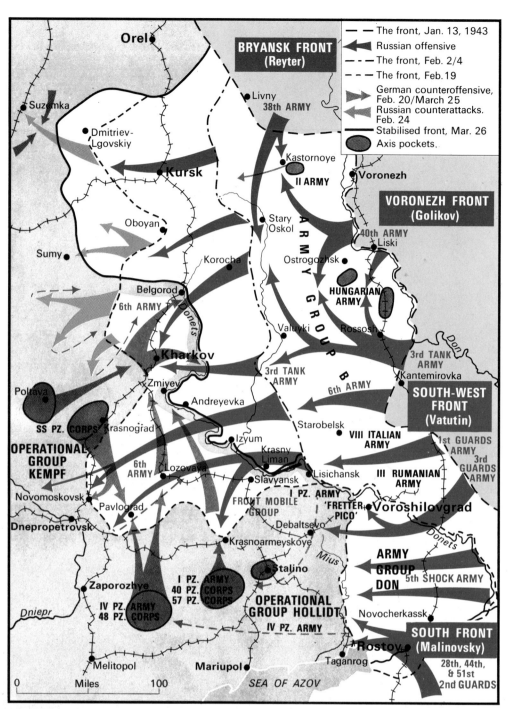

The front, Jan. 13, 1943
- ◄■ Russian offensive
- The front, Feb. 2/4
- The front, Feb.19
- ►► German counteroffensive, Feb. 20/March 25
- ◄◄ Russian counterattacks. Feb. 24
- Stabilised front, Mar. 26
- ⬭ Axis pockets.

BRYANSK FRONT (Reyter)

Orel

Suzemka

Dmitriev-Lgovskiy

Kursk

Livny
38th ARMY

Kastornoye
II ARMY

Voronezh

VORONEZH FRONT (Golikov)

Oboyan

Stary Oskol

40th ARMY
Liski

Sumy

Korocha

Ostrogozhsk

Belgorod
6th ARMY

HUNGARIAN ARMY

Rossosh

3rd TANK ARMY

Kharkov

Zmiyev

3rd TANK ARMY

6th ARMY

Kantemirovka

Poltava

Andreyevka

Valuyki

SOUTH-WEST FRONT (Vatutin)

SS PZ. CORPS

Krasnograd

Starobelsk

VIII ITALIAN ARMY

1st GUARDS ARMY

3rd GUARDS ARMY

OPERATIONAL GROUP KEMPF

6th ARMY

Lozovaya

Izyum

Krasny Liman

Slavyansk

Lisichansk

III RUMANIAN ARMY

Novomoskovsk

Pavlograd

FRONT MOBILE GROUP

I PZ. ARMY

'FRETTER PICO'

Voroshilovgrad

Dnepropetrovsk

Debaltsevo

ARMY GROUP DON

Krasnoarmeyskoye

Mius

Zaporozhye

I PZ. ARMY
40 PZ.
57 PZ.

ARMY CORPS

Stalino

5th SHOCK ARMY

IV PZ. ARMY
48 PZ. CORPS

OPERATIONAL GROUP HOLLIDT

IV PZ. ARMY

Novocherkassk

Dniepr

Melitopol

Mariupol

Rostov

SOUTH FRONT (Malinovsky)

Taganrog

28th, 44th, & 51st
2nd GUARDS

SEA OF AZOV

0 ——— Miles ——— 100

ARCTIC OCEAN

0 — Miles — 800

NORWAY
SWEDEN
FINLAND

Murmansk

Archangel

Ural Mountains

Leningrad

Perm

RUSSIA

Warsaw

Moscow

Kuybyshev

POLAND

Kiev

Stalingrad

HUNGARY

Kharkov

Astrakhan

RUMANIA

Rostov

YUG

BULGARIA

BLACK SEA

CASPIAN SEA

GREECE

TURKEY

Tiflis

- ▨ Axis territories before 'Barbarossa'
- ▧ Limit of German advance into Russia Nov. 1942
- ▢ Projected extent of the 'Greater German Empire' in Russia

Above: (1) The Nazi dream of a 'Greater German Empire' and the limits of their real achievement. The Germans had hoped to subjugate all of European Russia up to the Urals and down through the Caucasus. But they reached the end of their advance in the early winter of 1942. Even so, their achievement was astonishing, as was the Russian recovery.

Right: (2) January–March 1943. The Soviet four-front assault on Army Group B and Army Group Don. The Russians retook Kursk and Kharkov and were then halted by Manstein's brilliant and determined counter-attack against heavy odds.

Below: Already, by the autumn of 1942, relatively ill-equipped Russian troops had managed to thwart the German attempts to capture the oil-fields of the Caucasus.

Manstein Fights Back

Hitler's dreams of an eastern empire were destroyed in 1943 (map 1). On January 12, even before Paulus surrendered in Stalingrad, the Russians launched a massive counter-attack to regain the territories they had lost in the summer of 1942. They attacked on four fronts between Orel and Rostov (map 2). The Bryansk, Voronezh, South-west and South Fronts directed their assaults against Army Group B and Army Group Don, with the aim of recovering Kharkov and cutting off the German withdrawal from the Caucasus. Their advance was at first stunningly rapid.

Soviet forces had recaptured Kursk by February 8. By February 16, they had recovered Kharkov and Voroshilovgrad. By February 27, they had retaken Pavlograd, creating a salient on which the redoubtable Manstein turned suddenly with vigour and imagination. The Russians had over-reached themselves and underestimated the strength and skill of their opponent, even when he was in retreat.

Manstein launched his counterblow on February 20, having skilfully reorganized his reserves. Within a week, the Panzer spearheads had fought back to the Donets. Having trapped and destroyed Soviet 3rd Tank Army, Manstein massed four Panzer corps south-west of Kharkov on March 3 for a drive against the Voronezh Front. He retook Kharkov on March 15 and, three days later, recaptured Belgorod. The Russians were driven back to the east bank of the Donets but the spring thaw prevented any further German advance and left intact the huge Kursk salient.

To the south, Kleist's Army Group A had found itself in a hopeless situation. With the Russians threatening Rostov and with the Northern Group of the Trans-Caucasian Front attacking north-west of Ordzhonikidze, Kleist was forced to fall back from the Caucasus in the first week of January 1943 (map 3). Only I Panzer Army managed to escape through the corridor that Manstein tried to keep open to Rostov, which fell to the Russians on February 14. The remainder of Kleist's Army Group A was trapped in the Taman Peninsula. A combined assault from land and sea enabled the Russians to recapture Novorossiysk on September 16, 1943, and on October 9 Russian units reached the Kerch Strait (map 4). The North Caucasus was liberated.

Right: Out in the Russian steppe, a German 88-mm crew mans its post during the winter offensives of 1942–43.

Below left: (3) January–March 1943. Kleist's Army Group A is forced to withdraw towards Rostov and the Taman Peninsula. Manstein's efforts to keep the door to Rostov open were not sufficient to save all the Germans who had been fighting in the Caucasus.

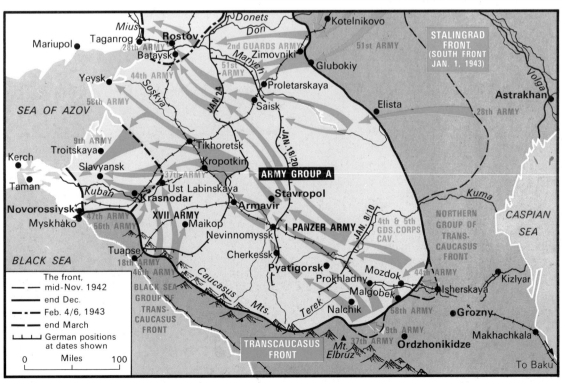

Above: (4) Six months after trapping the Germans in the Taman Peninsula, the Russians finally clear the peninsula and reach the Kerch Strait, September–October 1943.

The Battle of Kursk

The southern front stabilized between March and June 1943, while both sides prepared for the next assault (map 1). The Germans were determined to cut off the Kursk salient but the Russians had inside knowledge of their plans through the Lucy spy ring in Switzerland. They had prepared eight lines of anti-tank defences within the perimeter of the salient and were superior to the Germans in numbers of men, artillery, tanks and aircraft. The battle that ensued was to be the largest tank battle of the war and also a major battle for air supremacy. The Germans lost on both counts.

Operation Citadel opened on June 5, 1943 (map 2). In the north, IX Army advanced only six miles at great loss and after June 10 achieved no further advance (map 4). In the south, IV Panzer Army was at first more successful (map 3). The tightly bunched Panzers battled through concentric layers of anti-tank defences as Russian reserves flooded into the salient but after ten days and an advance of 25 miles IV Panzer Army was fought to a standstill.

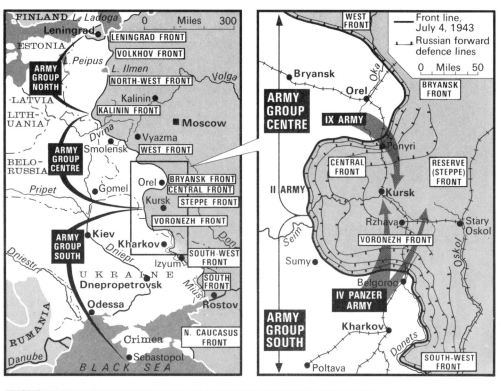

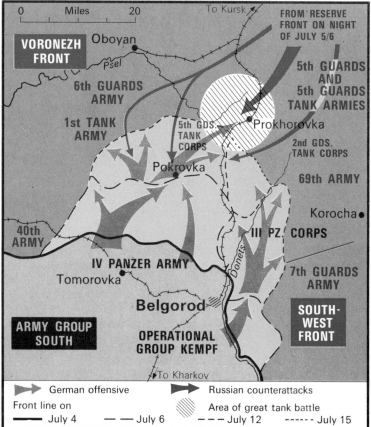

Far left: (1) The Eastern Front in the summer of 1943, with the Kursk salient bulging out between Orel and Kharkov.

Left: (2) For their third Russian offensive, the Germans concentrated their forces on pinching out the Kursk salient with assaults by IX Army in the north and IV Panzer Army in the south. They faced eight lines of defences.

Below left: (3) The southern sector of the Kursk salient, where IV Panzer Army was fought to a standstill after 10 days and 25 miles of desperate advance.

Below: A German Pzkw-III Special advances through steppe grass set on fire by Russian shells.

On July 15, the Russians counter-attacked and by July 23 the Germans had been forced back beyond their start lines (map 4). Orel and Belgorod were recovered by August 4–5, Kharkov by August 23. In the north, the Germans withdrew to the Hagen Line; in the south, Manstein fell back towards the Dniepr.

Above: Manstein considers how to cope with the Russian counter-offensive that followed immediately after Operation Citadel had been stopped in its tracks. He refused to obey Hitler and to allow his troops to be destroyed by the victorious Russians. Instead, he conducted another carefully controlled retreat westwards towards the Dniepr. Manstein's skill was shown repeatedly, not only in planning offensives, but in preventing retreats from becoming routs. The Russians were continually surprised by his resilience.

Right: (4) The limits of Operation Citadel's achievements and its collapse, as the Russians turn to the offensive and recover Orel in the north and Kharkov in the south. The salient disappeared, not because the Germans cut it off, as they had hoped to do, but because the Russians moved forward on either side of it.

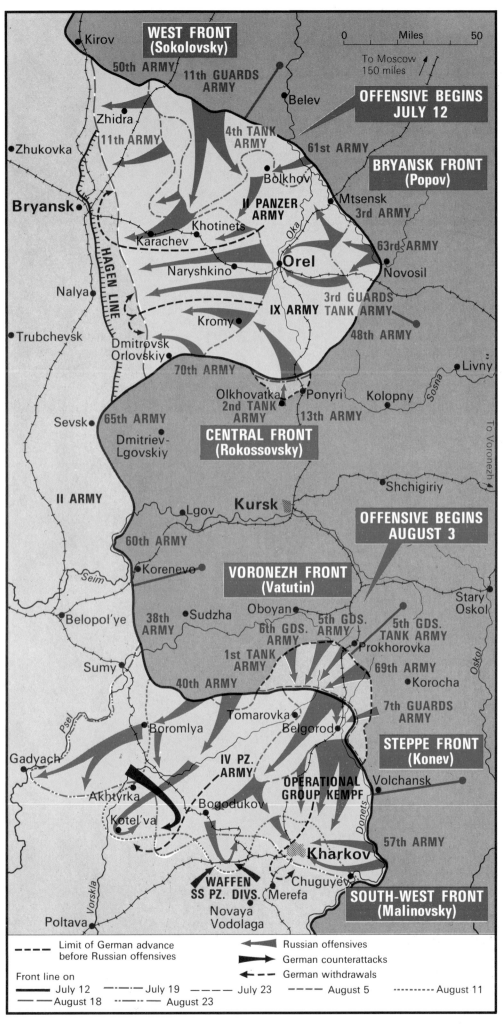

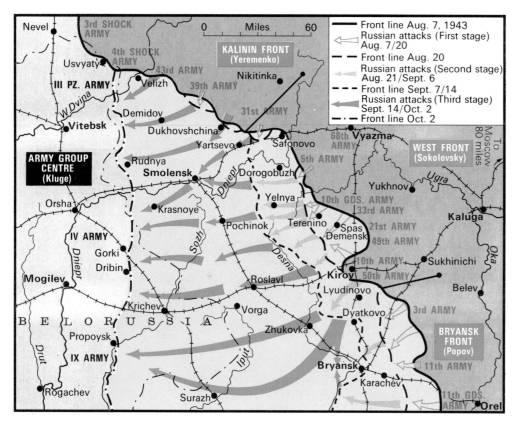

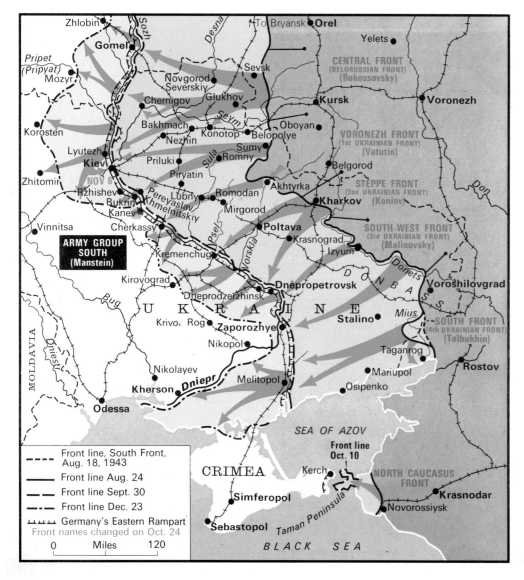

Left: (2) The central section of the front, where the Russians broke through the German defence lines, forcing back three German armies and liberating Smolensk. Soviet forces demonstrated that they had learnt the skills of their opponents in exploiting local superiority and maintaining the impetus of their advance, often pushing through an assault without waiting for support troops.

Bottom left: (3) The southern section of the autumn offensive, which aimed at liberating the ancient city of Kiev and crossing the Dniepr, a vital component of the Eastern Rampart on which the Germans relied heavily after their failure at Kursk. The Russians kept up their momentum across the river, often well in advance of their heavy equipment.

Below: (1) The Russian offensives to recapture Smolensk and to reach the Dniepr in the centre and south (autumn 1943) and to advance in the north (January–March 1944).

The Return to Smolensk and the Dniepr

The Soviet counter-attack in reply to Operation Citadel was only the beginning of a much larger Soviet offensive against Germany's Eastern Rampart from the Baltic to the Black Sea (map 1), aimed at reaching Smolensk and crossing the Dniepr. The swiftness of the Soviet advance, their greater numbers and the skills they had learnt in the penetration of defensive lines overwhelmed dogged German resistance.

The Soviet West Front launched its approach to Smolensk on August 7 (map 2) and on August 13 the Kalinin Front went on the offensive. The first task was to break through the German defence belt. On September 14–15 the two fronts moved forward towards Smolensk itself, which was liberated on September 25. By October 2, the offensive had come to an end on a line well to the west of Smolensk.

To the south, after Kharkov had been recaptured on August 23, the Red Army moved into the Eastern Ukraine, heading for the Dniepr (map 3). Russian forces crossed the Donets and

by September 22 the first units of the Central Front had reached and begun to cross the Dniepr south of Kiev. By September 30, the Russians had reached the Dniepr as far south as Zaporozhye, where the Germans retained a bridgehead that was wiped out in the second week of October. In that same week, the Soviet North Caucasus Front reached the Kerch Strait.

The Russian fronts were renamed on October 20. By October 23, Soviet forces had liberated the most southerly town of any significance on the Eastern Rampart, Melitopol, and by October 30 they had entered the Crimea, trapping the remaining German forces who had been ordered to hold fast by Hitler, against the advice of Manstein. The assault on Kiev began on November 3 and the last German forces moved out on November 6. By the end of the year, the Russians had established bridgeheads across the Dniepr and cleared the Germans from the east bank of the river at almost every point. There remained only a German bridgehead opposite Nikopol, in the south. The German High Command now began to fortify the Vistula Line and to prepare for the defence of the Balkans.

Left: Assault troops of the Red Army cross one of the many smaller rivers in their race to reach the Dniepr.

Below: The city of Kiev was one of the main objectives of the autumn campaign. The last Germans were driven out on December 6, 1943.

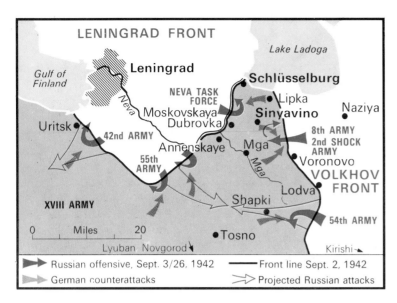

LENINGRAD FRONT

Above: Colonel-General Kuchler had been ordered to launch his own offensive against Leningrad in August 1942, but his immediate task was to repel the Soviet attack.

Above: General Govorov, Commander-in-Chief of the Leningrad Front, failed to join up with the Volkhov Front in 1942. He had more success in January 1943 and finally triumphed in January 1944.

Above: (1) Operation Sinyavino, August–September 1942. The first major attempt by the Volkhov and Leningrad Fronts to link up was resisted and thrown back by XVIII Army.

Right: (2) Having strengthened their siege lines during 1942, the Germans withdrew some of their forces to reinforce the line further south. It was then, in January 1943, that the Russians cleared a narrow corridor south of Lake Ladoga. Army Group North was pushed back from Leningrad and Novgorod in January 1944 and the stranglehold was broken.

The Relief of Leningrad

The siege of Leningrad continued throughout the fluctuations of German and Soviet offensives in 1942–43. Schlusselburg had been captured by the Germans in September 1941, cutting off the city from overland communication. Having failed to raise the siege in their winter offensive of 1941–42, the Russians failed again in August and September 1942. The Volkhov Front attempted to break through south of Lake Ladoga in Operation Sinyavino but was eventually forced back to its starting point (map 1).

On January 18, 1943, after another major effort, the Volkhov and Leningrad Fronts linked to form a corridor 5–7 miles wide south of Lake Ladoga but it was not until January 1944 that the final relief came (map 2). Three Soviet fronts attacked, led by 2nd Shock Army from the Oranienbaum bridgehead. By January 20, 2nd Shock and 42nd Armies linked west of Leningrad and 59th Army had captured Novgorod. By January 27, the Moscow–Leningrad railway was cleared. Army Group North withdrew east of Lake Chuskoye and established a line from Narva to Putoshka.

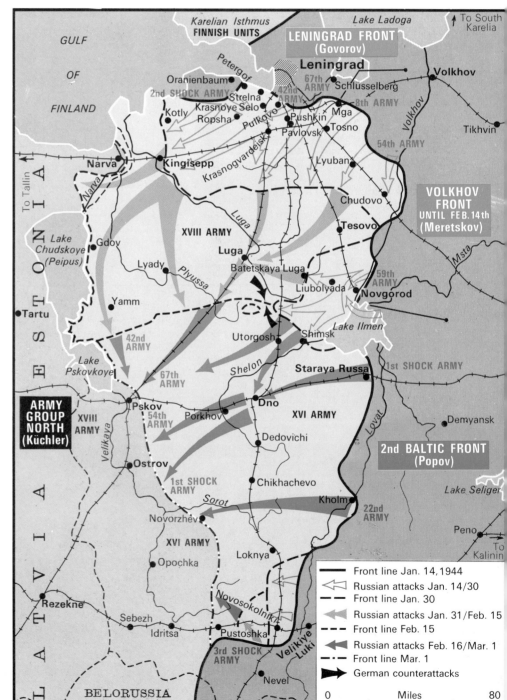

The Fight for the Ukraine

While the Volkhov Front prepared to relieve Leningrad, the pressure on the Germans farther south continued. By late December 1943 the Russians had established bridgeheads across the Dniepr. Before the year was out, 1st Ukrainian Front was pushing forward against Manstein's Army Group South (see map). On January 5, 1944, 2nd Ukrainian Front attacked Kleist's Army Group A. It was joined by 3rd and 4th Ukrainian Fronts on January 10 and 31.

By mid-February, I Panzer Army was encircled and only a brilliant rearguard action enabled it to escape. To the north, Manstein's counter-attacks were beaten back by the weather and the Russians. To the south, Kleist was forced back to Odessa, leaving behind units of VI and VIII Armies. He was driven out of Odessa on April 10. By mid-April, the Russians were across the Dniestr and up to the Carpathian foothills, also approaching the Polish border. In the Crimea, XVII Army was abandoned. It was cleared out by 4th Ukrainian Front and Sebastopol was retaken on May 12.

Hitler was furious. Manstein and Kleist were demoted. Model and Schorner were given Army Groups North and South Ukraine.

Above: Russian artillery firing amid deep snow in the foothills of the Carpathians after overwhelming the German defences in the Ukraine between January and April 1944.

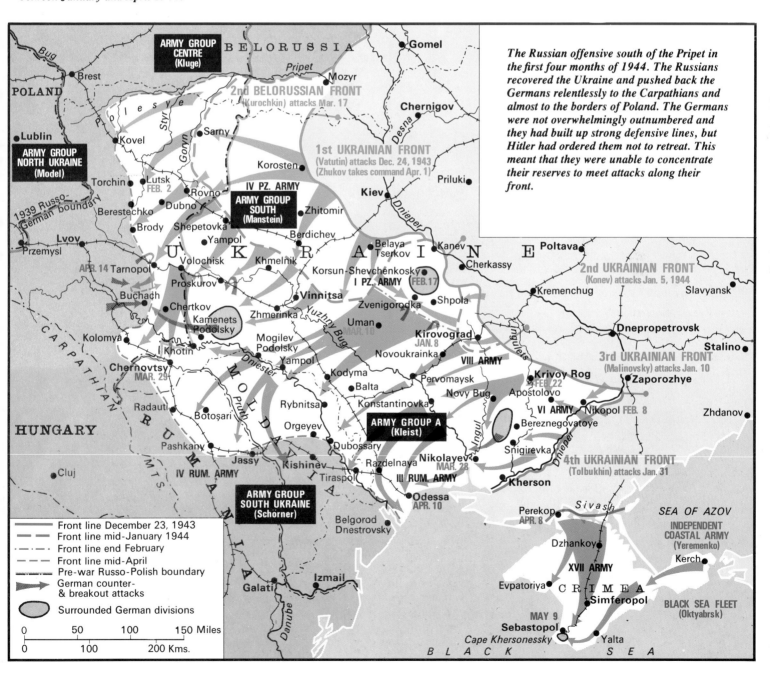

The Russian offensive south of the Pripet in the first four months of 1944. The Russians recovered the Ukraine and pushed back the Germans relentlessly to the Carpathians and almost to the borders of Poland. The Germans were not overwhelmingly outnumbered and they had built up strong defensive lines, but Hitler had ordered them not to retreat. This meant that they were unable to concentrate their reserves to meet attacks along their front.

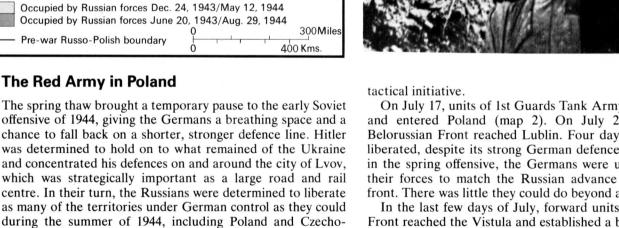

The Red Army in Poland

The spring thaw brought a temporary pause to the early Soviet offensive of 1944, giving the Germans a breathing space and a chance to fall back on a shorter, stronger defence line. Hitler was determined to hold on to what remained of the Ukraine and concentrated his defences on and around the city of Lvov, which was strategically important as a large road and rail centre. In their turn, the Russians were determined to liberate as many of the territories under German control as they could during the summer of 1944, including Poland and Czechoslovakia. Soviet confidence was growing daily.

The Red Army began its general summer offensive of 1944 in June and July (map 1). It ranged from the Baltic states to the Balkans. The campaign in the Ukraine sector was only a part of the wider assault and therefore affected to some extent by conditions elsewhere. Russian success further north, in Belorussia (see page 108), forced the Germans to take troops away from Army Group North Ukraine and thereby weakened the northern flank of their Ukraine defence. Moving with all the speed of a *Blitzkrieg* attack, the Russians exploited this advantage and repeatedly made good use of their strategic and tactical initiative.

On July 17, units of 1st Guards Tank Army crossed the Bug and entered Poland (map 2). On July 23, troops of 1st Belorussian Front reached Lublin. Four days later, Lvov was liberated, despite its strong German defences. Once again, as in the spring offensive, the Germans were unable to balance their forces to match the Russian advance along so wide a front. There was little they could do beyond an orderly retreat.

In the last few days of July, forward units of 1st Ukrainian Front reached the Vistula and established a bridgehead on the western bank. A German counter-attack by IV Panzer Army against the Stopnica area of the bridgehead between August 11 and 18 was held and the Russians began to break out of the northern sector of the bridgehead, advancing west. Further to the south, 4th Ukrainian Front attempted to seize the passes across the Carpathians but was stopped by determined German resistance, which continued unabated despite the setbacks. By then, in any case, the Red Army was suffering from supply problems after advancing more than 400 miles in two months. By the end of August, 1st Ukrainian Front had temporarily gone on the defensive.

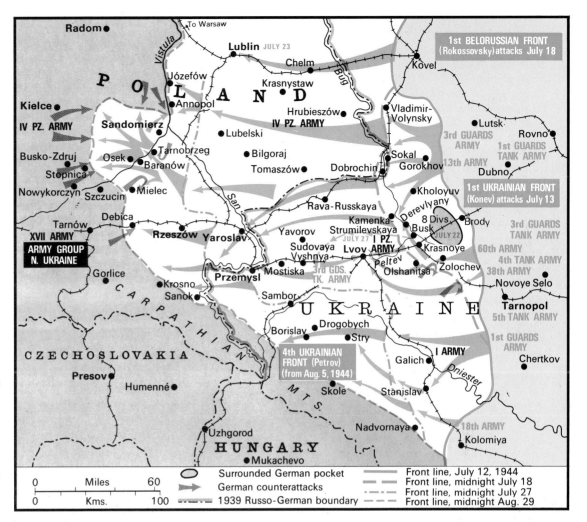

Radom

Vistula

To Warsaw

Lublin JULY 23

Chelm

1st BELORUSSIAN FRONT (Rokossovsky) attacks July 18

Kovel

Józefów

Krasnystaw

P O L A N D

Kielce

IV PZ. ARMY

Sandomierz

Annopol

Hrubieszów

IV PZ. ARMY

Vladimir-Volynsky

Lutsk

Rovno

3rd GUARDS ARMY

1st GUARDS TANK ARMY

Busko-Zdruj

Osek

Tarnobrzeg

Baranów

Lubelski

Bilgoraj

Sokal

13th ARMY

Dubno

Stopnica

Tomaszów

Dobrochin

Gorokhov

Nowykorczyn

Szczucin

Mielec

Kholoyuv

1st UKRAINIAN FRONT (Konev) attacks July 13

Debica

San

Rava-Russkaya

Derevlyany

8 Divs

Brody

3rd GUARDS TANK ARMY

Tarnów

XVII ARMY

ARMY GROUP
N. UKRAINE

Rzeszów

Yaroslav

Yavorov

Kamenka-Strumilevskaya

JULY 27

Busk

JULY 22

Krasnoye

60th ARMY

4th TANK ARMY

Gorlice

Przemysl

Sudovaya Vyshnya

I PZ. ARMY

Lvov

Peltev

Olshanitsa

Zolochev

38th ARMY

Novoye Selo

Krosno

Sanok

Mostiska

3rd GDS. TK. ARMY

Sambor

U K R A I N E

Tarnopol

5th TANK ARMY

C Z E C H O S L O V A K I A

Borislav

Drogobych

Stry

4th UKRAINIAN FRONT (Petrov)
(from Aug. 5, 1944)

Galich

I ARMY

Dniester

1st GUARDS ARMY

Chertkov

Presov

Humenné

C A R P A T H I A N

Skole

Stanislav

M T S.

Uzhgorod

Nadvornaya

18th ARMY

Kolomiya

H U N G A R Y

Mukachevo

| 0 | Miles | 60 |
| 0 | Kms. | 100 |

⬭ Surrounded German pocket
➤ German counterattacks
▬▬ 1939 Russo-German boundary

Front line, July 12, 1944
Front line, midnight July 18
Front line, midnight July 27
Front line, midnight Aug. 29

Opposite page, far left: (1) The final scope of the Russian offensives in the summer and autumn of 1944. The offensive by 1st Ukrainian Front against Army Group North Ukraine in July and August is covered in map 2, plus the text on the opposite page. Events in Belorussia and the Baltic, where the Red Army was also sweeping through the German defences, are covered on pages 90 and 91.

Opposite page, near left: Soviet troops go into the attack. Despite tactical improvements, the Russians were still careless of lives and relied on the bravery of the individual Russian soldier.

Left: SS Panzer Grenadiers rest during the long retreat out of the Ukraine. Manpower was the only thing in which the Germans were not hopelessly outnumbered in this sector of the front. The Russians had more than double the number of tanks and artillery and four times the number of aircraft.

Below: Troops of a Russian infantry battalion deploy to attack a German defence line. The Germans were continually surprised at the speed of the Red Army's reactions.

Above: (2) The thrust into Poland, July–August 1944. Soviet 1st Ukrainian Front advanced through Lvov and crossed the 1939 Russo-German boundary. This pushed Army Group North Ukraine back beyond Rzeszow and across the Vistula beyond Sandomierz. Then the Russians themselves were brought to a halt by supply problems.

At the Gates of Warsaw

While the Ukrainian Front thrust towards Sandomierz during the Soviet summer offensive of 1944, Zhukov's three Belorussian Fronts overwhelmed Army Group Centre and advanced through Minsk and Brest Litovsk towards Warsaw and through Lithuania towards the Baltic. Although Busch almost had the manpower to match the Russians, he did not have the resources of armour or aircraft to control such a massive front.

The offensive began on June 23, 1944 (map 1). The main forces of IV Army were trapped in the forests east of Minsk and Minsk itself fell on July 4. The Minsk pocket had been eliminated by July 11 and Hitler replaced Busch by Model. By the end of July, the Russians held Brest Litovsk and by the end of August they were within reach of Warsaw and stood along the frontiers of East Prussia.

The gallant Polish Home Army in Warsaw rose in rebellion against the German masters and fought throughout August and September in an effort to determine their own destiny. They expected immediate help from the Allies. The Russians, so close to the city, paused for breath as the Germans crushed the rebellion and destroyed Warsaw, leaving no possibility of national resistance to the subsequent advance of Communism. The Poles surrendered to the Germans on October 2.

The End of Army Group North

With its retreat to Germany threatened by the success of Zhukov's Belorussian Fronts, Army Group North faced a major offensive by the three Baltic Fronts, whose aim in the late summer of 1944 was to liberate the Baltic states of Estonia, Latvia and Lithuania.

The Baltic offensive began in July (map 2). While the Leningrad Front captured Narva, 3rd Baltic Front headed into Latvia and Estonia and 1st and 2nd Baltic Fronts swept towards Memel and Riga. Russian troops reached the Gulf of Riga but the Germans massed six Panzer divisions for a counter-attack in the middle of August. This reopened a land route to Riga.

The Russians renewed their offensive on September 14. 1st Baltic Front held fast; the other two fronts swung down from the north. Tallinn fell to the Leningrad Front on September 22. Riga was taken by October 15. 1st Baltic Front had already reached the Baltic Sea near Memel but the fight for the city dragged on until January 1945. Army Group North was finally cut off in the Courland Peninsula, where the majority remained blockaded until the end of the war. Some units were taken off by sea. North of the Gulf of Riga, the Moonsund Archipelago was cleared by November 24. The Baltic states had exchanged one master for another.

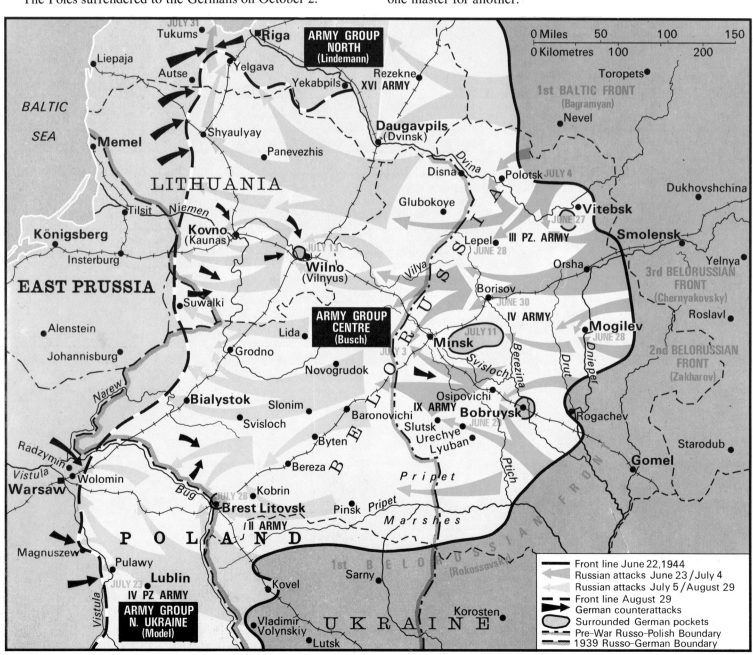

Opposite page: (1) The Belorussian offensive, June–August 1944. Army Group Centre was broken up as Russian armour swept through Minsk and Bobruysk towards Brest Litovsk, Bialystok and Warsaw, and through Wilno, towards Kovno and Riga. The Russians were within reach of the Polish capital when the Polish Home Army rose up in arms against the Germans. The bitterness of the Poles at the failure of the Russians to come to their aid left an indelible mark on their relationships with the Soviet Union.

Right: (2) The Baltic offensive, July–October 1944. Threatened from the south by 3rd Belorussian Front and relentlessly pushed back by the three Baltic Fronts and the Leningrad Front, Army Group North was finally trapped in the Courland Peninsula. This was in spite of a comparatively large scale counter-offensive by six Panzer divisions in the middle of August.

Below: A German Panther is repaired, as the six Panzer divisions prepare to reopen the road to Riga. By this stage in the war, the Wehrmacht was rarely able to mount any major offensives. Riga itself, protected by the German Sigulda Line, was not finally taken until the middle of October.

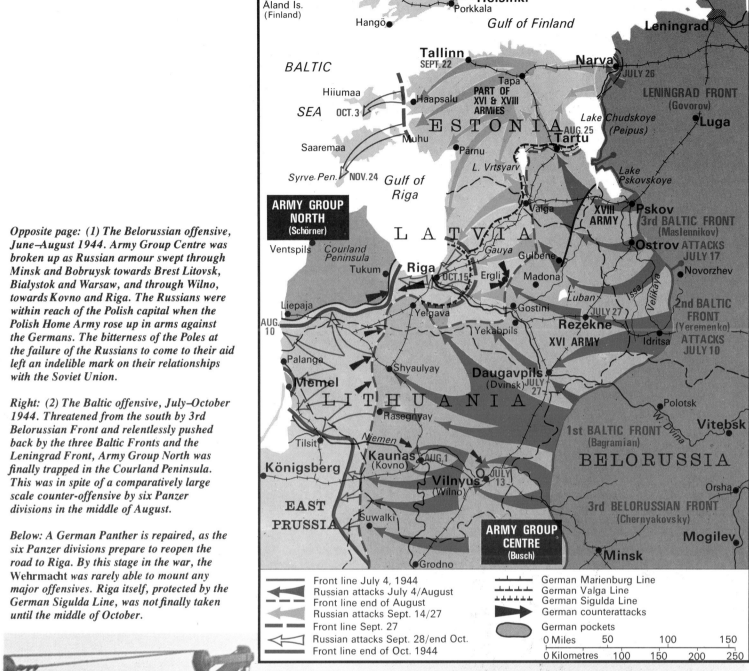

The End of the Arctic War

The Soviet summer offensive of 1944 extended in the extreme north to the Arctic Ocean. The Finns were taken by surprise. Having halted their own offensive of July and August 1941 as soon as they had won back the territory lost to the Russians in 1939–40, they had not expected that the Russians would bother to attack them. They believed that Russia would simply wait for Finland to be brought down in the final German collapse.

There was panic when the Soviet Karelian Front under Meretskov opened its offensive at the beginning of the second week in June 1944. The Soviet 21st and 23rd Armies, later joined by the 59th Army, swept through the VT Line defences on the Karelian Isthmus and captured Viipuri on the VKT Line on June 20 (map 1). On that and the following day, June 20 and 21, the Russians launched a second front north of Lake Ladoga and north of Lake Onega. Here the Finns were forced back to the U Line. Lack of co-ordination between the Soviet forces enabled the Finns to halt their advance at this point. It was something of a defensive victory.

Finland had few illusions about what the Russians could do if they put their mind to it. Peace was the best solution. But the Germans had put the Finns into a difficult position by demanding that they should not make a separate peace with the Russians. President Ryti had given his pledge to the Germans. On August 4, Mannerheim replaced him as president and made it clear that he would not keep Ryti's pledge. Finland accepted Russia's preliminary peace conditions on September 2 and a provisional peace treaty was signed on September 19. Meretskov then ordered the Soviet armies in the extreme north to begin operations against the Germans in Finland.

This third Russian front in Finland was opened by the Soviet 14th and 19th Armies (map 2). 19th Army had already broken through the German–Finnish defences in the first half of September and pushed back units of the German 20th Mountain Army near Salla, clearing them from Russian soil. 14th Army attacked farther north in early October, broke through the German defences on the Litsa, captured Petsano and, with the aid of amphibious operations, pushed 20th Mountain Army back into Norway by the end of the month.

Left: Marshal Mannerheim, who commanded the Finnish forces against the Russians. He succeeded Ryti as president in August 1944.

Right: (2) The northern offensive against the Germans in October.

Below: (1) The southern and central offensives in June and July 1944. The Russians failed to co-ordinate their attacks.

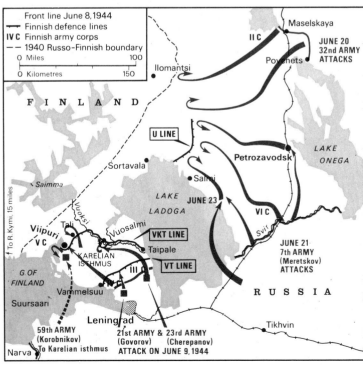

Clearing the Balkans

In the extreme south, near the Black Sea, the Soviet summer offensive of 1944 appeared to have lagged behind. Between April and August 1944, there were four months of tense quiet in this sector of the front. The quiet was broken on August 20, when 2nd and 3rd Ukrainian Fronts attacked Freissner's Army Group South Ukraine and trapped Rumanian III Army and German VI Army (see map below). Three days later Rumania surrendered and on August 29 the Russians reached the Danube. Moving on to Bucharest, they began to swing west and north, threatening to surround the remains of Army Group South Ukraine and to cut off Lohr's Army Group in Greece. The Germans were unable to hold the Transylvanian passes and the Russians had over-run Rumania by September 24.

On September 2, Soviet forces reached the Bulgarian border and crossed over six days later. Bulgaria was in Soviet hands by early October. The advance continued into Yugoslavia but was too slow to catch German Army Groups E and F, which managed to retreat under pressure to new defence lines in northern Yugoslavia. Helped by Tito's partisans, the Russians forced the Germans to evacuate Belgrade on October 19.

Further north, the Russians had over-extended themselves in their advance into Hungary. The Germans were to prove that they could still turn and fight. A massive tank battle around Debrecan between October 10 and 29 ended with the Germans withdrawing westwards and then counter-attacking to cut off and destroy three Soviet corps. The Russians were not to reach Budapest until the end of December and did not take the city until the middle of February 1945.

The Advance Towards Vienna

By Christmas 1944, the Russians had encircled Budapest, where a garrison of four German and two Hungarian divisions were forced to remain behind on Hitler's orders. In January 1945, IV SS Panzer Corps achieved a small dent in the Soviet line in an attempt to reach Budapest but was stopped after some early success. In the same month, the Soviets achieved a bridgehead across the Hron, north of the Danube. In the second week in February, the Budapest garrison made an attempt to break out of their prison-fortress. Only a mere handful succeeded in reaching the German lines. The majority were killed, wounded or taken prisoner.

The fall of Budapest was not the end of the Hungarian operation. Hitler was still obsessed with the importance of the Lake Balaton oil-fields and was determined to gain a prestige victory (as he had hoped to do at Kursk). Wohler's Army Group South prepared for Operation *Fruhlingserwachen*. VI SS Panzer Army was to break through the Russian front north of Lake Balaton and spread north towards Budapest and south towards Baja, to hold a line along the Danube, while II Panzer Army struck south of Lake Balaton and headed directly east towards the Danube. Another German strike was planned in the south to reach the Danube at Mohacs.

Hitler's last fling failed. The offensive began on March 6 but the Russians were already planning their counter-offensive, which began on March 16 (see map below). The collapse of the Hungarian III Army and lack of fuel forced Wohler to call a halt to Operation *Fruhlingserwachen*. By March 25, 2nd Ukrainian Front was advancing across the Hron and by March 28 Russian forces farther south had reached the Austrian border in the Koszeg–Szombathely sector. Two weeks later, on April 14, Vienna fell to the Russians. On May 7, 1945, Army Group South surrendered to the US 3rd Army, which had approached from the west.

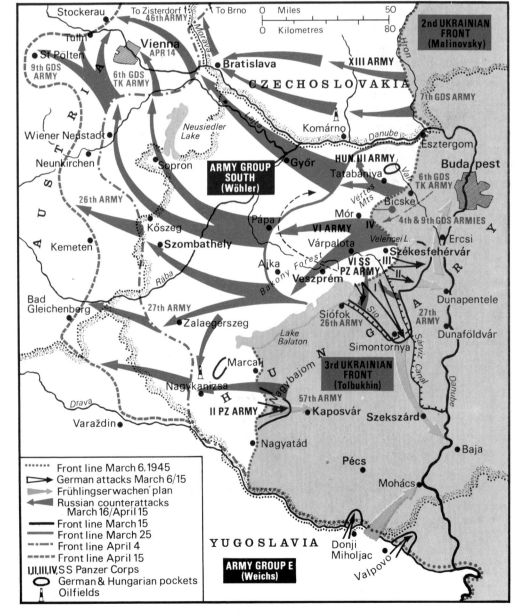

Above: The battle for Vienna. Hitler sent XXV Panzer Division and the 'Fuhrer' Grenadier Division to defend Vienna. They were in no position by then to make the sort of stand that had been made at Budapest. The fighting in the city lasted little more than a week, and was over by April 13–14.

Left: The Soviet advance from Budapest to Vienna, December 1944 to April 1945. The map also shows Hitler's final offensive, the ill-fated Operation Fruhlingserwachen *in early March 1945. German Army Group South fought on in Austria until May 7, when its commander (Rendulic had replaced Wohler at the beginning of April) surrendered most of his forces to Patton's US 3rd Army.*

The Russians Reach the Oder

The Russians opened a major new offensive into Germany in January 1945 (see map below). On January 12, Rokossovsky's 2nd Belorussian Front crossed the Narew north of Warsaw and struck II Army, then continued north-west towards Danzig. At the same time, 47th Army encircled Warsaw, which fell on January 17.

To the south of Warsaw, a massive assault was launched by 1st Belorussian and 1st Ukrainian Fronts, with 4th Ukrainian Front farther south. Completely outnumbered and outgunned, without adequate defensive lines, the Germans fell back through Poland into their homeland, leaving only pockets of resistance behind. The Russians moved in pursuit with remarkable swiftness. Zhukov's forces reached the Oder on January 31, after an advance of about 300 miles in less than three weeks. The offensive relieved the pressure on the Allies in the west after the German Ardennes offensive.

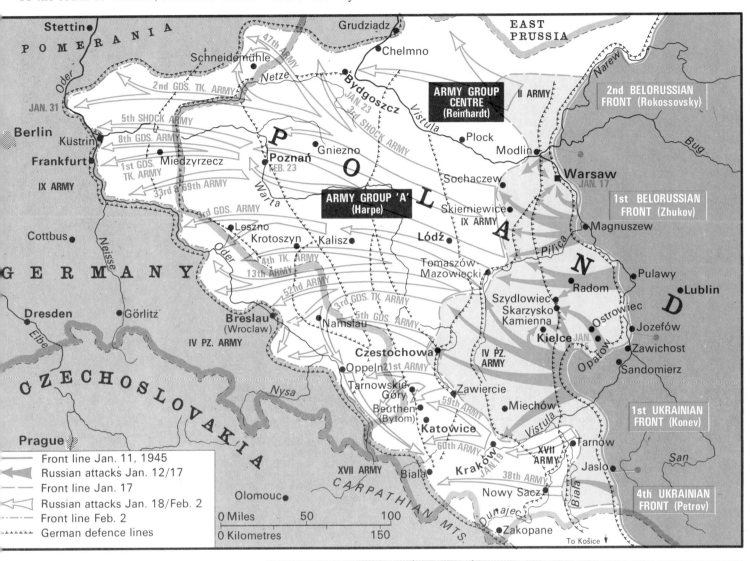

Above: The Soviet offensive, January 1945, through western Poland and into the Reich. Army Group A was swept back by the overwhelming onrush of the 'Bolshevik Horde'. Army Group Centre was cut off in the north and pushed remorselessly back towards the Baltic.

Right: Signs of things to come, as Russian signposts go up on the Polish–German frontier. The 'New Order' had arrived. The Russians were still pushing on towards Berlin to claim their final victory.

Operations in the E. Prussia area
— Front line January 13, 1945
▶ Russian attacks Jan. 13/18
▶ Russian attacks Jan. 19/26
▷ Russian attacks Jan. 27/Apr. 13
▷ Russian attacks Apr. 13/May 9

Operations in Silesia
— Front line February 1
▷ Russian attacks Feb. 8/24
--- Front line Feb. 24
▷ Russian attacks Mar. 15/31
--- Front line Mar. 31

Operations in Pomerania
— Front line February 1, 1945
▷ Russian attacks Feb. 10/20
—·— Front line Feb. 20
▷ Russian attacks Feb. 24/Mar. 31
— Front line Mar. 31

◖ German pockets
◣ German counterattacks
⚓ German naval bases
+++ Main Railways

MAY 9
GERMAN FORCES ON
HEILIGENBEIL & DANZIG
BEACHHEADS SURRENDER

BALTIC SEA

Samland Pen.

Königs

APR. 26
Pillau

Hel Peninsula

Puck

Bay of
Danzig

Heiligenbe

Frische
Nehrung

Braunsberg

Gdynia
MAR. 28

Sopot

Danzig
MAR. 30

Frisches
Haff

JAN. 27
FEB. 1

Stolpmünde

19th ARMY &
1st GDS. TK.
ARMY

II ARMY

Wormditt

Elbing
FEB. 10

Rügen

Peenemünde

Kolberg
MAR. 18

Köslin
MAR. 5

Deep

Treptow

1st POL

Belgard

Bublitz

Rummelsburg

Prechlau

Czersk

Tczew

Gniew

5th GDS.
TK. ARMY

Wartenbur

Allenst

Deutsch
Eylau

Swinemünde

Stettiner
Haff

III PZ. ARMY

1st GDS. TK.
ARMY

3rd SHOCK
ARMY

2nd GDS.
TK. ARMY

Gross
Radow

ARMY GROUP VISTULA
(Himmler)

Neustettin

Chojnice

Linde

70th

49th

65th

2nd SHOCK
ARMY

Grudziadz
APR. 6

Gilgenbu

Stettin

Gollnow
61st ARMY

III PZ. ARMY
(From Feb. 23)

Polzin

Falkenburg

Ratzebuhr

Sepolno

XI ARMY

2nd BELORUSSIAN

Prenzlau

Altdamm

Stargard

Deutsch
Krone

Schneidemühl
FEB. 14

19th
ARMY

Neustrelitz

Königsberg

47th
ARMY

Pyritz

Arnswalde

GERMAN
COUNTERATTACKS
FEB. 16/20

Bydgoszcz

Vistula

Zehden

Notec

Inowroclaw

Wloclawek

Bielsk

5th SHOCK ARMY

Berlin

Küstrin

IX ARMY

8th GUARDS
ARMY

1st BELORUSSIAN FRONT
(Zhukov)

Poznan
FEB. 23

FRONT LINE AFTER
VISTULA / ODER OPERATIONS
(1st BELORUSSIAN & 1st UKRAINIAN
FRONTS) JAN./FEB., 1945

Kolo

Kutno

Modl

ARMY GROUP

Frankfurt

Fürstenberg

Warta

Lübben

Guben

Oder

Grünberg

Leszno

2nd POL. ARMY

Kolo

Kalisz

Lodz

Cottbus

Forst

Glogau

Krotoszyn

Piotrkow

Sorau

Neisse

IV PZ. ARMY

13th ARMY
52nd ARMY
4th TK. ARMY

1st UKRAINIAN FRONT
(Konev)

Rothenburg

Bautzen

Penzig

Bunzlau

Steinau
3rd GDS. ARMY
6th ARMY

Dresden

Görlitz

Liegnitz

Bober

Lauban

Breslau
MAY 6

Ohlau

Brieg

4th TK. ARMY
(From right wing)

Czestochowa

Usti

Strehlen

5th GDS.
ARMY

21st ARMY

Grottkau

Oppeln

Zawiercie

ARMY GROUP CENTRE
(Schörner)

Neisse

Neustadt

Kosel

59th ARMY

Katowice

CZECHOSLOVAKIA

Elbe

Prague

Ratibor

60th ARMY

Krakow

Kolín

0 ———————— 80 Miles
0 ———————— 120 Kilometres

Opava

Opole

38th ARMY

PART OF I PZ ARMY

The map on the left shows labels:

Annexed by Germany from Lithuania 1939

LITHUANIA

1st BALTIC FRONT (Bagramyan)

43rd ARMY

Niemen

Tilsit

39th ARMY

5th ARMY

Pillkallen

Schirwindt

Kraupishken

28th ARMY

Pregel

Vilkaviškis

Insterburg

Stallupönen

Gumbinnen

Friedland

2nd GDS. ARMY

3rd BELORUSSIAN FRONT (Chernyakhovsky)

SSIA

Schippenbeil

Goldap

OUP CENTRE (NORTH JAN 25) nhardt)

Suwalki

Masurian

IV ARMY

ischofsburg

Augustow

Jikolaiken

Lakes

31st ARMY

burg

50th ARMY

Nowogrod

Narew

Bialystok

49th ARMY

N   D

Rozan

3rd & 48th ARMIES

2nd SHOCK ARMY

2nd BELORUSSIAN FRONT (Rokossovsky)

65th ARMY

70th ARMY

5th GDS. TK. ARMY

Serock

Warsaw

East Prussia, Pomerania and Silesia

After their rapid advance to the Oder, the Russians had to secure their flanks, in East Prussia and Pomerania to the north and in Silesia to the south, before their final attack on Berlin (see map). Rokossovsky's 2nd Belorussian Front, which had cut off Army Group Centre (renamed Army Group North) in January, was joined by 3rd Belorussian and 1st Baltic Fronts. By early February, the Germans were forced back into a few pockets of resistance along the Bay of Danzig. Those who were not evacuated by the German Navy surrendered on May 9.

The Russians advanced their flanks through Pomerania, against Army Group Vistula, and through Silesia, against Schorner's Army Group Centre. German counter-attacks in Pomerania, south of Stettin, between February 16 and 20, were contained and by the end of March the Russians stood on a line from Stettin south to Penzig, along the Oder and the Neisse.

Left and above: The Russian offensives through Poland into East Prussia, Pomerania and Silesia, January–March 1945.

Above: A German Volkssturm *(home guard) member receives anti-tank Panzerfaust instruction.*

Below: Fighting on German soil, the Russians advance through the streets of Breslau, capital of Silesia.

The Battle for Berlin

The Russians meant to reach Berlin before the western Allies, who were advancing towards the Elbe early in April 1945. The Soviet plan was for Zhukov's 1st Belorussian Front to advance directly west towards the city while Konev's 1st Ukrainian Front advanced south of a line established by Stalin which allowed Konev to swing north towards Berlin after Luben (map 1).

The Russian advance on April 16 met bitter resistance for two days. On April 25, the two Russian fronts met to the west of Berlin and on the same day elements of Bradley's 12th Army Group and Konev's 1st Ukrainian Front made contact at Torgau on the Elbe. Pockets of Army Group Vistula and Army Group Centre vainly attempted to surrender to the western Allies in preference to the Russians.

In Berlin, Zhukov fought his way through to the River Spree, while Konev came from the south through the *Tiergarten* (map 2). On April 30, the *Reichstag* fell and Hitler, appointing Doenitz as his successor, committed suicide in his command bunker in the garden of the Chancellery. On May 2, the two Russian fronts met in the *Tiergarten* and the last resistance was quelled.

To the north, 2nd Belorussian Front pursued III Panzer Army. To the south a large part of XII Army, pursued by 1st Belorussian Front, crossed the Elbe and had surrendered to the Americans by May 7. Resistance remained only in the city of Prague and among the survivors of Schorner's Army Group Centre, holding out in Bohemia.

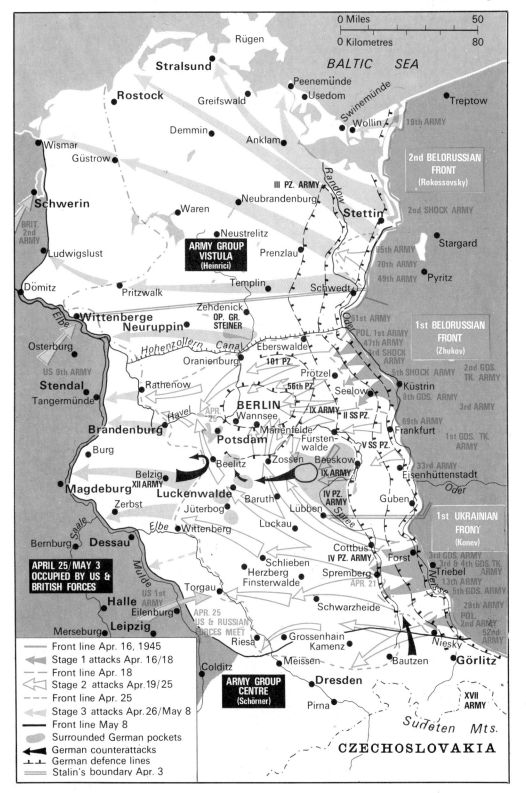

Above: Stalin directs the final assault on Berlin, determined to capture Hitler's capital before his western Allies.

Left: (1) With the western Allies on the Elbe, Zhukov's 1st Belorussian Front and Konev's 1st Ukrainian Front made the final drive for Berlin, April 1945. Rokossovsky meanwhile over-ran Army Group Vistula. German resistance was either overwhelmed or driven into the arms of western Allies.

Right: One sector of the massive Russian artillery line at the start of the final Berlin offensive. The Russians had an unprecedented artillery density of one gun every 13 feet, a ratio of four to one against the German tanks, and more than double the number of aircraft. Despite their great losses in the preceding months, the Germans were still able to put a million men into the defences around Berlin. These were pitted against the two-and-a-half million fielded by Zhukov and Konev.

Below: (2) The Battle for the Reichstag, in the last days of April 1945. It fell to Zhukov's 1st Belorussian Front. The Red Flag was hoisted above the ruins on April 30. The Tiergarten and the Chancellery, to the south of Charlottenburger Chaussee, were over-run by Konev's 1st Ukrainian Front.

Below: The last stand is over. One of the 2,600 surviving defenders of the Reichstag. Another 2,500 were killed in the fighting against Russian soldiers. Hitler killed himself before the last resistance ended.

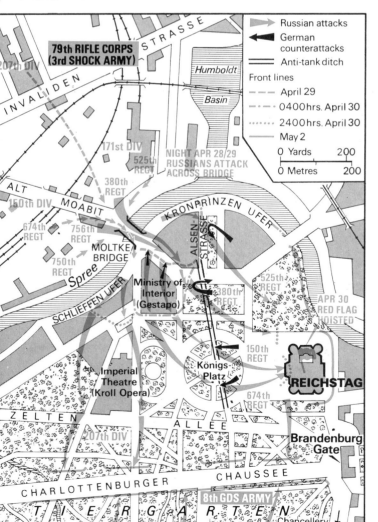

Czechoslovakia: the End of German Arms

With the fall of Berlin on May 2, 1945, and the surrender of the majority of the German forces, the only substantial German resistance was in Czechoslovakia, completely surrounded by the Russians and the western Allies.

Slovakia had not succumbed easily to German arms. As in France, Yugoslavia and Poland, resistance fighters had proved to be an effective irritant. The entry of German military units in August 1944, when Soviet 4th and 1st Belorussian Fronts were bearing down through Poland, had provoked a premature Slovak rising (map 1). Although the rising was planned with great efficiency, not all the Slovak garrisons joined the insurgents and German counter-moves were prompt and ruthless. The Germans attacked again in October (map 2), driving the rebels into the Tatra Mountains, where they linked up with the advancing Russians (map 3).

The Russian advance continued, with the help of the partisans, from January to April 1945. By the end of April, Schorner's Army Group Centre was desperately holding on to the Reich's last important industrial resource area (map 4). Schorner's position was hopeless and Konev's dash south after the fall of Berlin sealed his fate. On May 5, the insurgents in Prague seized the capital's key points and forced the *Reichprotektor* to negotiate. On May 8, the Russians launched a final offensive against Army Group Centre and on May 9 Prague was liberated. Schorner was forced to capitulate on May 11. The last sizeable German force in Europe laid down its arms, caught between Allied armies from east and west.

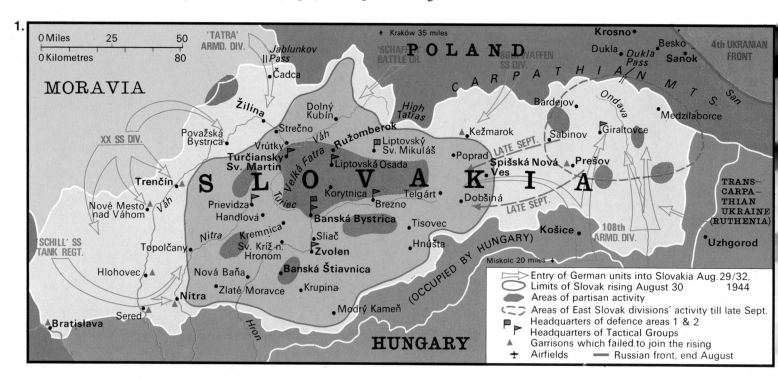

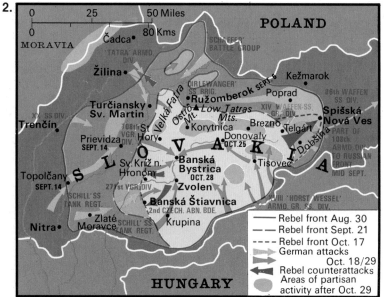

Above: (1) August 1944. The first phase of the Slovak rising in response to the movement of German forces into Slovakia. Below: (2) August–October 1944. The second phase of the rising, showing the German attacks during October. Below right: (3) September–November. The Russians enter Slovakia.

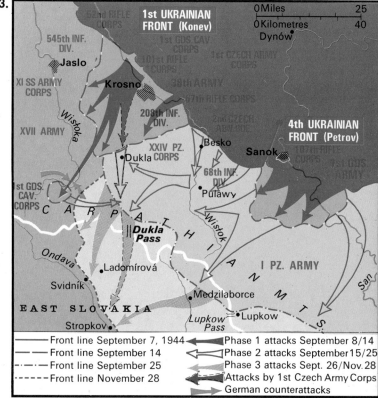

Below: (4) Schorner's Army Group Centre held on to Germany's last industrial resource until the bitter end. With substantial numbers of men and tanks, he was vastly outnumbered in guns and aircraft, and completely surrounded. It was only a matter of days before he, too, was forced to surrender.

Above: Prague was liberated on May 9, 1945. Here, the Red Army is welcomed into the city. There was immediate relief at the overthrow of the German aggressor. Few suspected what the future held in store.

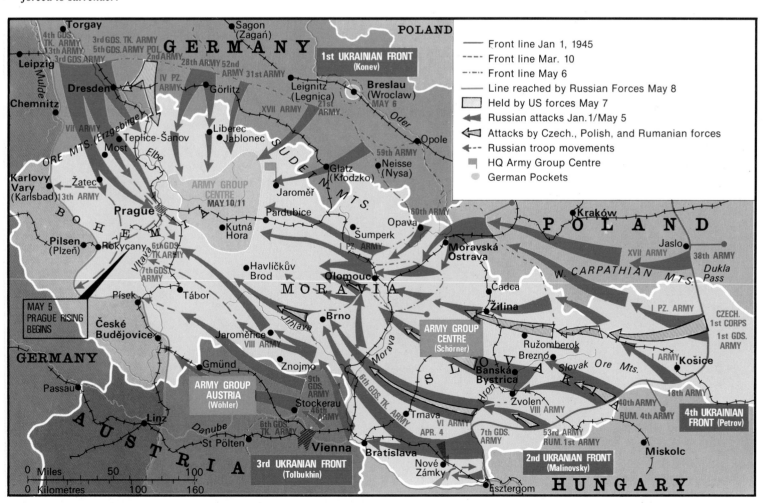

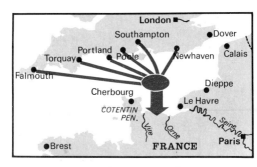

(1) *Calais was too far to the east for convoys based on the western ports. On the other hand, Normandy was approximately equidistant from all the major ports along the south coast of Britain.*

Above: One of the most common German defences along the invasion coast, these Tetrahydra were intended to disembowel and sink Allied landing craft when they came in over the beaches. Below: (5) Hitler's garrison in the West. Neither Rommel nor Hitler believed that the Allies would ignore the short crossing at the Pas de Calais. XV Army was strongest at this point.

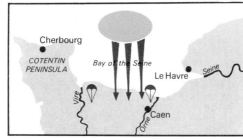

(2) The preliminary plan for the invasion of Europe envisaged only two airborne brigades to cover the flanks, and only three assault divisions to be landed on the sector between the Vire and the Orne.

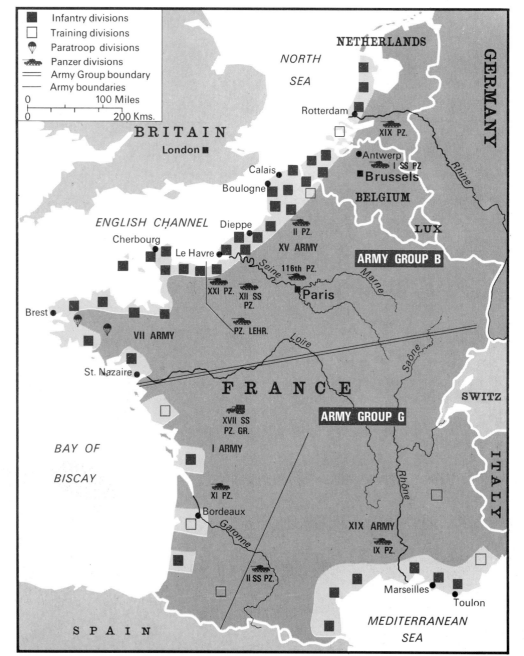

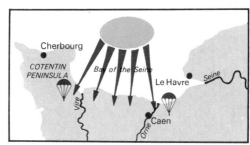

(3) Montgomery reacted unfavourably to the preliminary plan. He demanded five divisions instead of three, as well as two full-strength airborne divisions and separate sectors for US and British forces with a beach for each corps.

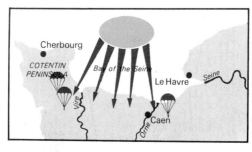

(4) Eisenhower's staff backed Montgomery's broadening of the assault plan and added a third airborne division. Build-up preparations were intensified. It was planned to get 18 divisions ashore by D+10.

The Allied Invasion of North-west Europe

While Hitler tried to stem the tide of the Russian advance through the Ukraine in the spring of 1944, he knew that an Allied attempt to force a landing on the coast of France was imminent. Fifty-eight divisions, under Rundstedt, were spread out from the Netherlands to the Italian frontier to await the invasion (map 6) but Hitler's own belief was that the blow must fall at the Pas de Calais, the narrowest stretch of water between France and England (map 5). This was therefore the strongest point of his much-vaunted 'Atlantic Wall'.

A disastrous 'reconnaissance in force' had been made by the Allies at Dieppe on August 19, 1942, but it had at least given them some idea of the strength and methods of the German defences. At the Trident Conference in May 1943, in Washington, Roosevelt and Churchill agreed to lay plans for a proper invasion in early summer 1944. The target was to be Normandy, between Cherbourg and Le Havre. There were several reasons for this choice. The area was close to Allied fighter bases in southern England and it provided the overall shortest distances to be covered by supplies and reinforcements from both south-east and south-west England. There were suitable beaches for landing and the countryside inland was favourable for fighting. Above all, German defences were not as strong as in the Pas de Calais. A complex deception plan was laid to persuade the Germans that the Pas de Calais was still the main objective and that the Normandy probe was merely a dummy.

Eisenhower was in command of the vast amphibious operation, with Montgomery in command of the Allied ground forces. Bradley's US 1st Army and Dempsey's 2nd Army were to land on five beaches, with their flanks protected by US 82nd and 101st Airborne Divisions and British 8th Airborne Division. This plan was eventually arrived at after several modifications (maps 1–4). Operation Overlord was to go into action the first week in June 1944, during the few days on which there were optimum conditions of moon and tide for the landings. In one way or another, nearly three million men were involved in the vital bid to regain a foothold on French soil.

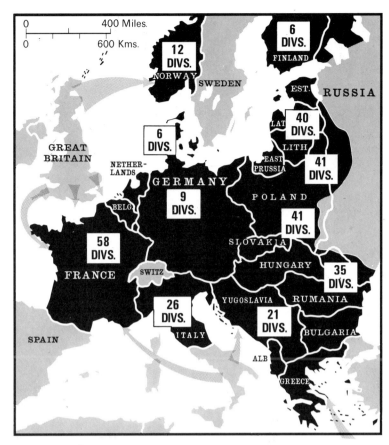

Above: (6) Hitler's guessing game. By spring 1944, the Germans were waiting for the Allies to open another front in the west. There were various points from which they expected assaults to be made (shown by the pink arrows) but the main blow, they knew, would be a cross-Channel invasion. There was still a large area to cover. Fifty-eight divisions were allocated to cover the frontier, divided into two army groups. The chain of command through Rundstedt was never clear because Hitler constantly interfered.

Below: Hitler's 'Atlantic Wall'. He saw it as an impregnable forest of entanglements backed by huge guns. However, the Pas de Calais apart, it consisted largely of scattered defences, as shown by these bunkers along the coast.

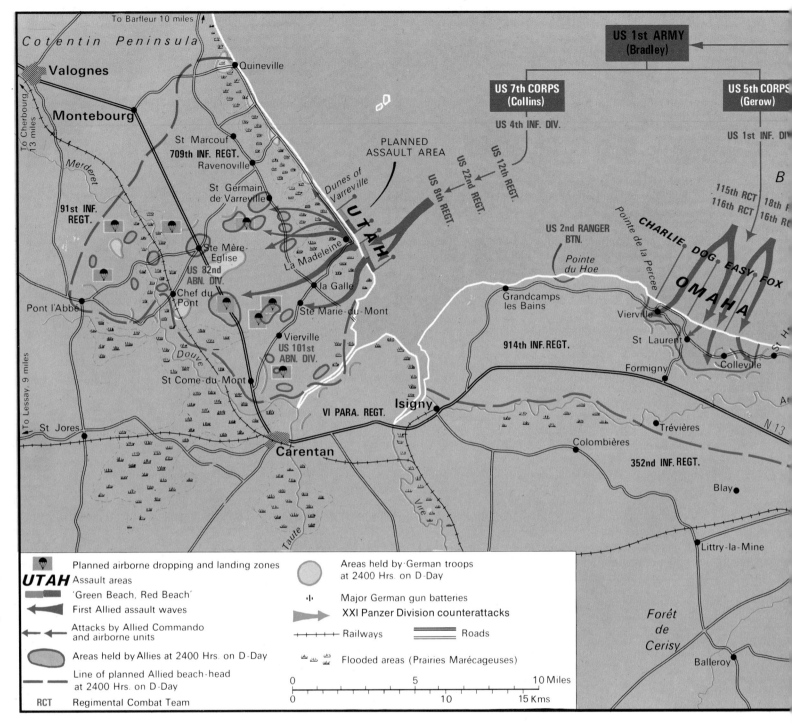

Map labels:

To Barfleur 10 miles

Cotentin Peninsula

Valognes

To Cherbourg, 13 miles

Montebourg

Quineville

St Marcouf
709th INF. REGT.
Ravenoville

Merderet

St Germain de Varreville

91st INF. REGT.

Dunes of Varreville

PLANNED ASSAULT AREA

UTAH

US 1st ARMY (Bradley)

US 7th CORPS (Collins)
US 4th INF. DIV.

US 5th CORPS (Gerow)
US 1st INF. DIV

US 12th REGT.

US 22nd REGT.

US 8th REGT.

Ste Mère-Eglise

La Madeleine

US 82nd ABN. DIV.

Pont l'Abbé

Chef du Pont

la Galle

Ste Marie-du-Mont

US 2nd RANGER BTN.

Pointe du Hoe

Pointe de la Percée

CHARLIE DOG EASY FOX

OMAHA

115th RCT   18th
116th RCT   16th R

Grandcamps les Bains

Vierville

St Laurent

Colleville

Formigny

Douve

Vierville
US 101st ABN. DIV.

St Come-du-Mont

914th INF. REGT.

St Jores

VI PARA. REGT.

Isigny

Trévières

Colombières

352nd INF. REGT.

N 13

To Lessay, 9 miles

Carentan

Taute

Vire

Blay

Littry-la-Mine

Forét de Cerisy

Balleroy

Legend:
Planned airborne dropping and landing zones
UTAH Assault areas
'Green Beach, Red Beach'
First Allied assault waves
Attacks by Allied Commando and airborne units
Areas held by Allies at 2400 Hrs. on D-Day
Line of planned Allied beach-head at 2400 Hrs. on D-Day
RCT Regimental Combat Team

Areas held by German troops at 2400 Hrs. on D-Day
Major German gun batteries
XXI Panzer Division counterattacks
Railways   Roads
Flooded areas (Prairies Marécageuses)

0   5   10 Miles
0   10   15 Kms

D-Day: Operation Overlord

Bad weather at the beginning of June threatened to disrupt the invasion of Europe. Taking advantage of a fair break, Eisenhower decided to go ahead on June 6. The assault force consisted of some 4,000 ships and landing craft carrying 176,000 troops and their *matériel*, escorted by 600 warships, with 2,500 bombers and 7,000 fighters and fighter-bombers overhead. The invasion was preceded by a heavy aerial bombardment. In the first hours of June 6, the American and British airborne forces went in on either flank, achieving complete tactical surprise. At dawn, aircraft and warships 'softened up' the beaches before the first soldiers landed at 0630 hours.

On the Allied right, US 7th Corps landed on Utah beach with negligible losses. They made contact with the airborne troops and quickly established a substantial bridgehead. To their left, US 5th Corps ran into serious trouble on Omaha beach. Lacking the necessary equipment to deal with the defences, the troops were pinned down on the beach with heavy losses. By midnight, they had achieved a bridgehead of no more

than a mile.

On the Allied left, British 30th Corps landed on Gold beach and British 1st Corps landed on Juno and Sword, with the Canadians taking Juno. The use of specialized armour to overcome the beach obstacles enabled the British and Canadians to break through stiff pockets of resistance and move swiftly forward off the beaches. By early afternoon, both beach-heads had advanced well inland.

It was at this point that the Germans attempted to counterattack. XXI Panzer Division attacked between Juno and Sword but withdrew when their retreat was threatened by reinforcements flown in to the airborne troops behind them. For the rest of the day, the weight of the German defensive armour was pinned down on the Allied left wing, giving the Americans on Omaha beach a chance to cling on to their precarious beach-head. Although the Allies did not achieve all their main objectives in the first day, by midnight four of the landings were secure and 5th Corps was still in position on Omaha. The foothold had been won on the mainland of Europe.

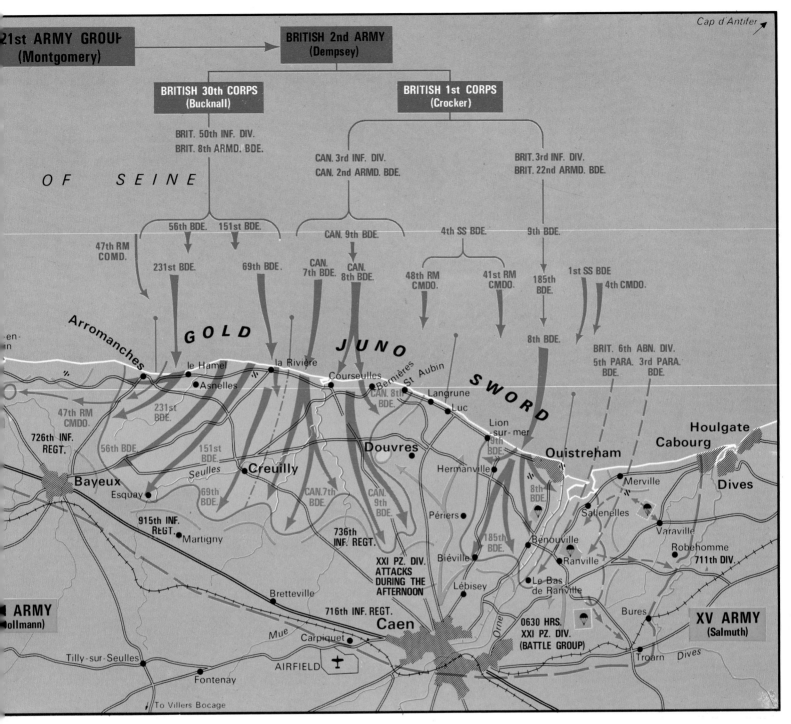

Cap d'Antifer

21st ARMY GROUP
(Montgomery) → BRITISH 2nd ARMY
(Dempsey)

BRITISH 30th CORPS
(Bucknall)

BRITISH 1st CORPS
(Crocker)

BRIT. 50th INF. DIV.
BRIT. 8th ARMD. BDE.

CAN. 3rd INF. DIV.
CAN. 2nd ARMD. BDE.

BRIT. 3rd INF. DIV.
BRIT. 22nd ARMD. BDE.

OF SEINE

56th BDE.   151st BDE.

CAN. 9th BDE.

4th SS BDE.   9th BDE.

47th RM
COMD.

231st BDE.

69th BDE.

CAN.
7th
BDE.

CAN.
8th
BDE.

48th RM
CMDO.

41st RM
CMDO.

185th
BDE.

1st SS BDE

4th CMDO.

Arromanches

GOLD

JUNO

SWORD

8th BDE.

BRIT. 6th ABN. DIV.
5th PARA. 3rd PARA.
BDE.   BDE.

le Hamel   la Rivière
Asnelles

Courseulles   Bernières   St. Aubin
CAN. 8th   Langrune
BDE.   Luc

Lion
-sur-mer

Houlgate
Cabourg

47th RM
CMDO.

231st
BDE.

726th INF.
REGT.

56th BDE.

151st
BDE.

69th
BDE.

Seulles

Creuilly

Douvres

Hermanville

9th
BDE.

Ouistreham

Merville

Dives

Bayeux
Esquay

915th INF.
REGT.
Martigny

CAN.7th
BDE.

CAN.
9th
BDE.

736th
INF. REGT.

Périers

8th
BDE.

185th
BDE.

Bénouville
Ranville

Sallenelles

Varaville

Robehomme
711th DIV.

XXI PZ. DIV.
ATTACKS
DURING THE
AFTERNOON

Biéville

Lébisey

Le Bas
de Ranville

Bures

XV ARMY
(Salmuth)

Bretteville

716th INF. REGT.

Caen

ARMY
(ollmann)

Mue   Carpiquet

0630 HRS.
XXI PZ. DIV.
(BATTLE GROUP)

Troarn   Dives

Tilly-sur-Seulles

AIRFIELD

Fontenay

To Villers Bocage

Above: Operation Overlord, D-Day, June 6, 1944. American 7th and 5th Corps landed on Utah and Omaha beaches to the west, while British 30th and 1st Corps, including the Canadians, landed on Gold,

Juno and Sword beaches to the east. XXI Panzer Division's counter-attack between Juno and Sword failed. The Germans were surprised by the sheer weight of the invasion and were slow to react.

Left: Commandos go ashore in the British sector. They were able to clear the beaches quickly and with minimum casualties.

Right: Ramps down, and American troops advance on to the open beach.

Cap de la Hague
● Auderville

JUNE 30
END OF GERMAN
RESISTANCE IN
COTENTIN PENINSULA

JUNE 29
US 7th CORPS TAKES
CHERBOURG

Cap Lévy

Pt. de Barfleur

Cherbourg

● Beaumont

● St Pierre-Eglise

● Barfleur

● St Croix

FORT DU
ROULE

● Brillevast

SITUATION JUNE 21

● Quettehou

US 4th DIV.

● St Vaast-la-Hougue

● Brix

● Les Pieux

Douve

SITUATION JUNE 19

709th DIV.

● Quinevile

Valognes

● Ozeville

US 4th
DIV.

US 9th DIV.

● Bricquebec

Montebourg

● Crisbecq

Merderet

US
79th DIV.

US 90th
DIV.

● Azeville

US 82nd
ABN. DIV.

US 9th DIV.

243rd DIV.

2400 HRS. D-DAY
APPROXIMATE PERIM
OF BEACH-HEAD

● Barneville-Carteret

St Sauveur ●

US 82nd ABN. DIV.

● Ste Mère-
Eglise

●UTAH BEAC

● Carteret

US 7th CORPS

91st DIV.

US 101st
ABN. DIV.

Gran
les B

77th DIV.

US 79th DIV.

NEWLY ARRIVED
US 8th CORPS

US 29t

● Portbail

353rd DIV.

US 7th CORPS

US 2nd
ARMD. DIV.

● Isign
JUNE 8

US 83rd DIV.

Carentan
JUNE 11

US 30th DIV.

US 3rd ARM

● La Haye
du Puits

NEWLY AR
US 19th C

XVII SS PZ. GR. DIV.
& VI PARA. REGT.

● St. Jean-
de-Daye

84th CORPS

● Lessay

Taute

Vire

● Périers

US 3

To Coutances 6 miles
& Avranches 40 miles

VII ARMY
(Dollmann)

352

To Coutances
5 miles

	Areas held by Allies 2400 Hrs. on D-Day		┼┼┼	Railways
▬ ▬	Front line morning June 10		▤▤▤	Roads
▬ ·▬	" " " June 18		⚏ ⚏	Flooded areas (Prairies Marécageuses)
▬▬	" " " July 25			Boundary between US 1st Army
➤	Allied attacks			& British 2nd Army
◄	German counterattacks			Allied corps boundaries

● Marigny

St Lô
JULY 18

II PARA. CORPS

0 ——— 5 ——— 10 Miles

0 ——— 10 ——— 15 Kilometres

The Battle of the Hedgerows

The movement of German forces to counter Operation Overlord had been made difficult by pre-invasion bombardments of rail communications. In any case, Hitler was unwilling to transfer reinforcements to the Normandy area when he was still convinced that the real invasion would come in the Pas de Calais. Even so, it was the third day before the Allies linked their beach-heads and they had to battle for every bit of ground.

German armour concentrated around Caen resisted all Allied attempts to push past it towards Falaise. To the west, the Americans advanced through the Cotentin Peninsula, towards Cherbourg, which was badly needed for its port facilities. They ran into strong opposition around Carentan, which they took on June 11, but by June 17 they had reached Carteret and Portbail on the west coast. Then a Channel storm destroyed the artificial Mulberry harbour on Omaha Beach and seriously damaged the one on Gold beach. Vital craft were lost and the flow of reinforcements and supplies was greatly reduced. It was not until a week after the storm that the Americans took Cherbourg and they found it left in ruins by the Germans.

US 7th Corps turned south and, joined by the newly arrived US 8th Corps, fought through the *bocage*, the checkerboard of fields and hedgerows that made ideal cover for the Germans. Bradley struck at VII Army and reached St Lô on July 18.

Progress had been very slow on the Allied left wing. Operations Epsom and Goodwood, in June and July, had both been held by German armour. Caen itself did not fall till mid-July. But by July 24, the Allies were ready for the breakout.

Rundstedt: 'As German C-in-C West, my sole prerogative was to change the guard in front of my gate.'

Rommel: repeatedly forced to postpone his decisive counter-attack, then almost killed by RAF fighter-bombers.

Von Geyr: his Panzer Group West failed to crush the first landings and was never given another chance.

Montgomery: he refused to be governed by the time-table in his conduct of the early battles in Normandy.

Bradley: charged with the early capture of Cherbourg and with the southward drive towards St Lô, a major objective.

Dempsey: as C-in-C British 2nd Army, he was accused of not trying hard enough to break through to Falaise.

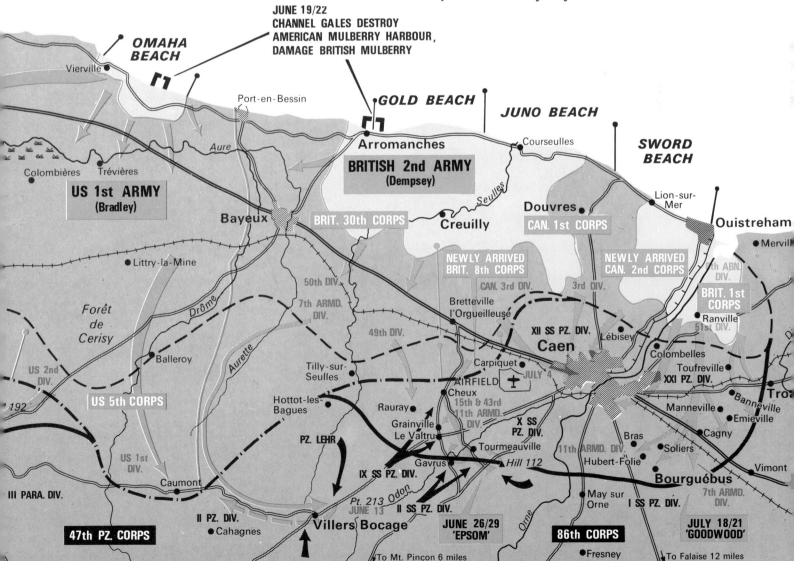

The Anvil Landings

It was the Americans who chiefly favoured the 'hammer' of the Normandy landings supported by the 'anvil' of a strike in southern France, in preference to renewed emphasis on the Italian Front. The landings between Cannes and Toulon on August 15, 1944, were immediately successful. Heavy toll was taken of the German XIX Army before it escaped north and Truscott's US 6th Corps and the French 2nd Corps succeeded in eliminating the German forces in southern France.

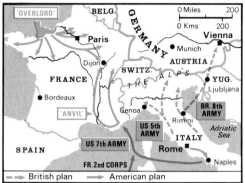

Left: The British argued that if the Italian Front had received the support given to the Normandy landings, it could have broken through to Vienna before the Russians. The Americans opted for Overlord and Anvil.

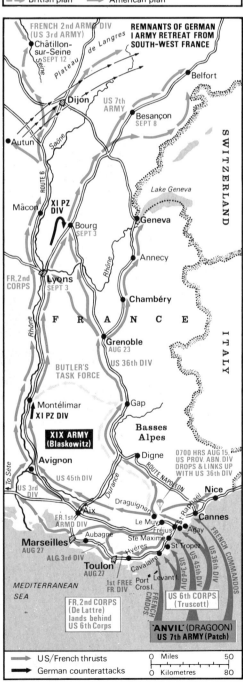

Bottom left: US 7th Army landed at Anvil against little resistance. French 2nd Corps passed through 7th Army and led the advance through Marseilles, Lyons and Dijon to link with US 3rd Army on September 12. On the right, Butler's Task Force turned west from Gap to Montelimar to cut off XIX Army.

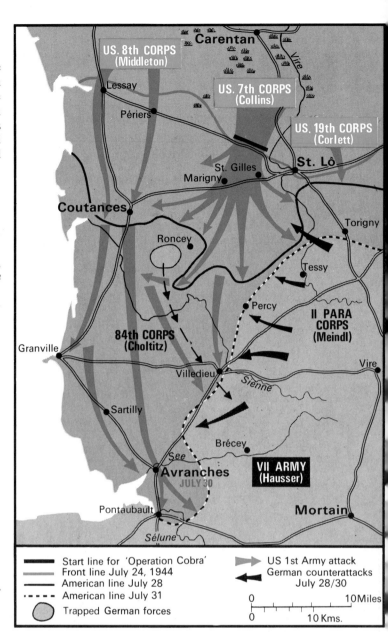

Start line for 'Operation Cobra'
Front line July 24, 1944
American line July 28
American line July 31
Trapped German forces

US 1st Army attack
German counterattacks July 28/30

0   10 Miles
0   10 Kms.

Above: (3) US 8th Corps was chiefly responsible for seizing the naval bases and ports of Brittany. These became of less importance once the Allies had pushed the front far to the east. Lorient and St Nazaire held out until the end of the war.

Below: (2) Operation Cobra was launched on July 25, after a massive air bombardment. The Americans reached Avranches in five days only. A German counter-attack on August 7–8 was repulsed.

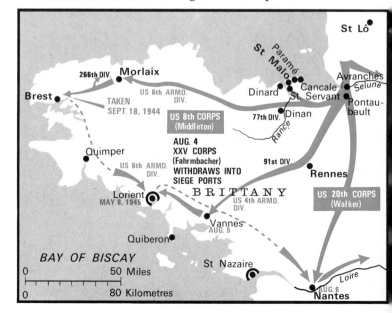

The Breakout from Normandy

Bradley's US 1st Army reached Avranches on July 31 (map 2). As US 8th Corps and US 20th Corps turned west and south into Brittany to seize the naval bases of Lorient, St Nazaire and Brest, as well as ports St Malo and Nantes [where they met resistance (map 3)], Patton's US 3rd Army also swept east towards Le Mans, Chartres, Orleans and the Seine (map 1). A Panzer attack ordered by Hitler went in towards Avranche on August 7–8 but was eliminated by August 10.

In late July and early August, US 1st Army, British 2nd Army and Canadian 1st Army formed a pincer movement with Patton's 3rd Army that forced the Germans into a salient between Falaise and Argentan (map 1). Kluge rescued most of his armour but more than 50,000 prisoners were taken before August 20. Patton reached the Seine at Fontainebleau and US 15th Corps established a bridgehead across the Seine. Paris was liberated on August 25.

Below: (1) The breakout from Normandy in August 1944. Four Allied armies (US 1st, British 2nd, Canadian 1st and US 3rd) closed on the Falaise gap and then pursued Kluge's Army Group B to the Seine. Paris was liberated on August 25.

Above: US infantry follow up the attack during Operation Cobra, the drive south from St Lô to Avranches in late July, 1944.

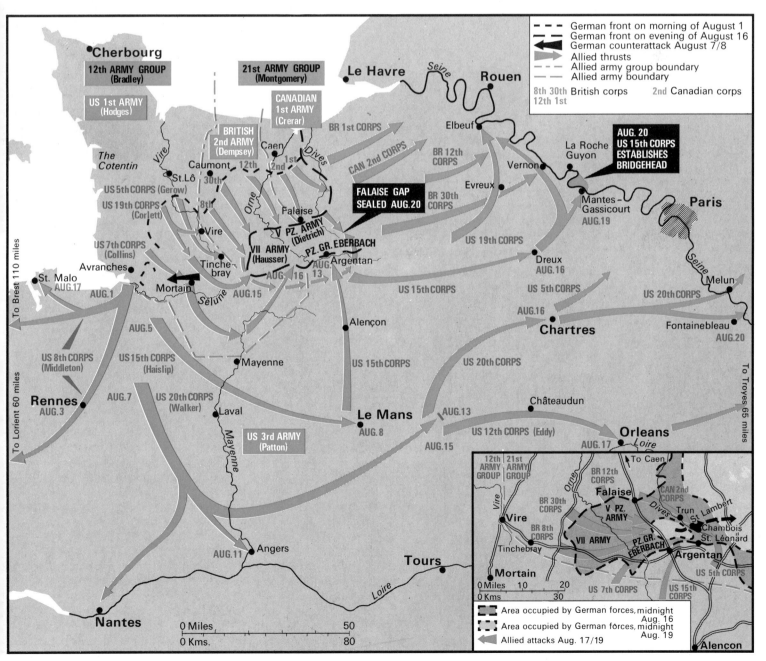

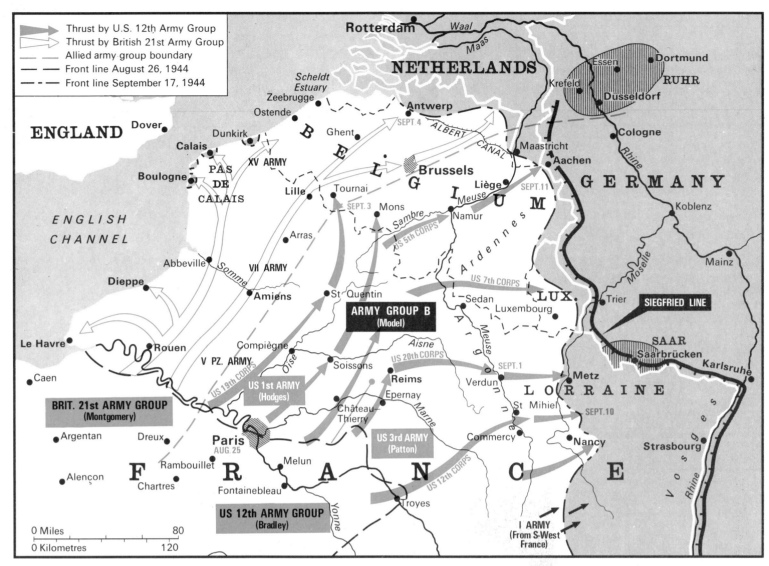

Above: (1) The Allied advance north of the Seine through France and into Belgium and Luxembourg. The broad front plan enabled Patton to cross the Meuse by the end of August. US 1st and 3rd Armies ran short of fuel and had to wait for Montgomery's 21st Army Group to clear the Channel ports and Antwerp, before Allied convoys could resupply the front line troops.

Below: (2) Although the Allies had captured Antwerp on September 4 (map 5), they were unable to bring convoys into the port until the Germans had been cleared from both sides of the Scheldt estuary. Germans and Allies suffered heavy losses in the fighting. This continued for more than a month, and had been delayed by Montgomery's Arnhem plan, as well as the commitment of the infantry to clear the Channel ports.

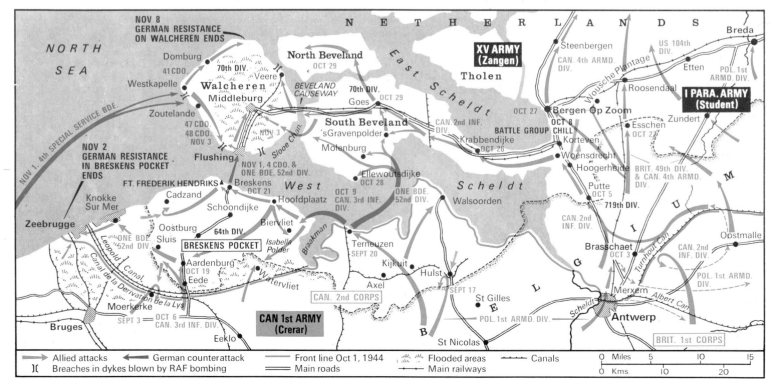

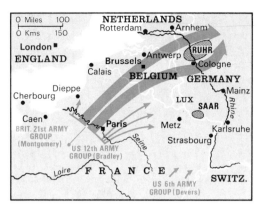

Above: (3) Montgomery and Bradley both favoured the narrow front. This meant a powerful thrust to the heart of the Ruhr.

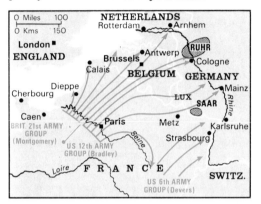

Above: (4) Eisenhower opted for a broad front that would give him time to secure the Channel ports and the Saar.

Below: GIs cross the 'Dragon's Teeth' defences of the Siegfried Line, Germany's much-vaunted Westwall.

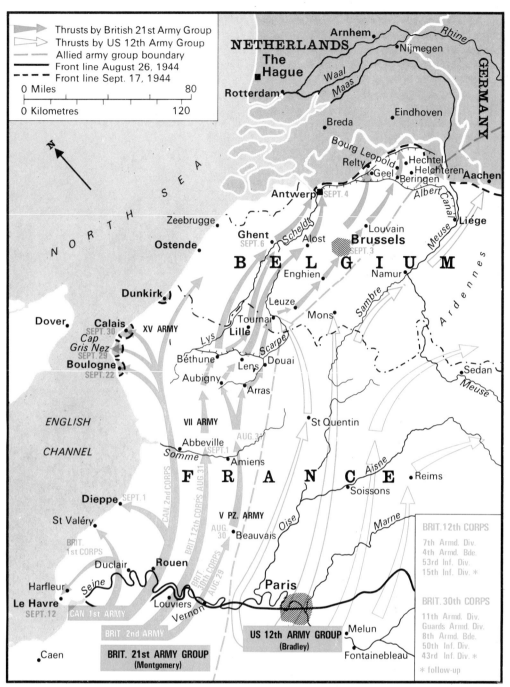

Above: (5) Montgomery's drive through northern France and Belgium reached Antwerp by September 4. Before clearing the Scheldt, Montgomery insisted on the priority of Operation Market Garden. There were also the Channel ports to clear to protect his rear, before sufficient troops were gathered to clear the estuary approach to Antwerp. One of the tasks of Canadian 1st Army was to over-run the V-1 missile sites in the Pas de Calais sector.

Clearing Northern France and Belgium

The Allies pressed on with their pursuit of the retreating German forces during September 1944. Montgomery and Bradley wanted a strong thrust on a narrow front (map 3) that would quickly encircle the Ruhr and move on to Berlin before the Russians. Eisenhower was more cautious and settled for a broad front (map 4) that would allow Patton's 3rd Army to maintain its impetus towards the Saar on one flank and would enable Montgomery to seize vital Channel supply ports on the other flank.

Pursuing the broad plan, British 2nd Army took Brussels on September 3 and captured Antwerp with its port facilities intact the next day (maps 1 and 5). On the right, Patton's 3rd Army crossed the Meuse on August 30. On September 3, Eisenhower took over direct command of all ground troops, leaving Montgomery to concentrate on 21st Army Group. But Montgomery had decided on a bold plan, Operation Market Garden, to drop three airborne divisions to seize the bridges north from Antwerp along the Eindhoven–Arnhem road and thus to create a narrow 60-mile corridor along which 30th Corps could advance to turn the northern end of the Siegfried Line. The drops in mid-September were successful at Eindhoven and Nijmegen but British 1st Airborne Division was badly mauled at Arnhem.

Operation Market Garden and the necessity for Canadian 1st Army to clear the Channel ports delayed Montgomery in clearing the Scheldt estuary (map 2), which was necessary before the port of Antwerp could be used. Walcheren Island and the South Beveland Peninsula were not finally secured until November 8 and the estuary was not cleared of mines until November 26.

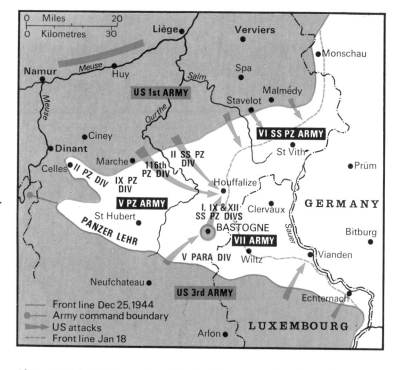

Left: (1) Hitler's Ardennes offensive, which burst on US 8th Corps on December 16, 1944, taking the Allies completely by surprise. Hitler's aim was to split the British and Americans, cross the Meuse, as he had done in 1940, and head through Brussels to Antwerp.

Above: (3) The Allied counter-offensive that squeezed out the Bulge during January 1945. The small 'squeeze' was favoured rather than the 'big' solution, to sever the Bulge completely. With Montgomery's reserve standing behind the Meuse, US 1st Army and US 3rd Army worked their way towards Houffalize.

Opposite page: (2) The German offensive was channelled between the Bastogne and St Vith sectors and finally stopped only four miles from the Meuse.

Below: Bastogne was the key to the Ardennes, a vital communications centre and the target for an all-out German attack. McAuliffe's 101st Airborne Division found itself trapped in the town and nearly gave up hope of emerging alive. When called on to surrender, McAuliffe's classic reply was 'Nuts!'.

The Battle of the Bulge

Having captured Aachen on October 21 and breached the Siegfried Line, the Allies were preparing to advance to the Rhine when they were struck by Hitler's counter-offensive in the Ardennes, aimed at breaking through to Brussels and capturing Antwerp in a last-ditch repeat of his 1940 success.

The Ardennes offensive opened on December 16, 1944, when poor visibility, low cloud, fog and snow hampered Allied aerial observation and capability. Eight Panzer divisions hit the weakest sector of the Allied line, the thinly-stretched US 8th Corps (map 1), taking it completely by surprise. As the Germans broke through 8th Corps and headed for the two important communications towns of St Vith and Bastogne (map 2), US 5th Corps halted its own offensive in the north and blocked the spread of the offensive northwards, while US 4th Division attempted to block a southward leak of the offensive. Patton's 3rd Army ceased its advance in the Saar and turned north towards the German left flank.

To the west, Eisenhower committed his reserves, 82nd and 101st Airborne Divisions, still recovering from Operation Market Garden. Ridgway's 82nd Airborne moved to the northern flank and McAuliffe's 101st went in to Bastogne, where it was trapped by the advancing Germans. Standing between the Meuse and the two main objectives of the German advance, Brussels and Antwerp, Montgomery carefully began to organize his own reserves and Eisenhower put him in overall command of the US troops north of the Bulge to hold the offensive until Patton was ready to strike from the south.

Fierce resistance in the Bastogne and St Vith areas forced the Germans to advance on a narrow front between the American breakwaters but, on December 22, US 7th Armoured Division had to withdraw from St Vith. Launching their last offensive towards the Meuse, II Panzer Division were turned back only four miles from the river by US 2nd Armoured Division on December 25. This was the high-water mark of the German advance. Delays at St Vith and Bastogne had seriously affected German plans, which relied above all on speed.

The US counter-offensive quickly gathered momentum (map 3). On December 26, US 4th Armoured Division reached Bastogne, although the last German attack was not beaten back until January 3–4. US 1st and 3rd Armies linked up at Houffalize on January 16 and the Bulge had disappeared by the end of the month. With it went Hitler's last reserve, his only hope for checking the Soviet spring offensive in the east. His gamble had failed, due partly to his inferiority in the air, partly to his own inability to adapt to the developing situation, partly to his failure to over-run the Allied fuel depots quickly enough to replenish his tanks. Due also to the courage and determination of the Americans who held out on the shoulders of the Bulge and in St Vith and Bastogne. The latter was one of the epic sieges of the war. On the Allied side, the offensive delayed operations by about six weeks. There were some 60,000 Allied and some 120,000 German casualties.

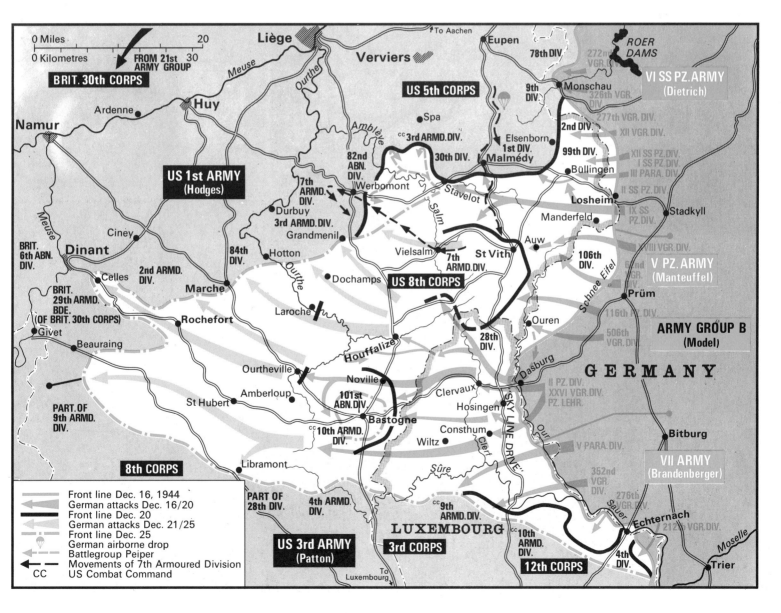

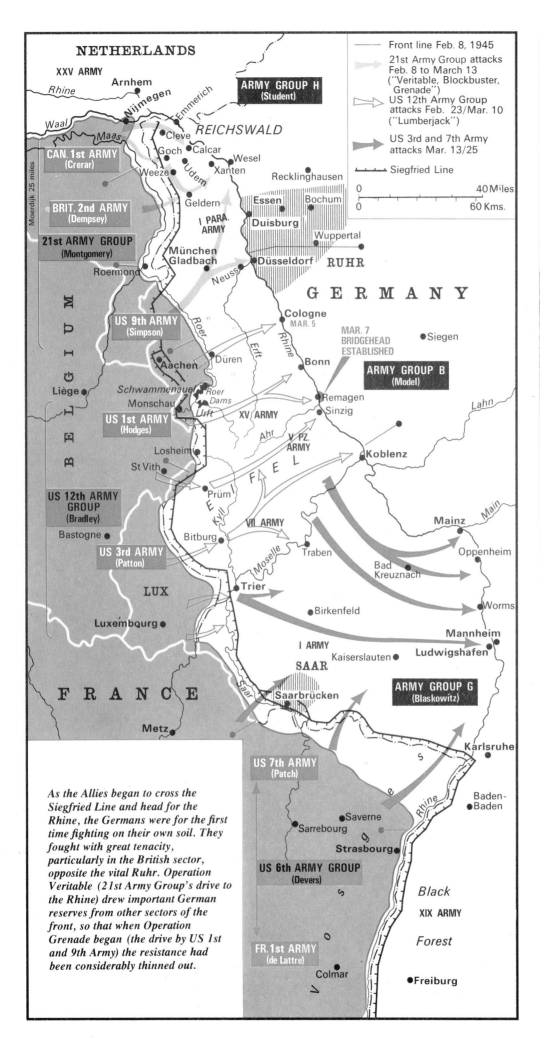

NETHERLANDS

XXV ARMY

Rhine

Arnhem

Nijmegen

Waal

Maas

Emmerich

ARMY GROUP H
(Student)

REICHSWALD

Cleve

Goch Calcar

Weeze

Udem Xanten

Wesel

CAN. 1st ARMY
(Crerar)

BRIT. 2nd ARMY
(Dempsey)

Geldern

Recklinghausen

Essen Bochum

21st ARMY GROUP
(Montgomery)

Roermond

München
Gladbach

I PARA.
ARMY

Duisburg

Neuss

Düsseldorf

Wuppertal

RUHR

GERMANY

B E L G I U M

US 9th ARMY
(Simpson)

Liège

Aachen

Monschau

Düren

Roer

Erft

Cologne
MAR. 5

Rhine

Siegen

MAR. 7
BRIDGEHEAD
ESTABLISHED

Bonn

ARMY GROUP B
(Model)

Lahn

Schwammenauel

*Roer
Dams*

Urft

US 1st ARMY
(Hodges)

Losheim

St Vith

XV ARMY

Remagen

Sinzig

Ahr

V PZ.
ARMY

Koblenz

**US 12th ARMY
GROUP**
(Bradley)

Bastogne

Prüm

Kyll

VII ARMY

E I F E L

Mainz

Main

US 3rd ARMY
(Patton)

Bitburg

Traben

Bad
Kreuznach

Oppenheim

LUX

Moselle

Trier

Birkenfeld

Worms

Luxembourg

I ARMY

Mannheim

SAAR

Kaiserslautern

Ludwigshafen

ARMY GROUP G
(Blaskowitz)

Metz

Saar

Saarbrücken

Karlsruhe

US 7th ARMY
(Patch)

Baden-
Baden

As the Allies began to cross the
Siegfried Line and head for the
Rhine, the Germans were for the first
time fighting on their own soil. They
fought with great tenacity,
particularly in the British sector,
opposite the vital Ruhr. Operation
Veritable (21st Army Group's drive to
the Rhine) drew important German
reserves from other sectors of the
front, so that when Operation
Grenade began (the drive by US 1st
and 9th Army) the resistance had
been considerably thinned out.

Saverne

Sarrebourg

Strasbourg

US 6th ARMY GROUP
(Devers)

Black

XIX ARMY

Forest

FR. 1st ARMY
(de Lattre)

Colmar

Freiburg

Legend

— Front line Feb. 8, 1945

⇉ 21st Army Group attacks
Feb. 8 to March 13
("Veritable, Blockbuster,
Grenade")

⇨ US 12th Army Group
attacks Feb. 23/Mar. 10
("Lumberjack")

➡ US 3rd and 7th Army
attacks Mar. 13/25

├┼┤ Siegfried Line

0 ——— 40 Miles
0 ——— 60 Kms.

Moerdijk 25 miles

FRANCE

*Above: An American infantryman advances
through an already devastated village as
Bradley's 12th Army Group advances to the
Rhine. The impetus of the Allied thrust had
been worn down by the Battle of the Bulge
and some redeployment was required before
the advance could continue with its former
strength.*

Above: (1) The strategic situation in March 1945: the Allies at the Rhine, the Russians on the Oder.

Across the Rhine

At the beginning of February 1945, the Allied flanks had reached the Rhine at Nijmegen in the north and Strasbourg in the south, but still had some way to go in the centre against stiff opposition and with little chance of finding the Rhine bridges intact (map 1). In the north, Crerar's Canadian 1st Army attacked south-east between the Maas and the Rhine through a maze of marshy rivers, while Simpson's US 9th Army attacked north-east across the Roer. The pincers met at Geldern on March 3 and within a week the last German bridgehead to the west of the Rhine vanished in this sector, opposite Wesel.

Further south, Hodge's US 1st Army reached Cologne on March 5, while Patton's US 3rd Army and Patch's US 7th Army co-ordinated their advance to sweep through to the west bank of the Rhine. On March 7, units of US 1st Army unexpectedly found the bridge at Remagen still intact (maps 1 and 2). Hodge's swift exploitation of the opportunity caused Eisenhower to make a southward shift in the emphasis of his attack, although the next crossing was not until March 22, when Patton's 3rd Army achieved a brilliant leap across the river at Nierstein. On March 23, Montgomery launched his major crossing on a 20-mile front near Rees and Emerlich. On March 24 US 9th Army started across at Dinslaken. By early April, the east bank of the Rhine was cleared.

Above: (2) The Allied crossings of the Rhine, March 1945. Having encountered stiff opposition to Operation Veritable, Montgomery approached the Rhine with caution. His Operation Plunder across the Rhine was a massive assault planned in detail, in contrast to the quick, imaginative advances of the Americans. Meanwhile, on the eastern front, just as the Allies were on the Rhine, the Russians were on the Oder, preparing for the advance to Berlin.

133

The Final Thrust to the Elbe

At the end of March 1945, Roosevelt and Eisenhower, not wishing to become embroiled in European politics, decided not to race for Berlin, to the dismay of the British. The Allies were to halt their advance on the Elbe. The plan was for 12th Army Group to advance towards Leipzig, while US 1st and 9th Armies encircled the Ruhr and British 2nd Army and Canadian 1st Army covered the left flank of the main advance by moving north-east towards Hamburg (map 2). Fearing a last-ditch National Redoubt in the German-Austrian Alps, Devers' 6th Army Group advanced south-east down the Danube.

There were pockets of brave resistance but most German units were only too anxious to surrender to the western Allies rather than to the Russians. On March 25–27, US 1st Army advanced out of its Rhine bridgehead and joined 3rd Army coming from the Oppenheim area. On April 1, units of 9th and 1st Armies linked at Lippstadt, completing the encirclement of the Ruhr, where the last resistance ceased on April 18. By April 4, US 9th Army made an assault crossing of the Weser. The first units of US 9th Army reached the Elbe near Magdeburg on April 12. This was the point at which the Americans missed their chance to make a direct drive for Berlin, almost half way between themselves and the Russians.

British 2nd Army reached the Elbe by

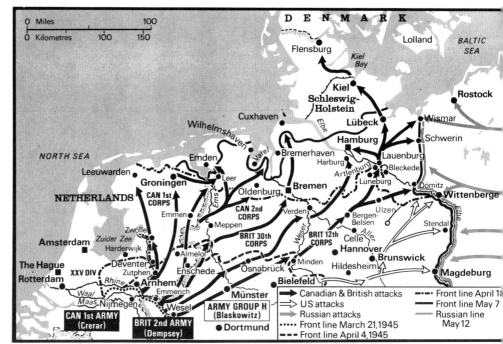

Above: (1) The last offensive of Montgomery's 21st Army Group, from the Rhine to the Elbe. Canadian 1st Army made a slow and painful advance through a series of parallel river barriers.

the end of April and had cleared Holland and North Germany by May 7 (map 1). Patton's 3rd Army occupied Linz on May 5 and units reached Pilsen on May 6, when Patton was stopped from advancing to Prague. Formal surrenders were completed by May 8 and Schorner's Army Group Centre laid down its arms on May 11.

Below: US 3rd Army enters a concentration camp. The lucky few could still stand up and cheer.

Above: For the second time in her life this old lady watched the collapse of Germany. This time, Allied troops stormed across German soil.

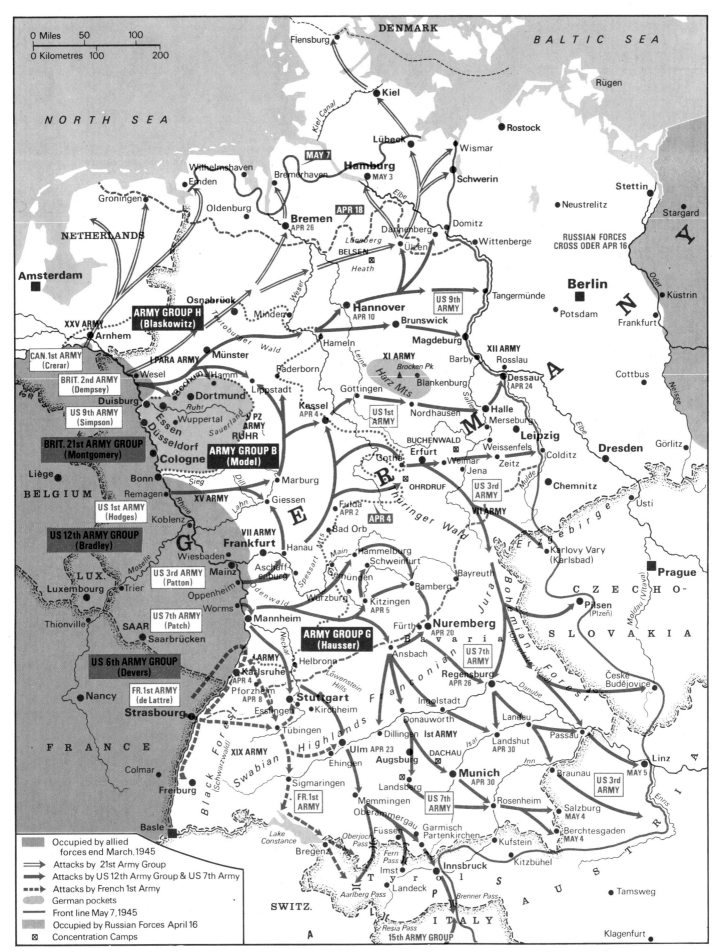

Scale

0 Miles 50 100
0 Kilometres 100 200

NORTH SEA

BALTIC SEA

DENMARK

Flensburg

Kiel
Kiel Canal
Lübeck
Wismar
Rostock
Rügen

MAY 7
Hamburg
MAY 3
Schwerin
Neustrelitz
Stettin
Stargard

Wilhelmshaven
Bremerhaven
Emden
Groningen
Oldenburg
Bremen
APR 26
APR 18
Dannenberg
Dömitz
Wittenberge
RUSSIAN FORCES
CROSS ODER APR 16

NETHERLANDS

Amsterdam

Lüneburg
BELSEN
Heath
Ülzen

US 9th
ARMY
Tangermünde

Berlin
Potsdam
Küstrin
Frankfurt
Cottbus

Osnabrück

ARMY GROUP H
(Blaskowitz)

Minden
Hannover
APR 10
Brunswick
Magdeburg

XI ARMY
Brocken Pk.
Blankenburg

Barby
Rosslau
XII ARMY
Dessau
APR 24
Halle
Merseburg
Leipzig
Colditz
Dresden
Görlitz

XXV ARMY
Arnhem

CAN. 1st ARMY
(Crerar)

BRIT. 2nd ARMY
(Dempsey)

US 9th ARMY
(Simpson)

BRIT. 21st ARMY GROUP
(Montgomery)

I PARA ARMY
Münster
Wesel
Bochum
Hamm
Dortmund
Lippstadt
Wuppertal
Duisburg
Essen
Sauerland
Düsseldorf
Cologne

ARMY GROUP B
(Model)

Paderborn

Kassel
APR 4
Göttingen
Harz Mts

Nordhausen

US 1st
ARMY

BUCHENWALD
Erfurt
Gotha
OHRDRUF

Weimar
Jena
Weissenfels
Zeitz

US 3rd
ARMY
Mulde

Chemnitz

Usti

Bonn
Remagen
Sieg
Liège

BELGIUM

US 1st ARMY
(Hodges)

US 12th ARMY GROUP
(Bradley)

XV ARMY
Marburg
Giessen
Fulda
APR 2
Bad Orb

Koblenz
Rhine
Lahn
Dill

VII ARMY
Frankfurt
Wiesbaden
Hanau

Fulda
APR 4
VII ARMY

Karlovy Vary
(Karlsbad)

Prague

CZECHO-
SLOVAKIA

Pilsen
(Plzeň)

LUX.
Luxembourg
Trier
Moselle

US 3rd ARMY
(Patton)
Mainz
Oppenheim
Worms

Aschaffenburg
Odenwald
Würzburg

Main
Hammelburg
Schweinfurt
Gemünden
Bamberg
Kitzingen
APR 5

Bayreuth

Thionville
SAAR
Saarbrücken

US 7th ARMY
(Patch)

Mannheim

ARMY GROUP G
(Hausser)

Fürth
Nuremberg
APR 20
Ansbach

Bavaria

US 7th
ARMY

Regensburg
APR 26

Danube

České
Budějovice

US 6th ARMY GROUP
(Devers)

Nancy

FR. 1st ARMY
(de Lattre)

Strasbourg

Neckar
Heilbronn
1 ARMY
Karlsruhe
APR 4
Pforzheim
APR 8

Löwenstein
Hills

Esslingen
Stuttgart
Kirchheim

Franconian

Helbronn

Ingolstadt
Donauwörth

Landshut
APR 30

Passau

Linz
MAY 5

Colmar

FRANCE

Freiburg

Black Forest
(Schwarzwald)

XIX ARMY

Swabian
Highlands

Tübingen

Ulm APR 23
Ehingen

Dillingen
DACHAU
Augsburg
Landsberg

1st ARMY
Isar

Munich
APR 30

Rosenheim

Braunau
US 3rd
ARMY

Salzburg
MAY 4
Berchtesgaden
MAY 4

Basle

Sigmaringen

FR. 1st
ARMY

Memmingen
Oberammergau

US 7th
ARMY

Inn

Kufstein

Kitzbühel

Tamsweg

Lake
Constance
Bregenz

Oberjoch
Pass
Füssen
Garmisch
Partenkirchen

Fern
Pass

SWITZ.

Aarlberg Pass
Imst
Landeck

15th ARMY GROUP

Innsbruck

Brenner Pass

Resia Pass

ITALY

TYROL

AUSTRIA

Klagenfurt

Legend

Occupied by allied forces end March, 1945
⇒ Attacks by 21st Army Group
→ Attacks by US 12th Army Group & US 7th Army
┅ Attacks by French 1st Army
German pockets
— Front line May 7, 1945
Occupied by Russian Forces April 16
⊠ Concentration Camps

Above: (2) The Allied aavance from the Rhine to join the Red Army on the Elbe. Most of the German forces surrendered and towns greeted the Allies with white flags. Model's Army Group B was encircled in the Ruhr on April 1; resistance ended by April 18. US 9th Army reached the Elbe, near Magdeburg, on April 12. The Russians could not understand why the Americans did not advance on Berlin at once. The decision was taken for military and political reasons. The Russians quickly took advantage of the delay.

The Key Bomber Raids against Germany

Allied bombing of Germany began in spring 1940. With only limited cover by fighter escorts and with general targets at first, it had little effect on the German war effort. The bombing offensive was stepped up towards the end of 1943, with the precision bombing of the US 8th Air Force on specific targets whose destruction helped to shorten the war. Massive pin-point raids wrecked the fuel and supply systems of the Reich and shattered her economy. (Statistics compiled by IWM.)

1940, May 15–16: RAF raid on the Ruhr
First strategic air raid, by 99 planes, with night precision attack on oil plants and marshalling yards. Negligible damage.

1940, December 16–17: RAF raid on Mannheim
Inaccurate bombing in first night area raid on industrial city, to disrupt war production and break morale. 134 planes, 3 lost.

1942, March 28–29: RAF raid on Lübeck
Night area raid including incendiary bombs. Extensive damage to houses and factories but production nearly normal after one week. 234 planes, 12 lost.

1942, April 17: RAF raid on Augsburg
Daylight precision raid on MAN diesel engine factory. Some damage but 7 out of 12 planes lost. No fighter cover.

1942, May 30–31: RAF raid on Cologne
First 'Thousand Bomber' raid (1,046 bombers) destroyed half the city and made 40,000 homeless. Swift reconstruction.

1942, August 17: 8th Air Force raid on Rouen
No loss to 12 B-17s in US 8th AF's first daylight precision raid on Sotteville marshalling yards. Temporary target damage.

1943, March 5–6: RAF raid on Essen
First use of 'Oboe' radar device helped overcome industrial

This map shows the main Allied bombing targets in Europe between 1942 and 1945. Unless otherwise specified, the cities listed below were general industrial targets.

Key Allied Airbases
A. Sunninghill Park
   (HQ US 9th Air Force)
B. High Wycombe
   (HQ RAF Bomber
   Command/HQ US 8th
   Air Force)
C. Bushy Park
   (HQ US Strategic Air
   Force)

1. Bordeaux
   (U-boats)
2. La Pallice
   (U-boats)
3. Lorient
   (U-boats)
4. St Nazaire
   (U-boats)
5. Nantes
   (aircraft)
6. Brest
   (U-boats)
7. Le Mans
   (aircraft)
8. Paris
9. Rouen
10. Martinvast
    (V-bombs)
11. Sottevast
    (V-bombs)
12. Siracourt
    (V-bombs)
13. Lottinghem
    (V-bombs)
14. Mimovecques
    (V-bombs)
15. Watten
    (V-bombs)
16. Wizernes
    (V-bombs)
17. Lille
18. Brussels
    (aircraft)
19. Rotterdam
20. Amsterdam
    (aircraft)
21. La Rochelle
22. Cherbourg
23. Le Havre
24. Boulogne
25. Dunkirk
26. Metz
27. Emden
    (U-boats)
28. Wilhelmshaven
    (U-boats)
29. Vegesack
    (U-boats)
30. Bremen
    (aircraft)
31. Hamburg
32. Flensburg
    (U-boats)
33. Kiel
    (U-boats)

34. Lübeck
35. Hannover
36. Brunswick
37. Magdeburg
38. Oschersleben
    (aircraft)
39. Dessau
    (aircraft)
40. Essen
41. Dortmund
42. Duisburg
43. Düsseldorf
44. Cologne
45. Bonn
46. Möhne Dam
47. Wuppertal
48. Eder Dam
49. Sorpe Dam
50. Kassel
    (aircraft)
51. Leipzig
    (aircraft)
52. Dresden
53. Liegnitz
54. Berlin
55. Rostock
56. Peenemünde
    (V-bombs)
57. Stettin
58. Danzig
    (U-boats)
59. Erfurt
60. Gotha
    (aircraft)
61. Schweinfurt
    (ball-bearings)
62. Fürth
63. Nuremberg
64. Regensburg
    (aircraft)
65. Augsburg
    (aircraft)
66. Munich
67. Ulm
68. Stuttgart
69. Ludwigshafen
70. Saarbrücken
71. Bochum
72. Karlsruhe
73. Friedrichshafen
74. Chemnitz
75. Prague
76. Wiener Neustadt
    (aircraft)
77. Frankfurt
78. Hanau
79. Aschaffenburg
80. Koblenz
81. Oberlahnstein
82. Giessen
83. Siegen
84. Schwerte
85. Soest
86. Hamm
87. Löhne
88. Osnabrück
89. Rheine
90. Bielefeld

91. Altenbecken
    Neuenbecken
92. Seelze
93. Lehrte
94. Hameln
95. Paderborn
96. Bebra
97. Stendal
98. Halle
99. Gera
100. Breslau
101. Oppeln
102. Heydebreck
103. Bohumin
104. Minden
105. Mulhouse
106. Freiburg
107. Offenburg
108. Rastatt
109. Karlsruhe
110. Heilbronn
111. Treuchtlingen
112. Pasing
113. Munich
114. Rosenheim
115. Salzburg
116. Strasshof
117. Würzburg
118. Mannheim
119. Darmstadt
120. Mainz
121. Bingen
122. Vienna
123. Münster
124. Wesseling
125. Reisholz
126. Dülmen
127. Gelsenkirchen
128. Salzbergen
129. Nienburg
130. Farge
131. Heide
132. Hitzacker
133. Dollbergen
134. Derben
135. Pölitz
136. Salzgitter
137. Lützkendorf
138. Leuna
139. Ruhland
140. Böhlen
141. Rositz
142. Mölbis
143. Zeitz
144. Brüx
145. Deschowitz
146. Blechhammer
147. Auschwitz
148. Neuburg
149. Freiham
150. Linz
151. Moosbierbaum
152. Korneuburg
153. Floridsdorf
154. Schwechat
155. Lobau
156. Budapest

haze in night area attack on Krupp works. Heavy damage. 442 planes.

1943, May 16–17: RAF Dams raid
Precision bombing by 19 Lancaster 'Dam Busters'. Mohne and Eder dams breached, Sorpe damaged. 8 planes lost. Severe floods and 1,000 drowned. No appreciable effect on war economy.

1943, July 24–25: RAF raid on Hamburg
791 planes in night area raid on city centre confused German defences by dropping 'Window' (strips of tinfoil). Extensive fires and residential damage. Heavy raids on nights of July 27, 29 and August 2 left city in ruins. Estimated 42,000 killed.

1943, October 14: 8th Air Force raid on Schweinfurt
One of 16 Schweinfurt raids on ball-bearing works. 291 planes, 60 lost and 138 damaged. Daylight raids curtailed thereafter.

1943, November 18–19: RAF raid on Berlin
First of 16 mass raids on Berlin. 444 planes in night area raid. Damage believed to be heavy but planes hampered by distance, weather and the strength of the defences.

1944, March 30–31: RAF raid on Nuremberg
Bomber Command's heaviest defeat. 795 planes, 95 lost and 71 damaged, in night area raid on city centre. Lacked air superiority.

1944, September 23–24: RAF Canal raid
Eleven 'Tallboy' bombs (12,000 lbs each) dropped in night precision raid by 141 planes on Dortmund–Ems Canal. Canal breached and six-mile section drained.

1945, February 13–14: RAF raid on Dresden
In the war's most destructive, controversial European raid, 805 planes caused a firestorm, killing 35,000–135,000 civilians.

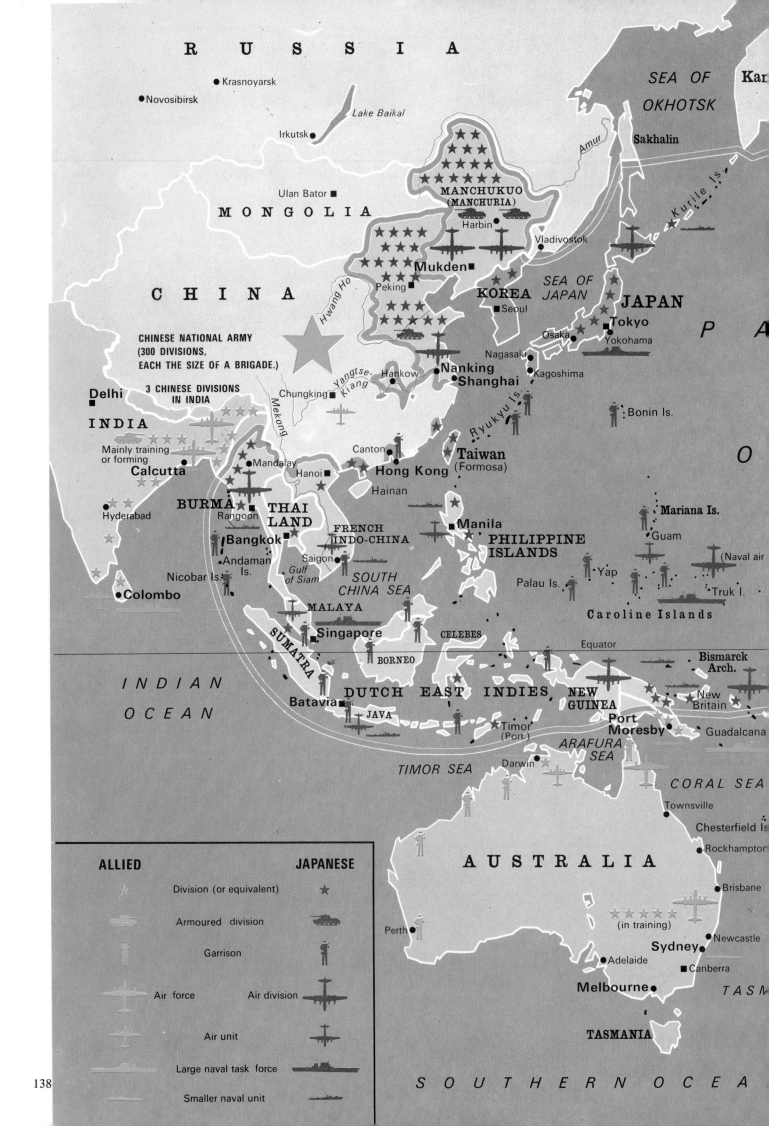

RUSSIA

• Krasnoyarsk

• Novosibirsk

Lake Baikal

Irkutsk •

MONGOLIA

Ulan Bator ■

SEA OF
OKHOTSK

Kar

Amur

Sakhalin

Kurile Is.

MANCHUKUO
(MANCHURIA)

Harbin •

Vladivostok •

CHINA

Peking •

Mukden

SEA OF
JAPAN

KOREA

Seoul •

JAPAN

Tokyo

Osaka •

Yokohama

CHINESE NATIONAL ARMY
(300 DIVISIONS,
EACH THE SIZE OF A BRIGADE.)

Hwang Ho

*Yangtse-
Kiang*

Hankow •

Nanking
Shanghai

Nagasaki •

Kagoshima

3 CHINESE DIVISIONS
IN INDIA

Delhi ■

Chungking ■

Mekong

INDIA

Mainly training
or forming

Calcutta

• Mandalay

Hanoi ■

Canton •

Taiwan
(Formosa)

Hong Kong

Hainan

Bonin Is.

Ryukyu Is.

Hyderabad

BURMA

Rangoon •

**THAI
LAND**

**FRENCH
INDO-CHINA**

Manila

**PHILIPPINE
ISLANDS**

Mariana Is.

• **Bangkok**

• Andaman
Is.

Saigon •

*Gulf
of Siam*

*SOUTH
CHINA
SEA*

Guam

(Naval air

Nicobar Is.

• Yap

• Truk I.

Colombo

Palau Is.

MALAYA

Caroline Islands

SUMATRA

Singapore

CELEBES

Equator

BORNEO

**Bismarck
Arch.**

*INDIAN
OCEAN*

DUTCH EAST INDIES

**NEW
GUINEA**

New
Britain

Batavia

JAVA

Timor
(Port.)

**Port
Moresby**

Guadalcana

*ARAFURA
SEA*

Darwin •

TIMOR SEA

CORAL SEA

• Townsville

Chesterfield Is

• Rockhampton

AUSTRALIA

Perth •

(in training)

• Brisbane

• Newcastle

Sydney ■

• Adelaide

■ Canberra

Melbourne •

TASM

TASMANIA

SOUTHERN OCEAN

ALLIED

JAPANESE

Division (or equivalent)

Armoured division

Garrison

Air force   Air division

Air unit

Large naval task force

Smaller naval unit

138

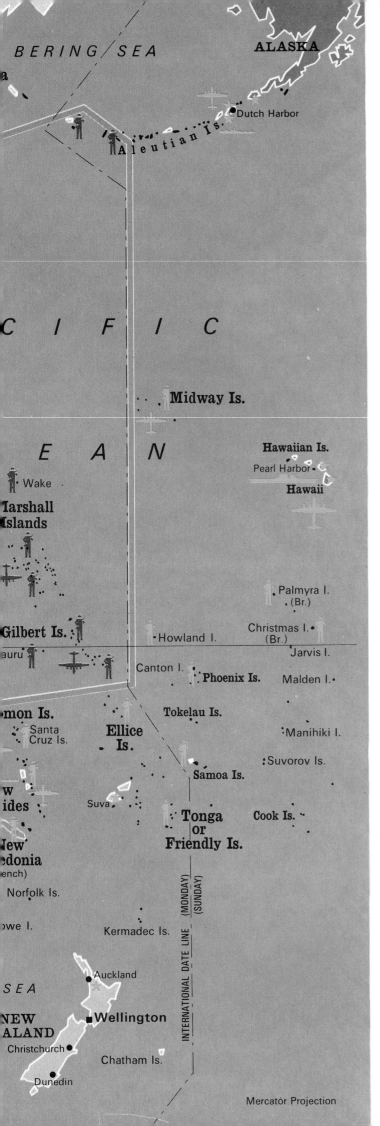

B E R I N G / S E A

ALASKA

Dutch Harbor

Aleutian Is.

C I F I C

Midway Is.

E A N

Hawaiian Is.

Pearl Harbor

Hawaii

Wake

Marshall Islands

Palmyra I.
(Br.)

Gilbert Is.

Christmas I.
(Br.)

Howland I.

Jarvis I.

auru

Canton I.

Phoenix Is.

Malden I.

mon Is.

Tokelau Is.

Santa Cruz Is.

Ellice Is.

Manihiki I.

Suvorov Is.

Samoa Is.

Suva

w ides

Tonga or Friendly Is.

Cook Is.

New edonia (ench)

Norfolk Is.

INTERNATIONAL DATE LINE (MONDAY) (SUNDAY)

owe I.

Kermadec Is.

Auckland

S E A

NEW ALAND

Wellington

Christchurch

Chatham Is.

Dunedin

Mercator Projection

The War in the Orient

The Japanese war had its origins in Japan's search for the equivalent of Hitler's *Lebensraum*, the Greater East Asia Co-Prosperity Sphere. In July 1937, Japan invaded China and, in September 1940, Japanese forces moved into French Indo-China, in direct contradiction of American warnings. The Berlin–Rome–Tokyo Axis was formed on September 27, 1940 and in October 1941 Tojo became premier and formed a militaristic government.

The secret Japanese plans for a simultaneous attack against the US fleet at Pearl Harbor and against British Malaya, the American Philippines, and the Dutch East Indies were prepared in November 1941. To conceal their intentions, the Japanese continued negotiations in Washington over their presence in Indo-China even after their I Air Fleet, including six aircraft carriers, supported by battleships, heavy cruisers and submarines, had left the Kurile Islands in absolute secrecy on November 26 bound for Pearl Harbor. The Americans should have anticipated trouble, but they believed that any action would occur in Malaya or in the American Philippines.

On December 7, 1941, Japanese planes caught Pearl Harbor completely by surprise (map below). The US Pacific Fleet was crippled and it was only by sheer chance that the three US carriers, *Enterprise*, *Lexington* and *Saratoga*, were absent at the time of the attack. The Japanese moved on to Wake Island, which they attacked on December 8 and took on December 23. They also overwhelmed Guam on December 10. Britain, America and the Netherlands declared war on Japan on December 8, 1941.

Before the attack on Pearl Harbor, Japan controlled the islands from Taiwan to the Kurile Island, as well as the Marianas, Caroline Islands, Marshall Islands and Bonin Islands. Guam and Wake were both occupied by Americans. Within six months of December 1941, Japan had gained vast territories and the raw materials that went with them (map opposite). Guam, Wake Island, the Philippines, French Indo-China, Burma, Thailand, Malaya, the Dutch East Indies, three-quarters of New Guinea and Papua, the Bismarck Archipelago and parts of the Solomon Islands and the Gilbert Islands were all in Japanese hands. Their plan to seize a wide perimeter by surprise attack had succeeded. Now they had to hold that perimeter.

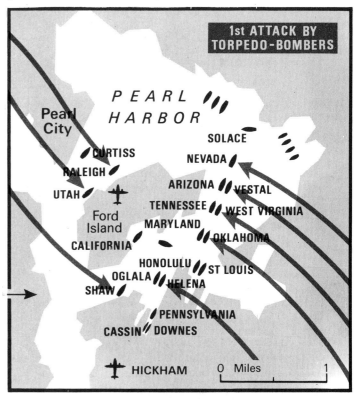

1st ATTACK BY TORPEDO-BOMBERS

PEARL HARBOR

Pearl City

CURTISS

RALEIGH

UTAH

Ford Island

SOLACE

NEVADA

ARIZONA VESTAL

TENNESSEE WEST VIRGINIA

MARYLAND

CALIFORNIA

OKLAHOMA

HONOLULU ST LOUIS

OGLALA HELENA

SHAW

PENNSYLVANIA

CASSIN DOWNES

HICKHAM

0 Miles 1

The Conquest of Malaya and Singapore

As one Japanese fleet made for Pearl Harbor, another made for southern Thailand and northern Malaya. At dawn, on December 8, 1941, after intensive air attacks on RAF bases in Malaya and Singapore, three divisions of Yamashita's XXV Army landed on the Malay Peninsula and the Isthmus of Kra, while XV Army invaded Thailand from Indo-China (map 2). Japanese V and XVIII Divisions landed unopposed at Singora and Patani, while the Takumi Force fought its way ashore at Kota Bharu.

Lieutenant-General Percival's garrison was ill-prepared, expecting any attack on Singapore to come from the sea and believing the jungle impenetrable. The Japanese demonstrated otherwise. On December 10, naval Force Z (which left Singapore on December 8 to intercept the Japanese convoys landing on the Peninsula) was attacked by Japanese aircraft. The battleship *Prince of Wales* and the battle-cruiser *Repulse* were sunk.

The British were quickly forced back from their northern positions, outflanked by Japanese amphibious landings farther down the coast. As the Takumi Force hugged the south-east coast, V and XVIII Divisions swept all western defences before them. They had crossed the Slim river by the first week of 1942. They took Kuala Lumpur on January 11. Australian 8th Division and 91st Indian Division reinforced the Muar river defences. By January 31 the last British and Empire forces had withdrawn to Singapore Island, partly destroying the adjoining causeway.

On February 8, after a feint across Pulau Ubin, the Japanese launched their main attack in the west (map 1). Percival surrendered on February 15. 130,000 prisoners were taken and 9,000 men killed. Yamashita had conquered Malaya and Singapore; Japanese attention had already turned north towards the conquest of Burma.

Above: (1) The attack on Singapore Island, February 7–15, 1942. A feint to the east was followed by the main attack in the west. Tengah airfield fell almost at once. When the reservoirs were also captured, Singapore quickly capitulated.

Left: (2) The Japanese advance through Malaya, December 1941–January 1942. When Yamashita's divisions landed on December 8, the British were preparing to rush into Thailand to forestall any Japanese invasion. They were too late. Taken by surprise by the swiftness of the Japanese moves, the British soon lost what little air cover they had and were forced into retreat. The Japanese were provided with ample seaborne support as they drove down the coast and met no effective checks.

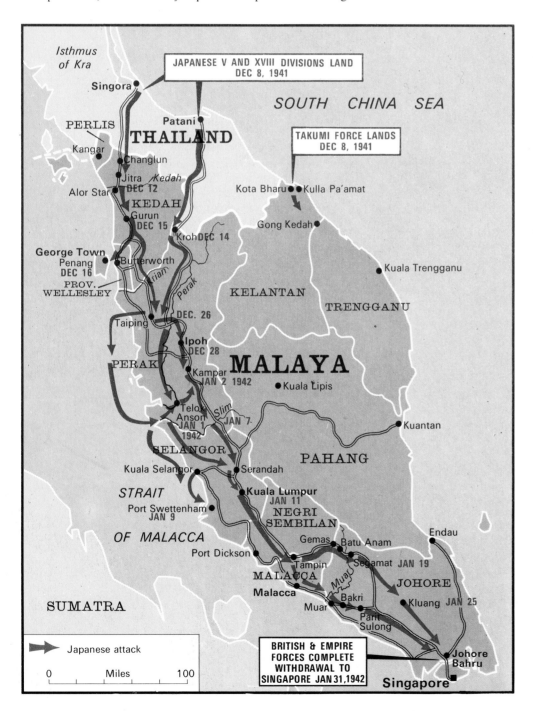

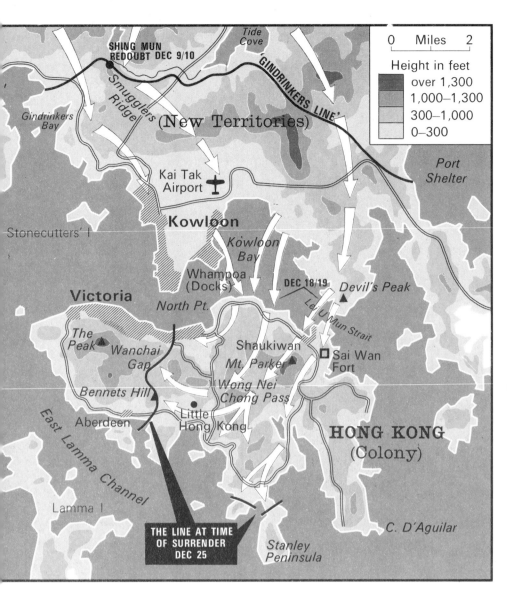

Above: (1) The area of the British colony of Hong Kong, showing the two main towns of Victoria on Hong Kong Island and Kowloon on the mainland, in the New Territories. Japan invaded December 8, 1941.

Left: (2) The Japanese attack on Hong Kong, December 1941. The Gindrinkers Line was broken in the west at the Shing Mun Redoubt on the night of December 9–10. The defenders were outnumbered by about two-to-one and had no hope of reinforcement, although there were rumours that the Chinese were sending a relief force by land. Without any air cover of their own, they suffered from constant Japanese air and artillery bombardment.

Above: Japanese soldiers in the captured city after the fall of Singapore. Nearly 140,000 casualties were inflicted on the Allies.

Below: The fight for Malacca, as the Japanese sweep down through Malaya. A Japanese attack clears a main street. But it was the jungle that provided the Japanese with their surprise approach.

The Fall of Hong Kong

The Japanese 38th Division launched its attack on the British colony of Hong Kong from the mainland of China on the morning of December 8, 1941 (map 1). The colony was not considered by the British to be of great strategic value and was clung to more for reasons of prestige and a determination to refuse the enemy the use of the harbour. The Japanese had a massive superiority in numbers over Maltby's garrison and Maltby's only hope was that the Gindrinkers Line, barring the entrance to the New Territories, could briefly sustain the Japanese attacks.

The five obsolete aircraft at Kai Tak airport were quickly destroyed on the ground, leaving the colony with no air defence at all. On the evening of December 9–10, the second evening of the campaign, the Japanese breached the Gindrinkers Line at what was supposedly its strongest point, the Shing Mun Redoubt (map 2). The British were forced to rapidly evacuate the New Territories. The evacuation was completed on December 13 and the Japanese at once ordered the surrender of the island, threatening a severe artillery and aerial bombardment. Maltby and the governor refused.

After an intensive bombardment, the Japanese crossed Kowloon Bay on a wide front on the night of December 18-19, having sent a second demand for surrender on December 17, which had also been rejected. Despite dogged resistance and several counter-attacks, the British were forced back from the east and south of the island and their efforts steadily became less co-ordinated. Pushed remorselessly to the western end of the island, the British finally surrendered unconditionally in the afternoon of Christmas Day, December 25. Some 4,500 British and Indian soldiers were killed and some 6,500 more were taken prisoner. The Japanese suffered about 2,750 casualties.

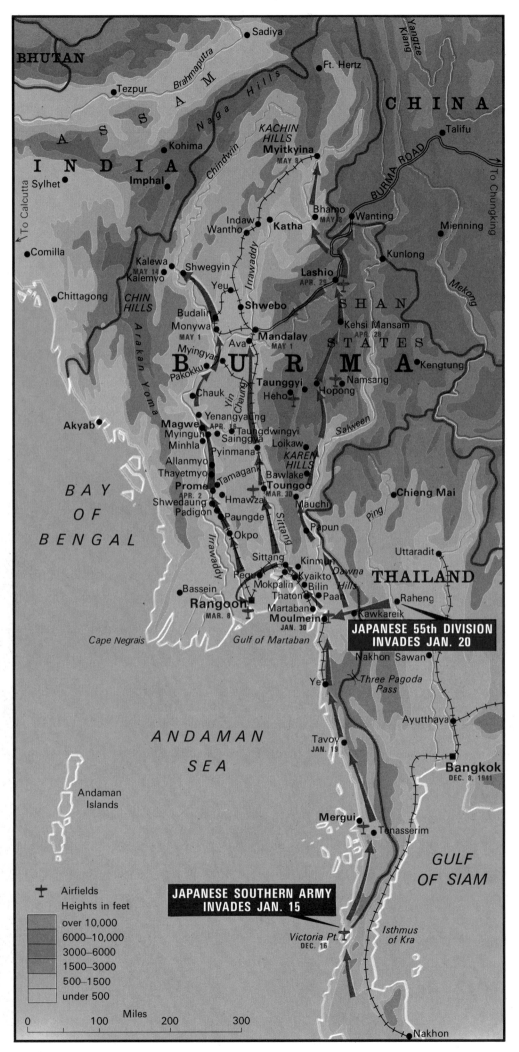

JAPANESE 55th DIVISION INVADES JAN. 20

JAPANESE SOUTHERN ARMY INVADES JAN. 15

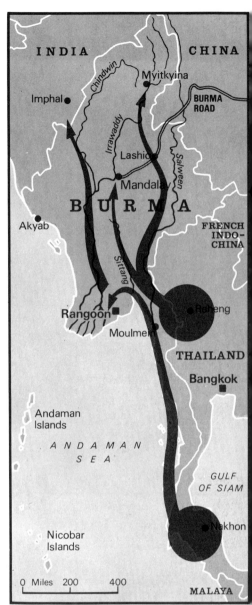

Above: (1) Japanese grand strategy in Burma was a development of the campaign in Malaya. Having occupied the Kra Isthmus on December 8–10, 1941, the Japanese southern army had established a sufficiently secure position in Malaya to strike north into Burma, joining 55th Division from Thailand.

Left: (2) The Japanese performed a brilliant series of outflanking moves to drive the British and Chinese from Burma in a four months campaign. It was a long and hard retreat for the British and a disaster for the Chinese forces.

Right: Japanese infantrymen break cover and charge, as a machine-gun crew prepare to support the attack.

Far right, top: A Japanese 70-mm howitzer dismantled for the march.

Far right, bottom: Japanese 70-mm howitzer in action in Burma.

The Retreat through Burma

The defences of Burma had been as much neglected by the British as those of Malaya and Singapore, for it was thought unlikely that Burma would ever be invaded overland. But Burma was important to Japanese strategy. Its occupation was necessary for the protection of the north-west flank of the Greater East Asia Co-Prosperity Sphere. The campaign in Burma was a triumph for the Japanese and a disaster for the British and Chinese. It involved the British army in the longest retreat in its history, all the way back to the Indian border.

Japanese XV Army had entered Thailand on December 8, 1941, and had occupied the country without much trouble. By mid-January, it was able to turn its attention to Burma. One detachment of XV Army seized an air-base at Victoria Point, at the southernmost tip of Burma, to cut off British air communications between India and Malaya. This detachment then moved north through Mergui and Tavoy to join the main invasion force, which attacked from Raheng on January 20, 1942 (maps 1 and 2).

In the last days of January, Hutton's under-strength, ill-equipped force of British, Burmese and Indian troops was driven out of Moulmein and had to retreat across the Salween. It was the beginning of a very long road. Retreating further, across the Sittang, the force lost all its heavy equipment. Alexander arrived in Rangoon on March 5 and barely escaped when the Japanese occupied the city on March 8. The British garrison hastily withdrew.

The British had already accepted an offer of help from Chiang Kai-shek, who sent his two under-strength 5th and 6th Armies as an expeditionary force under the command of his new American Chief-of-Staff, Stilwell. Alexander planned to hold the line between Prome and Toungoo, with the British Burma Corps (under Slim, from mid-March) on the right, Chinese 5th Army in the centre and Chinese 6th Army on the left. A renewed Japanese attack forced the Chinese to retreat. The British were forced to withdraw from Prome by the end of March, to avoid being cut off from their retreat to India.

Slim and Stilwell were reinforced by Chinese 66th Army but this advantage was neutralized when the Japanese were also reinforced by two divisions from Malaya. The Japanese attacked the British Burma Corps at Yenangyaung in mid-April and Slim barely escaped encirclement as he fought desperately to protect the Yenangyaung oil-fields without success. At the same time, the Japanese hit Chinese 66th Army near Taunggyi, once again threatening the British left and rear. Lashio fell to the Japanese at the end of April and Alexander decided to abandon Mandalay. He withdrew across the Irra-waddy.

Hard-pressed by the pursuing Japanese, Slim made a last stand at Kalewa in the middle of May and then withdrew across the Chindwin and over the border into India, while the scattered units of Chinese 5th and 6th Armies fended as best they could. The Japanese completed the conquest of Burma by May 15 and ceased pursuit partly because of the onset of the monsoon season. It was to be three years before Slim returned through Burma in pursuit of the Japanese and raced to seize Rangoon before another monsoon, three seasons later, threatened to deny him the prize he had to fight so long and patiently to recapture.

The Fall of the Dutch East Indies

The Japanese took this area (map below) and the Philippines (map opposite) using units that were usually outnumbered by the defenders. These co-ordinated forces achieved their objectives within five months of Pearl Harbor.

On January 10, 1942, the Allies in the south-west Pacific set up ABDA (American, British, Dutch, Australian) with Wavell as commander. On January 11, the Japanese Central and Eastern Forces attacked Tarakan and Manado. They controlled the Java and Flores Seas by February 10. Singapore surrendered. Western Force landed on Sumatra at Bali and at Timor. Western and Eastern Forces combined to land on eastern Java, repelling Allied ships in the Battle of the Java Sea, February 27. The Dutch East Indies Government surrendered unconditionally on March 8, 1942.

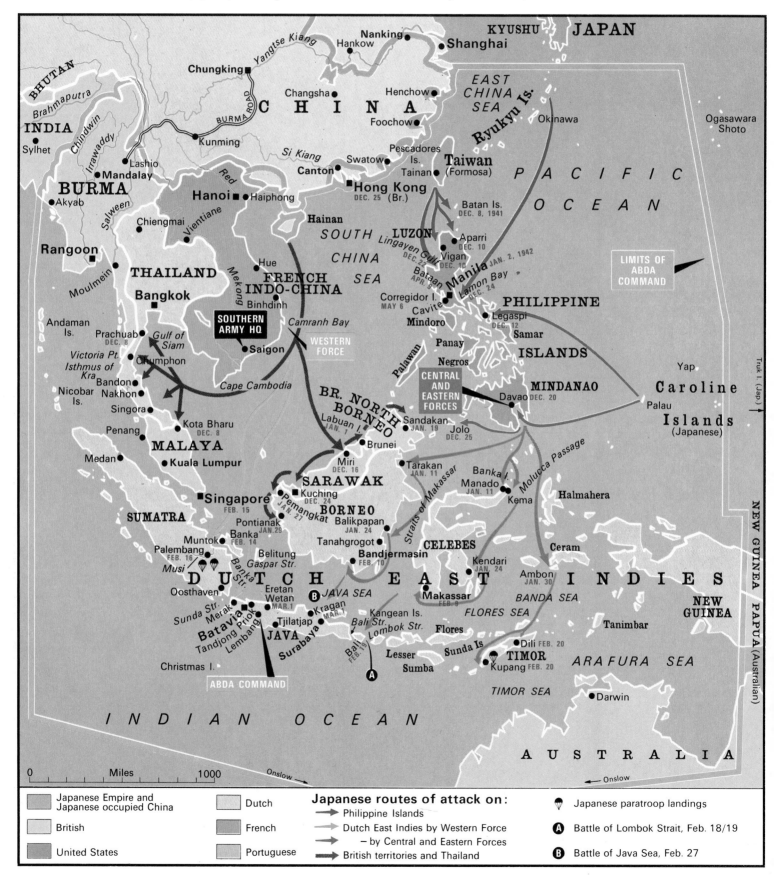

Japanese Empire and Japanese occupied China	Dutch	**Japanese routes of attack on:**
British	French	→ Philippine Islands
United States	Portuguese	→ Dutch East Indies by Western Force
		→ – by Central and Eastern Forces
		→ British territories and Thailand

Japanese paratroop landings

Ⓐ Battle of Lombok Strait, Feb. 18/19

Ⓑ Battle of Java Sea, Feb. 27

Match-box labels circulated by the Japanese as propaganda against the Allies; particularly against Churchill and Roosevelt.

Japan Attacks the Philippines

The Japanese took a calculated risk with their first landings on Luzon. The largest unit to open the campaign was only a regiment and Homma was given only two divisions in all from XIV Army with which to tackle eleven divisions of Americans and Filipinos commanded by MacArthur. The Japanese did, however, have three times the number of aircraft and their troops were better trained and equipped than the Allies.

Heavy air attacks on December 8, 1941, and in the following two days crippled US air power by the time the Japanese landed in the north of the island at Vigan and elsewhere (map on right). A further Japanese detachment captured Legaspi in the extreme south. The main landings occured on December 22 in Lingayen Gulf (inset map). After establishing a strong beach-head, the Japanese advanced south, meeting only limited pockets of stiff resistance.

MacArthur realized that the Japanese assessment of his weakness was painfully accurate. He withdrew from Manila into the Bataan Peninsula on December 23 and declared Manila an open city. The Japanese entered Manila on January 2, 1942 and then confronted MacArthur at the northern end of the Bataan Peninsula. The American forces held out for another three months in the peninsula.

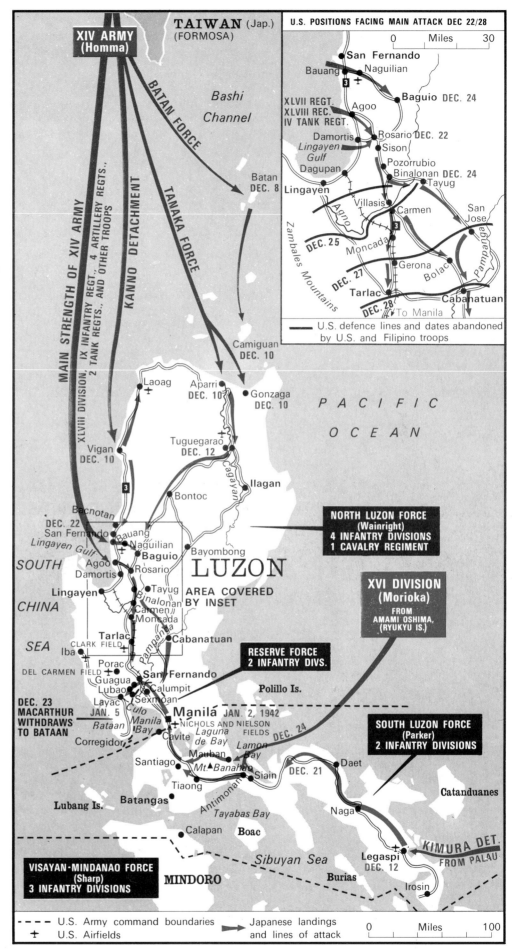

The Battle of the Java Sea

In February 1942, while MacArthur and the Japanese were stalemated in the Bataan Peninsula, the Japanese Western and Eastern forces were moving swiftly through the Dutch East Indies (see page 144). In a last desperate bid to stop the Japanese convoys reaching Java, Dutch Admiral Doorman attacked the Eastern force in the later afternoon of February 27. The Japanese had an escort of two light and two heavy cruisers and 14 destroyers; they also had better co-ordination and communications. Doorman had the two Dutch light cruisers *De Ruyter* and *Java*, with the *Exeter*, *Perth* and *Houston*, six US destroyers and three other destroyers, the *Encounter*, *Electra* and *Jupiter*. His men were tired and his ships had not worked together before.

Throughout the battle, the Japanese escort kept between Doorman's force and the convoy. An opening gunnery duel between the cruisers was followed by a Japanese torpedo attack which failed (map 1). The first major casualty was the *Exeter*, put out of action by an 8-inch shell. The second torpedo attack sank the *Kortenaer*. Doorman counter-attacked and lost the *Electra* (map 2). Both sides withdrew. Doorman tried again to get round the Japanese force to attack the convoy but failed. He sent his US destroyers back to Surabaya. At 2125 hours, the *Jupiter* suddenly blew up (map 3), possibly after hitting a mine. The remaining destroyer *Encounter* was detached to pick up survivors from the *Kortenaer*. Just before 2300 hours, Doorman's cruisers engaged the Japanese cruisers *Nachi* and *Haguro*. The *Java* was hit and sank immediately. Two minutes later, Doorman's own *De Ruyter* was hit and sank within two hours. *Perth* and *Houston* withdrew to Batavia.

From Batavia, *Perth* and *Houston* sailed again and attempted to slip through the Sundra Strait. They ran straight into the Japanese Western Force, which was disembarking its troops. The two cruisers attacked at once and inflicted heavy damage on the Japanese destroyers and transports on the evening of February 28, but both cruisers were sunk. Meanwhile, after quick repairs in Surabaya, the *Exeter* sailed again, also on February 28, with the *Encounter* and *Pope*. The ships were sighted by the Japanese at approximately 0930 hours on March 1. All three ships were sunk. Of Doorman's original force, only four US destroyers managed to escape to Australia. Unconditional surrender of the Dutch East Indies was agreed on March 8, 1942.

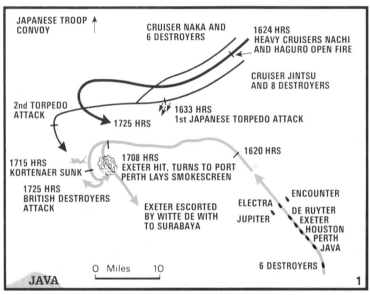

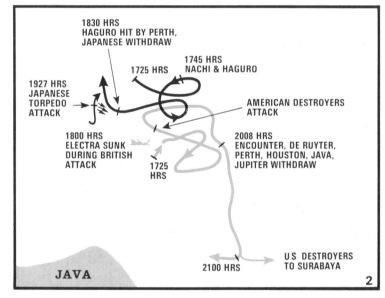

Above: (1) Doorman's cruisers and destroyers engage the Japanese escort force of the invasion convoy. The first Japanese torpedo attack failed. Exeter *was severely damaged by shellfire. The second torpedo attack sank the destroyer* Kortenaer.
Below: (3) Jupiter, Java *and* De Ruyter *were sunk in the night action.*

Above: (2) Electra *is sunk and* Haguro *hit by* Perth. *Both sides draw off after Doorman fails to manoeuvre round the escort to reach the Japanese convoy.*
Below: The end of the Exeter. *Damaged on February 27, she was repaired in Surabaya and put to sea the next day only to be sunk.*

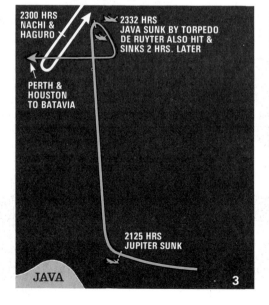

The Raid on Ceylon

The swift victory of the Japanese in the Dutch East Indies opened their way to the Indian Ocean (map 4), where the island of Ceylon became of crucial strategic importance. An Eastern Fleet was built up under the command of Admiral Somerville although most of its capital ships were old. Against them, the Japanese deployed their most powerful naval force, 1 Air Fleet, under Nagumo, with a raiding force under Ozawa. Somerville's plan was to protect Ceylon while avoiding a fleet action.

On April 2, 1942, Somerville ordered the majority of his fleet to return to Addu Atoll in the Maldives to refuel, thinking that the Japanese had postponed their attack. He sent only the heavy cruisers *Dorsetshire* and *Cornwall* to Colombo and the light aircraft carrier *Hermes* to Trincomalee. On April 4, the Japanese were sighted and a fighter-bomber force struck Colombo at dawn on April 5, before Somerville could intercept. *Dorsetshire* and *Cornwall* were caught at sea and sunk. Trincomalee was the next target, with the *Hermes*, a destroyer and several other ships falling victim. Nagumo then withdrew; so did Ozawa's raiding force, which had destroyed 23 ships. The Eastern Fleet was also withdrawn.

The Invasion of Madagascar

After the Japanese attack on Ceylon, it seemed to the British that the next Japanese objective might well be the island of Madagascar, part of the Vichy French Empire and an excellent base for the Japanese from which to cut the Allied supply route round the Cape of Good Hope.

A substantial Combined Operations raid was launched in May, 1942 (map 5). The first landings were made on May 5 at Diego Suarez in the north of the island. This objective was taken within two days but continued fear of a Japanese base on the island kept the force on the alert. On the night of May 30, a Japanese midget submarine torpedoed an oiler, which sank, and the battleship *Ramillies*, which had to be docked at Durban for repairs. It was decided to over-run the rest of the island.

The Vichy French proved tough to beat (just as they had shown surprising resistance to the attempted landings at Dakar, on the west coast of Africa, in September 1940). The Madagascar operation was renewed four months after the first landings. The Vichy French Governor surrendered at Fort Dauphin on November 5, 1942.

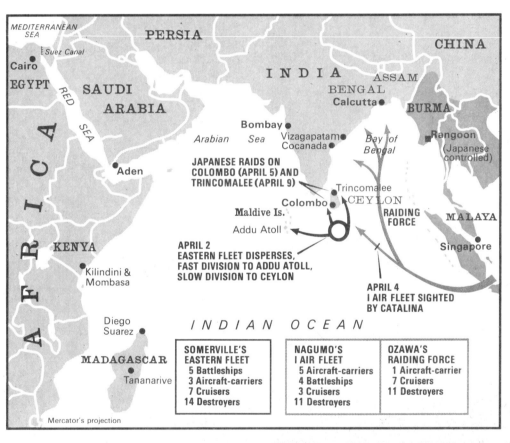

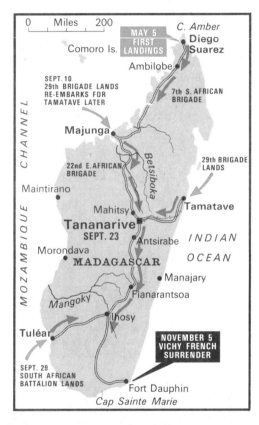

SOMERVILLE'S EASTERN FLEET	NAGUMO'S I AIR FLEET	OZAWA'S RAIDING FORCE
5 Battleships	5 Aircraft-carriers	1 Aircraft-carrier
3 Aircraft-carriers	4 Battleships	7 Cruisers
7 Cruisers	3 Cruisers	11 Destroyers
14 Destroyers	11 Destroyers	

Above left: (4) The Japanese attacks in the Indian Ocean, April 1942, and the positions of the ineffectual Eastern Fleet under Somerville.

Above right: (5) Combined Operations raid on Madagascar, May 1942, and the clearing operation, September to November.

Right: The end of the old, lightweight carrier Hermes, *off Trincomalee, April 1942. The two heavy cruisers,* Dorsetshire *and* Cornwall *were also lost. Japanese planes, launched from carriers, proved their superiority.*

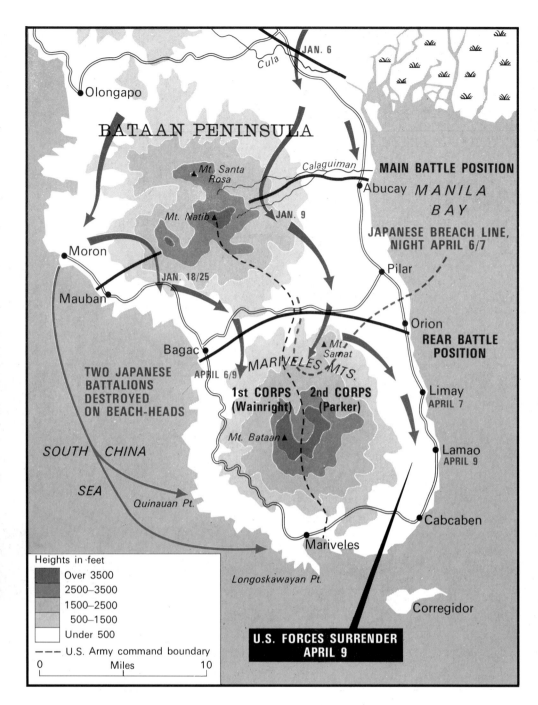

BATAAN PENINSULA

Olongapo

Cula JAN. 6

Mt. Santa Rosa

Calaguiman

MAIN BATTLE POSITION

Abucay MANILA BAY

Mt. Natib JAN. 9

JAPANESE BREACH LINE, NIGHT APRIL 6/7

Moron

Pilar

Mauban

JAN. 18/25

Orion

REAR BATTLE POSITION

Bagac

MARIVELES MTS.

APRIL 6/9

Mt. Samat

TWO JAPANESE BATTALIONS DESTROYED ON BEACH-HEADS

1st CORPS (Wainright)

2nd CORPS (Parker)

Limay APRIL 7

SOUTH CHINA SEA

Mt. Bataan

Lamao APRIL 9

Quinauan Pt.

Cabcaben

Mariveles

Longoskawayan Pt.

Corregidor

Heights in feet
Over 3500
2500–3500
1500–2500
500–1500
Under 500
— — — U.S. Army command boundary
0   Miles   10

U.S. FORCES SURRENDER APRIL 9

Left: (1) The Bataan Peninsula was believed by the Americans to be easily defensible. Large quantities of ammunition and fuel had been stored there. The Americans resisted the first Japanese rush but were forced back to their rear battle position at the end of January, after which there was stalemate until the final Japanese assault in early April.

Right: The end of Corregidor and the Philippines campaign as men of the Allied garrison swarm out of Malinta Tunnel in surrender. Some 15,000 American and Filippino troops surrendered to a landing force of 1,000 Japanese.

Below: General Douglas MacArthur commanded the defence of Bataan and Corregidor until replaced by Wainwright on March 12. Having been US Chief-of-Staff, he retired in 1935 to become advisor to the Philippine Government. When Filippino armed forces were incorporated into the US forces in July 1941, Roosevelt nominated MacArthur as C-in-C. He later assumed command of Allied forces in the Pacific Theatre.

Below: (2) The last Allied foothold off Luzon. Corregidor held on for another month after the fall of Bataan.

Below: (3) The island fortress of Corregidor was believed to be invulnerable; the 'Gibraltar of the East'. After months of bombardment, the Japanese launched a determined assault and took the island within twelve hours of establishing a beach-head. The defenders were forced back to the Malinta Tunnel.

Bataan

MANILA BAY

Mariveles

North Channel

CORREGIDOR (Ft Mills)

CABALLO (Ft Hughes)

EL FRAILE (Ft Drum)

CARABAO (Ft Frank)

Ternate

Catumpan

0 Miles 8

Cavite

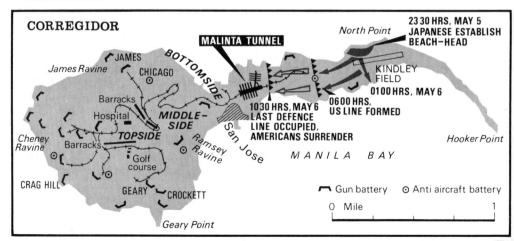

CORREGIDOR

MALINTA TUNNEL

North Point

23 30 HRS, MAY 5 JAPANESE ESTABLISH BEACH-HEAD

JAMES

BOTTOMSIDE

James Ravine

CHICAGO

KINDLEY FIELD

Barracks

Hospital

MIDDLE-SIDE

0100 HRS, MAY 6

10 30 HRS, MAY 6 LAST DEFENCE LINE OCCUPIED, AMERICANS SURRENDER

06 00 HRS, MAY 6 US LINE FORMED

Cheney Ravine

TOPSIDE

Barracks

San Jose

Ramsey Ravine

Hooker Point

MANILA BAY

CRAG HILL

Golf course

GEARY

CROCKETT

⌐ Gun battery   ⊙ Anti aircraft battery

Geary Point

0   Mile   1

The Conquest of Bataan and Corregidor

MacArthur withdrew into the Bataan Peninsula on December 23, 1941, after the Japanese had swept through the north and south of Luzon. He had with him 80,000 troops in Bataan, securely situated behind strong defensive lines based on Mount Santa Rosa in the north of the peninsula.

The first main Japanese attack on these defences was an impetuous rush on January 9, 1942 (map 1). There were heavy casualties on both sides but the Japanese were rebuffed. Two days later, an attempt to outflank the line was also repulsed. It was not until January 23 that the Japanese succeeded in exerting enough pressure on the eastern sector of the line to force the Americans back to their reserve line, running across the peninsula from Bagac to Orion.

More than once, in the last week of January, the Japanese attempted amphibious landings against the south-west coast of Bataan, but two Japanese battalions were destroyed on their beach-heads. Almost two months of stalemate followed, during which both exhausted sides suffered from disease and insufficient food. MacArthur was flown out from his headquarters on Corregidor on March 12 and replaced by General Wainwright.

By April 3, the Japanese had been reinforced sufficiently to launch another attack, preceded by a heavy artillery bombardment. On April 4, they forced a way through the centre of the line and turned the flank of 2nd Corps. By April 7, they had penetrated four miles beyond the line and both 1st and 2nd Corps had to retreat rapidly. The forces on Bataan finally surrendered on April 9. More than 70,000 were forced to make the 65-mile-long 'death march' from Mariveles north to San Fernando. Only about 2,000 escaped to Corregidor.

Japanese aircraft had made their first heavy raid on the island fortress of Corregidor on December 29, 1941 (map 2). On January 1, 1942, with MacArthur trapped in the Bataan Peninsula and the prospect of a siege increasing daily, the garrison was put on half rations. From the end of March, the Japanese began a regular artillery bombardment of the island, which increased after the surrender in Bataan on April 9. By the end of the month, most of the defenders' own artillery had been destroyed by enemy fire. The Japanese launched their attack on May 5 and established a beach-head at North Point (map 3). The last defence in the Malinta Tunnel area was broken on May 6 and the survivors were forced to surrender. The 'invulnerable fortress' had fallen.

The Battle of the Coral Sea

The two naval battles that halted Japanese expansion in May and June, 1942, were in the Coral Sea and at Midway. Midway offered a base within striking distance of Hawaii; the Coral Sea was the gateway to Port Moresby, control of which would have enabled the Japanese to isolate Australia. Vice-Admiral Inouye had overall command of Operation 'MO': the Port Moresby Invasion Group of 11 transports; a smaller Invasion Group for setting up a seaplane base at Tulagi; a Support Group to create a base in the Louisiades; a Covering Group, with the carrier *Shoho*, four heavy cruisers and a destroyer, to cover the Tulagi and Port Moresby landings; and a Striking Force, under Takagi, with the carriers *Shokaku* and *Zuikaku*, to counter US opposition (maps 1 and 2).

Nimitz, C-in-C US Pacific Fleet, directed Fletcher's Task Force 17, with the carrier *Yorktown*, to be joined by Fitch's Task Force 11, with the carrier *Lexington*, and Crace's Task Force 44, with Australian and US cruisers and destroyers, all to be in the Coral Sea on May 4. But the Japanese attack began on May 3, with the occupation of Tulagi. After striking at the landings with *Yorktown*'s planes on May 4, Fletcher turned south and joined the *Lexington*. Throughout May 5 and 6, the opposing forces searched for each other without success. On May 7, the Japanese located Crace's Force 44, which had moved up to harass the Port Moresby Invasion Group. An unsuccessful air attack was made on Crace at 1358 hours. Two hours earlier, another Japanese air strike had sunk the destroyer *Sims* and damaged the tanker *Neosho* to the south.

At 1100 hours on May 7, planes from *Yorktown* and *Lexington* located the Covering Group and bombed the *Shoho*, which sank later. Takagi's Striking Force launched an air attack on Force 17 on the night of May 7–8. This failed and the majority of his aircraft were shot down. The next morning, shortly after 0800 hours, both forces located each other. In the ensuing air strikes, the *Shokaku* was disabled and the *Lexington* was severely hit. She was later abandoned and had to be sunk by torpedoes. The Japanese abandoned any immediate attempt on Port Moresby. They were to try again by land two-and-a-half months later.

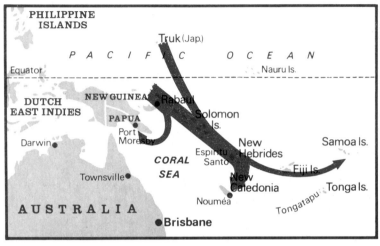

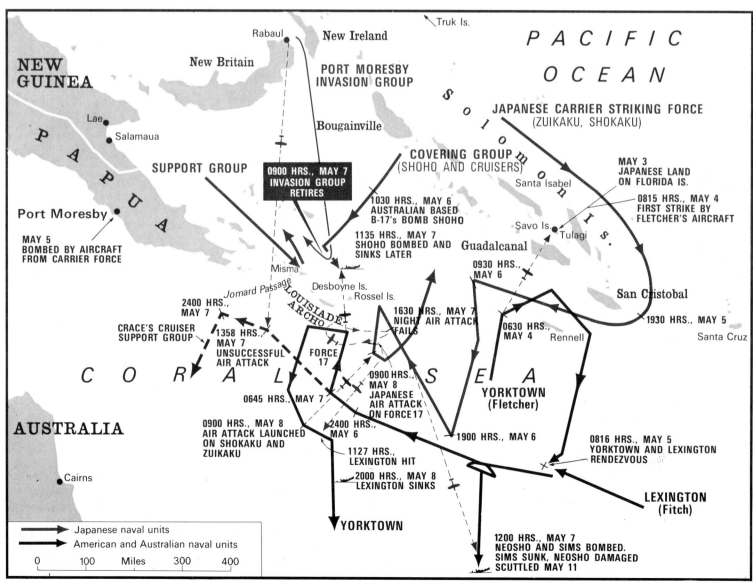

150

Above: A Japanese photograph of the action in the Coral Sea, showing the heavy cruisers of Fletcher's Task Force 17 taking evasive action in the face of Japanese air attack. For the four or five days of the battle, no ship on either side made visual contact with an enemy ship. The battle was fought from the air.

Left: Lexington's 40 mm flak crews hit back at a Japanese air strike.

Left: The Lexington being abandoned by her crew, as a destroyer comes alongside to assist. Lexington and Yorktown were attacked at 1118 hours on May 8. At 1120 hours, Lexington was hit by a torpedo but continued to receive aircraft on her deck. At 1247, there was a major explosion on board the Lexington and at 1710 she was abandoned.

Below: The Lexington was finally blown up and sunk by torpedoes from the destroyer Phelps at 1956 hours on May 8. The Americans suffered heavier ship losses than the Japanese in the battle but, in return, the Japanese suffered greater loss of aircraft. Their strategic plan was destroyed.

Left, upper map: (1) Japanese strategy in the South Pacific: an attempt to outflank New Guinea and seize Port Moresby, from which the Japanese hoped to isolate Australia. While the Invasion Group took the transports to Port Moresby, the Carrier Striking Force was to cruise into the Coral Sea, past the Solomon Islands and ward off any US interference.

Left, lower map: (2) The manoeuvres of the Japanese and US forces in the Coral Sea between May 3 and 8, 1942. The Japanese landed on Tulagi but the Invasion Group for Port Moresby was recalled before it reached the Jomard Passage. The Japanese lost the carrier Shoho from their Covering Group, while Force 11 lost the carrier Lexington. It was the first victory for the US in the Pacific.

The Battle of Midway

Wrongly believing that the *Yorktown* as well as the *Lexington* had gone down in the Coral Sea and that the *Hornet* and *Enterprise*, had remained in the South Pacific after covering the battle, Admiral Yamamoto, C-in-C Japanese Combined Fleet, saw his chance to attack Midway while it was apparently undefended. A northern force was to launch a diversionary attack on the Aleutian Islands, drawing off US ships, while three other forces attacked Midway and drew any remaining US ships onto their big guns: these were Nagumo's First Carrier Strike Force, with the *Kaga*, *Akagi*, *Soryu* and *Hiryu*, the Midway Occupation Force and a powerful Main Force with 7 battleships.

Nimitz had advance warning of Yamamoto's plan. Fletcher's Task Force 17, with *Yorktown*, and Spruance's Task Force 16, with *Hornet* and *Enterprise*, were already at sea when the attack on the Aleutians began on June 3. The US Task Forces tried to make contact with Nagumo's Strike Force, while avoiding the Japanese Main Force. At 0430 hours on June 4, 1942, Nagumo launched what he hoped would be his only air strike against Midway, to soften the island for the Occupation Force landings. The strike hit Midway at 0616 hours (map, position 1). US land-based planes suffered heavy losses but forced the Japanese to prepare for a second strike. While Nagumo was organizing this, his Zero fighters repelled an attack by US bombers from Midway. At 0820, Nagumo received news of the carrier force to the north-east. He changed direction to meet this new threat (map, position 2), causing the first US carrier strike to miss its target. The US dive-bombers

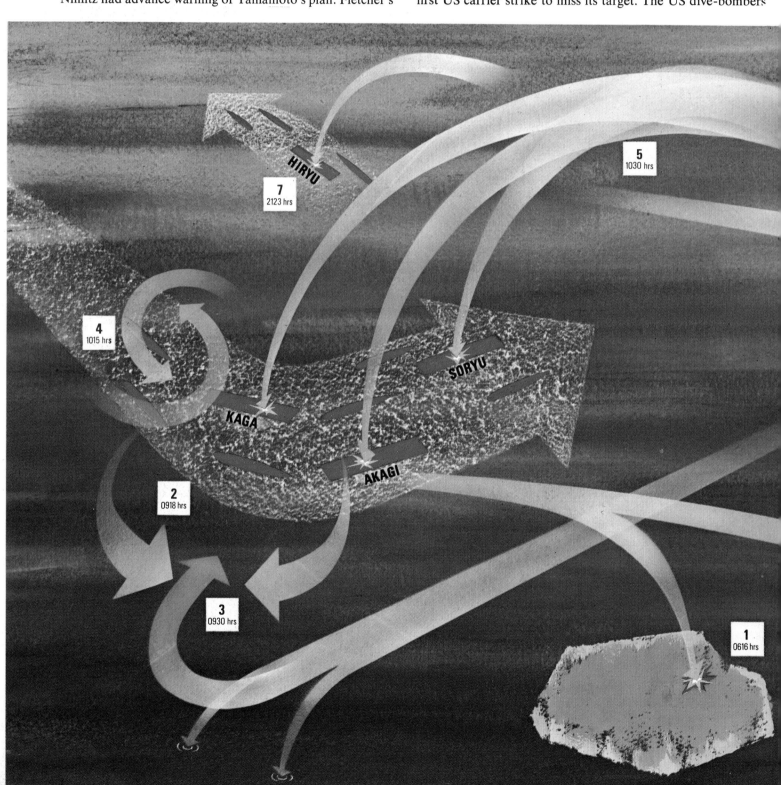

from *Hornet* turned south and the fighters ran out of fuel. At 0930 (map, position 3) and 1015 (map, position 4), torpedo-bombers struck Nagumo's force but lacked fighter cover and suffered heavily from the Zeros. At 1030, when Nagumo's decks were crowded with planes ready for their second strike at Midway, dive-bombers from all three US carriers struck (map, position 5). Within five minutes, the *Kaga, Akagi* and *Soryu* were sunk. The *Hiryu* counter-attacked and hit the *Yorktown* (map, position 6), which was abandoned and later sunk by a submarine. Aircraft from the *Enterprise* continued to attack the *Hiryu* (map, position 7), which was scuttled the next day. The US force withdrew before Yamamoto's Main Force. The initiative in the Pacific, both at sea and in the air, had passed from the Japanese to the Americans.

Right: After surviving the Coral Sea, Yorktown *was crippled at Midway. Hit by dive-bombers from* Hiryu, *her fuel tanks were torn open and flooding caused a 26-degree list. Abandoned, she was reboarded the next day and taken in tow. Two days later, a Japanese submarine torpedoed and sank her.*

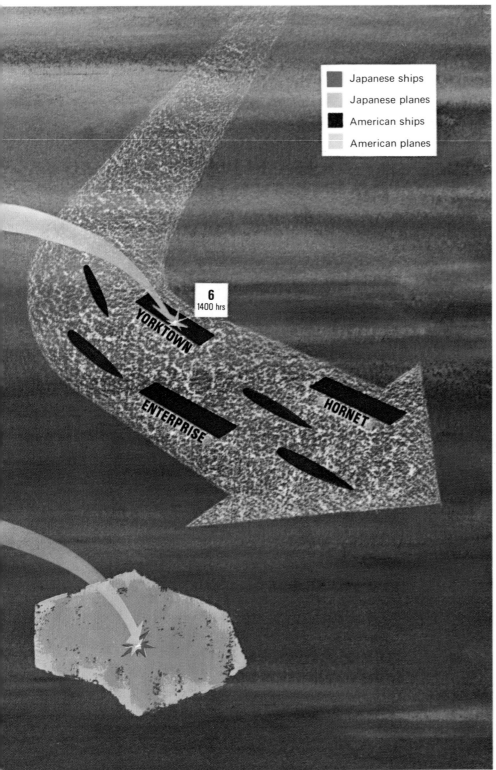

Legend:
- Japanese ships
- Japanese planes
- American ships
- American planes

6
1400 hrs

YORKTOWN
ENTERPRISE
HORNET

Left: The action between the US carriers and Nagumo's Strike Force, which opened with an air strike against Midway and concluded with the loss of all four Japanese carriers and the Yorktown.

Below: Akagi *takes evasive action as 35 US dive-bombers arrive unseen and in five minutes destroy three Japanese carriers.*

153

The War in New Guinea

Frustrated by their failure to take Port Moresby from the sea [after their defeat in the Battle of the Coral Sea in early May, 1942 (page 150)] the Japanese were still determined to win this important base. From it they would be able to isolate Australia and secure their own defensive perimeter. Little more than two months later, therefore, they launched a bold attempt to take Port Moresby by an overland route, striking across the island from the north (map 1).

On the night of July 21–22, elements of Horii's XVIII Army landed at Buna and Gona (map 2) and advanced inland up the narrow Kokoda Trail into the Owen Stanley Mountains that formed a ridge down the centre of the island. Pushing back American and Australian opposition, Horii seized the key passes over the range by August 12 and continued to advance against increasingly stiff resistance. He was within 30 miles of his objective by the second half of September, when at last he was halted by the Australians, who were backed by local air superiority. The Japanese were gradually driven back over the mountains.

Horii's withdrawal was partly under Allied pressure and partly under defensive instructions from his superiors. His retreat was not a rout. By November 1942, Horii had established a jungle fortress around Buna and Gona, where he had originally landed. Untrained in this type of warfare, tired out, ridden with disease, short on artillery and rations, the Australians and Americans were soon bogged down, unable to prise the Japanese from their dug-in positions on the edge of the jungle. MacArthur drove his local commander ruthlessly. 'Bob,' he told Robert Eichelberger, 'I want you to take Buna, or not come back alive.'

Eichelberger set about restoring the men's morale and on December 9 the Australians on the Allied left stormed Gona. It was not until the fourth week in January 1943 that a combined frontal attack and flanking movement along the north-east coast of the peninsula finally enabled the Allies to capture Buna as well.

MacArthur then turned his attention north-west, to lever the Japanese out of the 'tail' of New Guinea (map 3). His immediate objectives were the key Japanese airfield at Lae and control of the coastline facing New Britain so that Rabaul could be isolated. At the end of January 1943, an airlift to Wau (map 4) threatened the Japanese in Salamaua, which was not finally taken until September 12. Lae fell four days later. Co-ordinated land and sea attacks continued along the Huon Peninsula. By the end of the year, the Allies had landed on New Britain.

Above: (1) Papua-New Guinea. Port Moresby offered the perfect base from which the Japanese might apply pressure on Australia, across the Torres Strait.

Below: (2) July–November 1942. The Japanese advance along the Kokoda Trail and the Allies counter-attack.

Above: Japanese reinforcements climbing up the Kokoda Trail from Buna and Gona in the late summer of 1942. They were within 30 miles of Port Moresby before they were stopped by the Australians and Americans.

Below: Australian troops climbing up the southern end of the Kokoda Trail to counter the Japanese offensive. In September and October 1942 they began to prove for the first time that they were equal to the Japanese in the jungle.

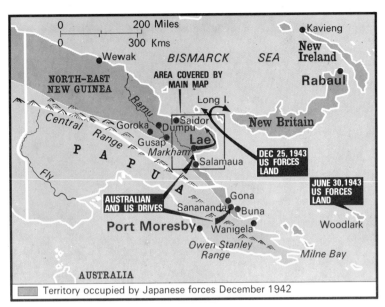

Above: (3) Papua-New Guinea 1942–43. Once the Allies had prised the Japanese out of Buna, Gona and Sanananda, they advanced north-west to recapture the airport at Lae and to clear the coastline opposite New Britain. It took them nearly a year of dogged fighting to flush the Japanese out of the Huon Peninsula.

Above: American 37-mm anti-tank gun crew in action on the beach near Buna, in the long and painful battle to drive the Japanese out of their beach-head and to recover Buna, Gona and Sanananda. Driven hard by MacArthur, who showed little sympathy for their suffering in the appalling conditions, the Allies rapidly learnt from their experiences and showed themselves to be a match for the fanatically determined Japanese.

Right: (4) Australian and American landings and attacks in north-east New Guinea during 1943.

January 22: The Allies prepare for the drive to the north-west. January 29: Japanese begin retreat from Wau, at the head of the Bulldog Track.

February–March: Allied transport problems and lack of aircraft force a halt. March 3: Allied air strikes neutralize the main Japanese airfield at Lae. May: Australians begin attacks against the Japanese forces holding Lae. June–July: Japanese eventually retreat on Mount Tambu. August 12–16: Australians encircle Mount Tambu. August 19: Japanese abandon Mount Tambu. September 4–5: Allied landings prepare the way for the capture of Lae. September 11–12: Allies capture Salamaua. September 15–16: Allies capture Lae. September 22: Allies begin co-ordinated land and sea attacks on Huon Peninsula. October 2: Australian troops capture Finschhafen on Huon Peninsula. December 25: Allies cross to New Britain.

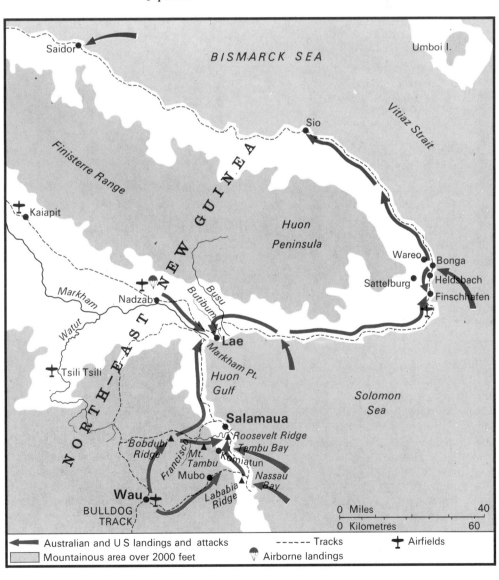

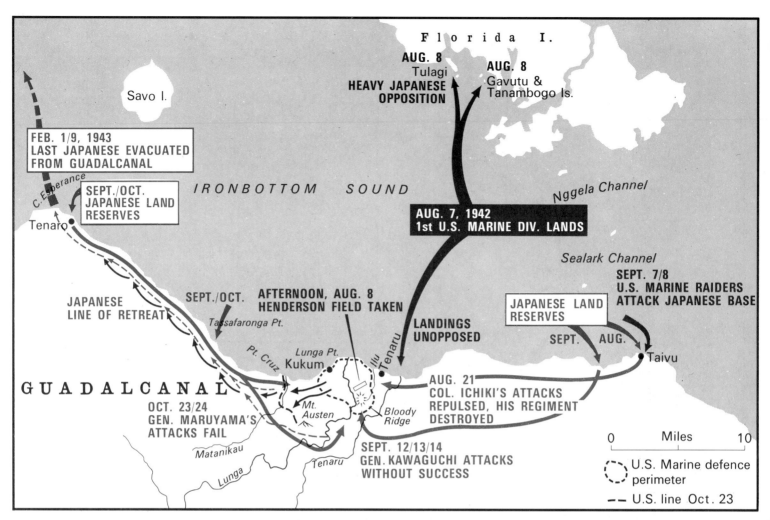

F l o r i d a   I.

AUG. 8
Tulagi
HEAVY JAPANESE OPPOSITION

AUG. 8
Gavutu & Tanambogo Is.

Savo I.

Nggela Channel

FEB. 1/9, 1943 LAST JAPANESE EVACUATED FROM GUADALCANAL

I R O N B O T T O M   S O U N D

SEPT./OCT. JAPANESE LAND RESERVES

C. Esperance

AUG. 7, 1942 1st U.S. MARINE DIV. LANDS

Tenaro

Sealark Channel

SEPT. 7/8 U.S. MARINE RAIDERS ATTACK JAPANESE BASE

JAPANESE LINE OF RETREAT

SEPT./OCT.

AFTERNOON, AUG. 8 HENDERSON FIELD TAKEN

Tassafaronga Pt.

LANDINGS UNOPPOSED

JAPANESE LAND RESERVES

SEPT.   AUG.

Taivu

Lunga Pt.
Pt. Cruz   Kukum

Ilu   Tenaru

AUG. 21 COL. ICHIKI'S ATTACKS REPULSED, HIS REGIMENT DESTROYED

G U A D A L C A N A L

OCT. 23/24 GEN. MARUYAMA'S ATTACKS FAIL

Mt. Austen

Bloody Ridge

Matanikau

SEPT. 12/13/14 GEN. KAWAGUCHI ATTACKS WITHOUT SUCCESS

Lunga   Tenaru

0   Miles   10

- - - U.S. Marine defence perimeter

— — U.S. line Oct. 23

Above: (1) The six-month battle for Guadalcanal, showing the repeated Japanese attempts to prise US 1st Marine Division from their hold on the crucial Henderson Field. The Americans were once more on the offensive, eight months to the day after the disaster at Pearl Harbor.

Right: A US platoon crosses the River Lunga, which ran through the Marine defence perimeter in their beach-head at Henderson Field. Disease and tropical storms added to the difficulties faced by the Americans in their hard-won struggle.

The Fight for Guadalcanal

News that the Japanese were constructing a vital airfield on Guadalcanal in the summer of 1942 hastened the Allied plans to move back into the southern Solomons. On August 7, 1942, an amphibious force landed Vandergrift's reinforced 1st Marine Division on Guadalcanal (map 1). The marines achieved tactical surprise on the main island, at Tenaru, but encountered stiff opposition on the neighbouring islands of Tulagi and Gavutu. All landings were successfully achieved by August 8 and Henderson Field was abandoned by the Japanese.

On August 8–9, Japanese vessels forced the marine transport ships to withdraw and on August 18 the first Japanese reinforcements landed at Taivu. This was a regiment commanded by Colonel Ichiki. The marines had received their first aircraft by the time Ichiki launched his attack on August 21 across the

Tenaru river and they were able to counter-attack and drive Ichiki's regiment into the sea. Ichiki committed hara-kiri.

On September 7, US marine raiders attacked the Japanese base at Taivu, captured stores and equipment and gained intelligence of an impending Japanese attack, which was launched on September 12–14 by General Kawaguchi and beaten back with heavy Japanese losses. The Japanese rushed in reinforcements to Tenaro, west of Henderson Field, during September and October. These included II Division and the headquarters of XVII Army. Vandergrift's exhausted 1st Marines were meanwhile reinforced by US 7th Marines and 164th Infantry Regiment.

General Maruyama's planned attack on Henderson Field was delayed by a Japanese naval setback off Cape Esperance

Japanese Empire, 1937
Territory occupied by
Japanese forces, 1937–1942
Pacific Command Areas
Subdivisions of
Pacific Ocean Areas
South–West Pacific Area,
after July 1942
Final attacks on
Japanese homeland

Mercator Projection

The Pacific Drive

but on October 23–24 he launched two attacks to the south. These attacks were not properly co-ordinated and the marines were able to defeat them piecemeal. Maruyama suffered 3,500 casualties. In early December, 14th Army Corps replaced the battle-weary marines. Appalled by their own losses, the Japanese were beginning to plan their withdrawal from Guadalcanal by the end of the month. By February 9, the 'Tokyo Express' removed the remnant of XVII Army. The marines had won an outstanding victory, both in psychological and material terms. They had proved that the Japanese could be beaten and they had denied them an important air base. The Allies now stood ready to advance up the chain of Japanese-held islands.

Once Japanese attention focused on consolidating their swiftly-won empire, the Allies turned their own attention to the recapture of the Pacific Islands, which would end, they hoped, in the defeat of Japan.

MacArthur (South-West Pacific Area) was to outflank the fortress of Rabaul and approach the Philippines from the south. Halsey (South Pacific Area) was to co-operate with MacArthur in isolating Rabaul and to drive north-west from Guadalcanal along the Solomon Islands. Nimitz (Central and North Pacific Areas) was to feed adequate resources to the other two commanders while supervising the central drive. The final attacks on the Japanese homeland were to come from the Philippines through Okinawa, from the Marianas through Iwo Jima and from the Aleutians.

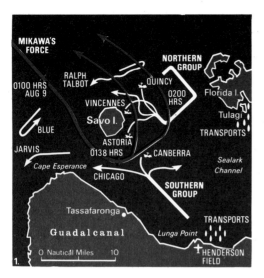

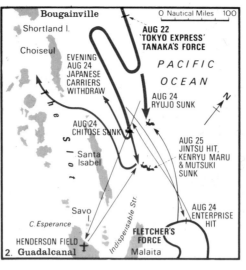

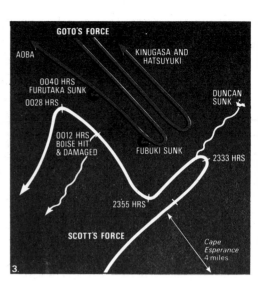

(1) Savo Island, August 8–9, 1942. (2) Eastern Solomons, August 23, 1942. (3) Cape Esperance, October 11–12, 1942. (4) Santa Cruz, October 24–26, 1942. (4) Comparative losses in the four naval actions.

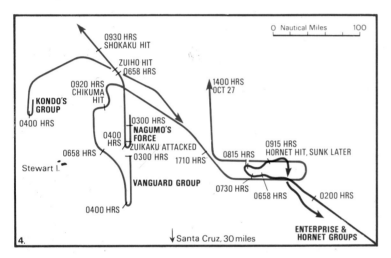

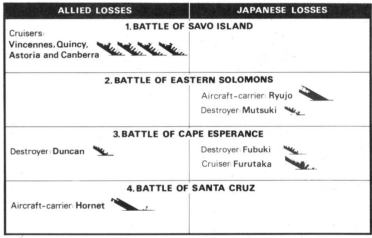

ALLIED LOSSES	JAPANESE LOSSES
1. BATTLE OF SAVO ISLAND	
Cruisers: Vincennes, Quincy, Astoria and Canberra	
2. BATTLE OF EASTERN SOLOMONS	
	Aircraft-carrier: Ryujo
	Destroyer: Mutsuki
3. BATTLE OF CAPE ESPERANCE	
Destroyer: Duncan	Destroyer: Fubuki
	Cruiser: Furutaka
4. BATTLE OF SANTA CRUZ	
Aircraft-carrier: Hornet	

Guadalcanal: the Sea Battles

The naval actions that took place in the Solomon Islands at the same time as the Marine landings on Guadalcanal played an important part in the fortunes of the opposing sides between August and November 1942. The first action took place near Savo Island on the night of August 8–9 (map 1). Vice-Admiral Mikawa's cruisers, intending to attack US transports unloading off Guadalcanal, encountered Crutchley's cruiser force patrolling the approaches around Savo Island. Mikawa slipped past Crutchley's outlying destroyers in the dark and disabled the cruisers *Canberra* and *Chicago*. Turning north-east, Mikawa crippled the cruisers *Vincennes*, *Quincy* and *Astoria*; he then withdrew, leaving four cruisers sinking.

The Japanese attempted to run supplies to reinforce their troops on Guadalcanal, supported by the carriers *Ryujo*, *Shokaku* and *Zuikaku*, but on August 23 these ran into Fletcher's Task Force 61, patrolling east of the Solomons (map 2). Fletcher launched an air strike but the Japanese reversed course rapidly. Fletcher sighted the *Ryujo* again and sank her. The *Enterprise* was subsequently disabled in a counter-strike. Both carrier forces withdrew but the Japanese Transport Group continued towards Guadalcanal. Dive-bombers from Henderson Field hit the *Jintsu* and *Kenryu Maru* on August 25. The destroyer *Mutsuki* was sunk later. The Japanese stopped daytime reinforcement runs and concentrated instead on the 'Tokyo Night Express' from Bougainville.

On the night of October 11–12, off Cape Esperance, at the northern end of Guadalcanal (map 3), a US supply convoy escorted by Scott's cruiser squadron encountered a Japanese convoy, also with a cruiser squadron, coming down 'The Slot', the narrow channel between the eastern and western Solomons (see map 2 for 'The Slot'). In the confusion of sudden contact at night, the Japanese *Aoba* and *Furutaka* were severely damaged and the US destroyer *Duncan* was sunk. The Japanese withdrew, damaging the cruiser *Boise* and losing the destroyer *Fubuki*.

Later in the month, General Maruyama planned a major attack on Henderson Field, to be supported by planes from the Japanese Combined Fleet north of Guadalcanal. On October 24, US Task Forces 16 (*Enterprise*) and 17 (*Hornet*) were ordered to patrol the area around the Santa Cruz Islands to intercept Japanese forces approaching Guadalcanal (map 4). The clash came on the 26th. As the Japanese launched their first strike from the *Zuiho*, *Shokaku* and *Zuikaku* at 0658 hours and prepared for their second strike, dive-bombers from the *Enterprise* disabled the *Zuiho*. Between 0730 and 0815, *Enterprise* and *Hornet* launched three small strikes and at 0822 *Shokaku* and *Zuikaku* launched their second strike. At 0915 hours, the first Japanese strike hit the *Hornet*. At 0930 hours, the *Shokaku* was severely damaged by US dive-bombers. It was the turn of the *Enterprise* to be hit by the Japanese second strike. The US force then withdrew, leaving the *Hornet* a burning hulk which was later sunk by the Japanese. US ships had suffered heavily but so had Japanese air crews.

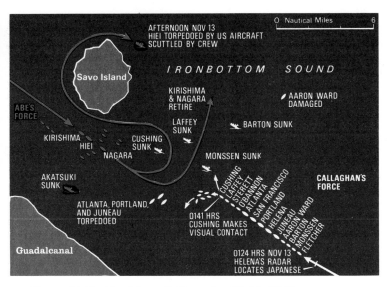

Above: (1) '1st Guadalcanal', November 12–13, 1942.

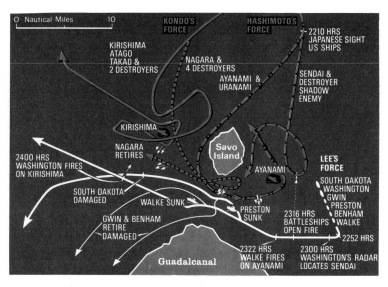

Above; (2) '2nd Guadalcanal', November 14–15, 1942.

Guadalcanal: the Final Actions

Despite the terrible losses suffered by Maruyama's land forces in their attacks on Henderson Field toward the end of October 1942, the Japanese seemed determined to hang on to Guadalcanal. During November, Japanese reinforcements were still being sent in to the island, while US cruisers tried desperately to intercept them. On the night of November 12–13, Callaghan's cruisers and destroyers blundered into Abe's squadron of battleships, cruisers and destroyers, which was acting as cover for a troop transport convoy (map 1). In the confused fighting that followed, four US cruisers were crippled (*Juneau* and *Atlanta* later sank) and four destroyers sunk. Callaghan himself was killed aboard the *San Francisco*. The Japanese *Akatsuki* was also sunk and next morning the battleship *Hiei* was hit by torpedo-bombers and scuttled. The US cruiser force was eliminated but the Japanese troops were prevented from landing.

At dawn on November 14, a Japanese cruiser squadron bombarding Henderson Field was attacked by US torpedo-bombers. One cruiser sank. US planes also struck at a Japanese convoy in 'The Slot' and sank seven transports. Kondo then moved up to bombard Henderson and cover the remaining transports with one battleship, four cruisers and nine destroyers. He was intercepted by Lee's US Task Force 64 (two battleships, four destroyers) at 2300 hours on the night of the 14th (map 2). In a brief action, the US destroyers *Preston* and *Walke* were sunk and the *Gwin* and *Benham* retired damaged. The battleship *South Dakota* was put out of action but the *Washington* sank the battleship *Kirishima* and one destroyer and dispersed the other destroyers.

On November 30, at the Battle of Tassafaronga (map 3), eight destroyers under Tanaka were surprised by Wright's force of cruisers and destroyers. Radar contact was made with the Japanese at 2306. When Wright finally opened fire, Tanaka turned to attack. The destroyer *Takanami* was sunk but in turn the Japanese sank the cruiser *Northampton* and severely damaged three more cruisers. Although the Japanese had once again shown their superiority at night-fighting, this was the last major clash before they pulled out of Guadalcanal.

Below: (3) The Battle of Tassafaronga, November 30, 1942, the last major clash around Guadalcanal. The Japanese had shown incredible determination in pushing their supplies down 'The Slot' for four months in their attempts to reinforce the garrison in Guadalcanal. The battle for the island had cost both sides heavily, in men and in ships.

Below: Comparative losses in the three final actions. Throughout the four months of the naval actions, between August and November, the Japanese had shown themselves masters of night-fighting and the Americans had so far failed to make the best use of their one potential advantage, the radar that was later to be of such service to them.

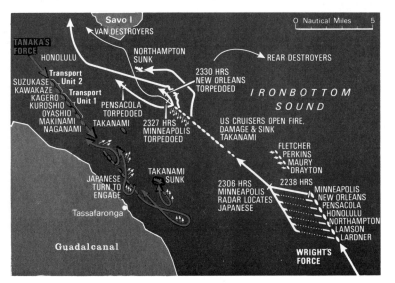

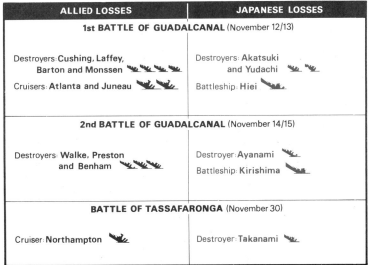

ALLIED LOSSES	JAPANESE LOSSES
1st BATTLE OF GUADALCANAL (November 12/13)	
Destroyers: Cushing, Laffey, Barton and Monssen	Destroyers: Akatsuki and Yudachi
Cruisers: Atlanta and Juneau	Battleship: Hiei
2nd BATTLE OF GUADALCANAL (November 14/15)	
Destroyers: Walke, Preston and Benham	Destroyer: Ayanami
	Battleship: Kirishima
BATTLE OF TASSAFARONGA (November 30)	
Cruiser: Northampton	Destroyer: Takanami

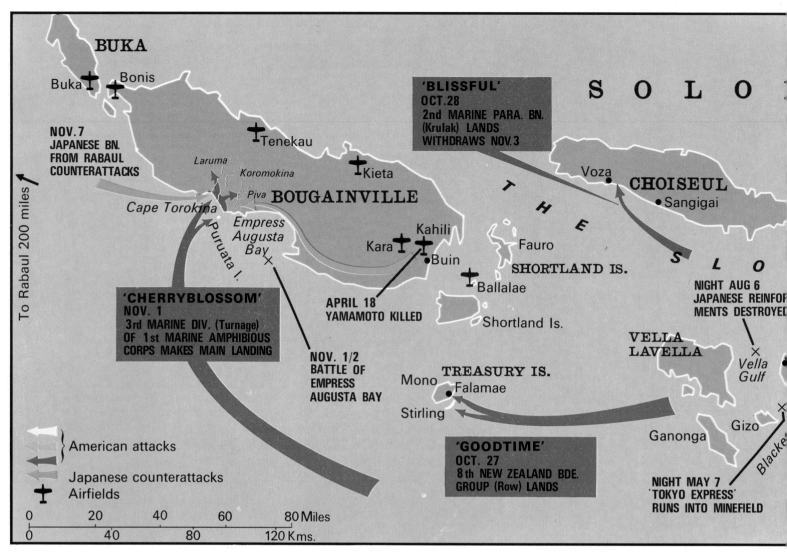

'BLISSFUL'
OCT.28
2nd MARINE PARA. BN.
(Krulak) LANDS
WITHDRAWS NOV.3

SOLO

BUKA

Buka ✈ ✈ Bonis

NOV.7
JAPANESE BN.
FROM RABAUL
COUNTERATTACKS

✈ Tenekau

Laruma
Koromokina
✈ Kieta
Piva BOUGAINVILLE

Cape Torokina

Empress
Augusta
Bay

Puruata I.

Voza
CHOISEUL
● Sangigai

THE

S

L O

Kara Kahili
✈ ✈
Buin ●

Fauro

SHORTLAND IS.

✈ Ballalae

Shortland Is.

NIGHT AUG 6
JAPANESE REINFOR
MENTS DESTROYED

VELLA
LAVELLA

Vella
Gulf

'CHERRYBLOSSOM'
NOV.1
3rd MARINE DIV. (Turnage)
OF 1st MARINE AMPHIBIOUS
CORPS MAKES MAIN LANDING

APRIL 18
YAMAMOTO KILLED

NOV. 1/2
BATTLE OF
EMPRESS
AUGUSTA
BAY

TREASURY IS.
Mono ● Falamae

Stirling

Gizo

Ganonga

Blacke

'GOODTIME'
OCT. 27
8th NEW ZEALAND BDE.
GROUP (Row) LANDS

NIGHT MAY 7
'TOKYO EXPRESS'
RUNS INTO MINEFIELD

⬅ American attacks
⬅ Japanese counterattacks
✈ Airfields

| 0 | 20 | 40 | 60 | 80 Miles |
| 0 | 40 | 80 | | 120 Kms. |

To Rabaul 200 miles

Above: Through the Solomons, from Guadalcanal to Bougainville, February–December 1943. The island-hopping operations were planned to capture key air bases ahead of the advance and to strangle isolated islands while the build-up continued.

Below: By August 1943, the north-east and south-east outposts of the Japanese Empire had been driven in.

Below: Fighting through the Solomons, the Allies move inland from the beaches. The going was often made all the more difficult by calf-deep seas of mud in the plantations.

160

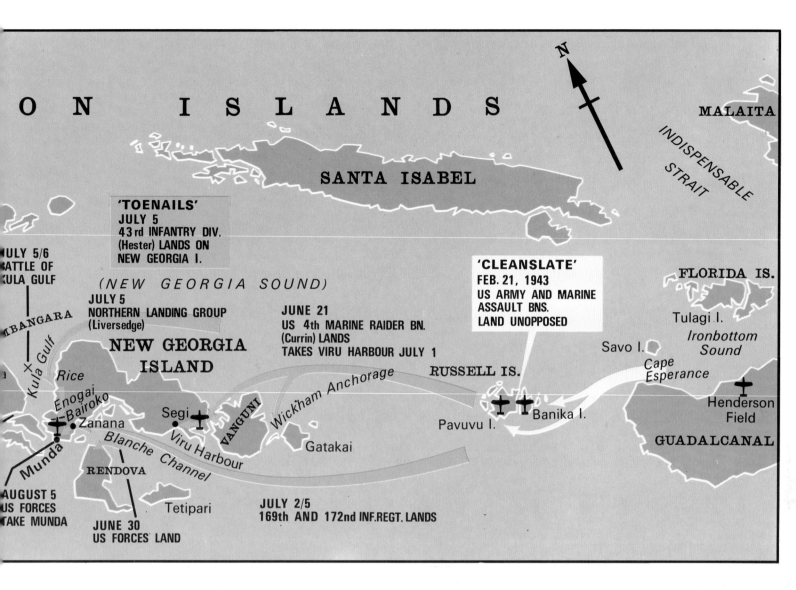

On the map:

O N I S L A N D S

N

MALAITA

SANTA ISABEL

INDISPENSABLE STRAIT

JULY 5/6
BATTLE OF
KULA GULF

'TOENAILS'
JULY 5
43rd INFANTRY DIV.
(Hester) LANDS ON
NEW GEORGIA I.

(NEW GEORGIA SOUND)

'CLEANSLATE'
FEB. 21, 1943
US ARMY AND MARINE
ASSAULT BNS.
LAND UNOPPOSED

FLORIDA IS.

JULY 5
NORTHERN LANDING GROUP
(Liversedge)

JUNE 21
US 4th MARINE RAIDER BN.
(Currin) LANDS
TAKES VIRU HARBOUR JULY 1

Tulagi I.

Ironbottom
Sound

KOLOMBANGARA

NEW GEORGIA
ISLAND

Savo I.

Cape
Esperance

Kula Gulf

Rice

RUSSELL IS.

Wickham Anchorage

Henderson
Field

Enogai
Bairoko

Zanana

Segi

VANGUNI

Banika I.

Munda

Viru Harbour

Gatakai

Pavuvu I.

GUADALCANAL

Blanche Channel

RENDOVA

AUGUST 5
US FORCES
TAKE MUNDA

Tetipari

JULY 2/5
169th AND 172nd INF. REGT. LANDS

JUNE 30
US FORCES LAND

The Battle for the Solomons

Guadalcanal was only the beginning of the battle for the Solomon Islands. Further advance along the island chain to seal off Rabaul from the south-east set the pattern for ensuing operations in the Pacific War. Key air bases were seized by outflanking moves, to provide an overlapping system of controlled air space. Intermediate enemy-held islands were mopped up while preparations were made for the next advance. The New Georgia Group and Bougainville were the prime objectives in the Solomons.

There was a breathing space between February and June 1943, while Admiral Halsey prepared for his assault on New Georgia. The Russell Islands, between Guadalcanal and New Georgia, were seized in an unopposed operation (Cleanslate) by US Army and Marine assault battalions on February 21. On April 18, Yamamoto, Japan's foremost strategist, was shot down when flying from Rabaul to Bougainville. At the end of April, MacArthur issued his final Elkton Plan for Operation Cartwheel, a co-ordinated drive in the South and South-West Pacific towards Rabaul.

On June 21, US Marines opened the campaign for the Central Solomons with landings at Segi, New Georgia, with Munda air field as the main target (Operation Toenails). US forces landed at Rendova on June 30. Between July 2 and 5, troops landed to attack Munda from north and south. Since this was the principal Japanese air field in the Solomons, it was fiercely defended and it was not taken until August 5. Japanese reinforcements were destroyed in the Vella Gulf on the night of August 6. By August 20–22 the Japanese had evacuated northern New Georgia and by August 25 all resistance in New Georgia was ended.

In mid-August, a US combat team had landed on Vella Lavella, east of New Georgia, and established an advance air base, leap-frogging Kolombangara. New Zealand troops replaced the US troops on Vella Lavella in mid-September and cleared the remnants of the Japanese garrison from the island. This forced the Japanese to withdraw from Kolombangara as well and by the end of the first week in October the campaign in the Central Solomons was completed.

On October 27, a small Marine detachment made a feint assault on Choiseul, to the north of New Georgia (Operation Blissful). This was quickly withdrawn on November 3 but served to obscure the main Allied intent of a simultaneous (October 27) attack on the Treasury Islands (Operation Goodtime) to provide a staging post for the assault on Bougainville. Operation Cherryblossom opened on November 1, when US 3rd Marine Division went ashore at Empress Augusta Bay and met only light resistance. The Japanese from Rabaul counter-attacked on November 7 but by the end of the year the Allies had established a substantial defensive perimeter and had turned Empress Augusta Bay into an Allied naval base with three airstrips in operation. Even though much of Bougainville was still in the hands of the Japanese, Admiral Halsey's eastern arm of the pincer movement was now outstretched and ready for operations against Rabaul. Landings by MacArthur's south-west force on New Britain itself and the capture of the Admiralty Islands and the St Matthias Group of Islands north-west of New Britain completed the trap.

The Gilbert and Marshall Islands

During the summer and autumn of 1943, Admiral Nimitz assembled vast numbers of men, ships and aircraft for the atoll-to-atoll struggle in the Central Pacific (map 1). After heavy bombardment from November 13–20, Makin Atoll in the Gilberts was cleared with little difficulty but Tarawa Atoll contained the Japanese stronghold of Betio, which offered stiff opposition (map 2). The battle lasted from November 20–23 and ended with a suicidal attack by the Japanese.

Operation Flintlock opened against Kwajalein Atoll in the Marshalls on February 1, 1944 (maps 3 and 4). A marine force attacked Roi and Namur, while an infantry force attacked Kwajalein itself, where the battle went on for four days. Eniwetok Atoll was the final target (map 5). Engebi fell on February 19. Parry and Eniwetok itself fell by February 23, with no survivors out of 2,000 defenders.

Closing the Trap on Rabaul

By February 1944, the South and South-West Pacific Forces were ready to pinch out Rabaul, with the capture of the Admiralty and St Matthias Islands (maps 6 and 8). On February 29, a reconnaissance in force by US 1st Cavalry Division turned swiftly into a full-scale attack on Los Negros Island in the Admiralties (maps 7 and 8). On March 12 and 15, reinforcements arrived to attack Manus Island and the outlying islands (map 7). On March 20, marines landed in the Matthias group and by the end of March the islands were secured.

More marines had landed in New Britain on March 6, strengthening the Allied position at the western end of the island. With advance air bases established in the Admiralties and in the St Matthias Islands, the main Japanese bases at Rabaul and Kavieng, at the northern tip of New Ireland, were successfully isolated and remained so until the end of the war.

Above: (1) The strategic situation in the Pacific in February 1944, with the taking of the Gilbert and Marshall Islands but before the trap closed completely on Rabaul.

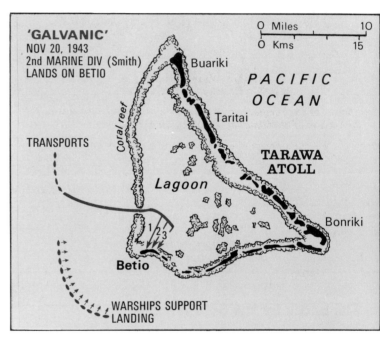

Above: (2) Tarawa Atoll in the Gilbert Islands, where the US invasion fleet had to negotiate coral reefs before passing the lagoon entrance under fire. Fanatical resistance by the Japanese resulted in only 100 prisoners being taken out of a total of 4,700 defenders.

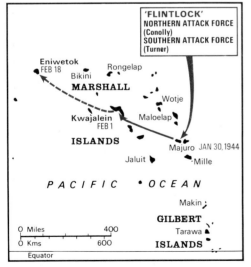

Above: (3) The Marshall Islands, showing the positions of the two main atolls, Kwajalein and Eniwetok.

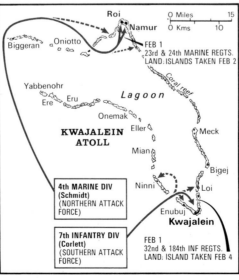

Above: (4) Kwajalein Atoll in the Marshalls required two attacks, 50 miles apart.

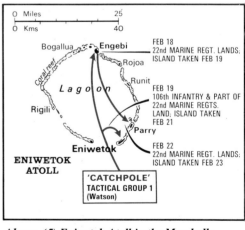

Above: (5) Eniwetok Atoll in the Marshalls, 325 miles north-west of Kwajalein, was attacked only two weeks later. As on Kwajalein, this was a combined infantry–marine operation.

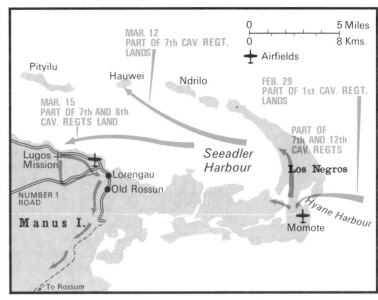

Above: (6) *The Pacific, March 1944, with Rabaul securely sealed off by the capture of the Admiralty and St Matthias Islands.*

Above: (7) *The assault on Los Negros and Manus Islands in the Admiralties by the US Army. By the time resistance ceased on Los Negros, ten Japanese had been killed for every one American. By the fourth week in March, the islands were safely in the hands of the Allies.*

Below: (8) *The assaults on the Admiralty Islands, the St Matthias group and New Britain, between December 1943 and March 1944. This was the finale of MacArthur's Elkton Plan.*

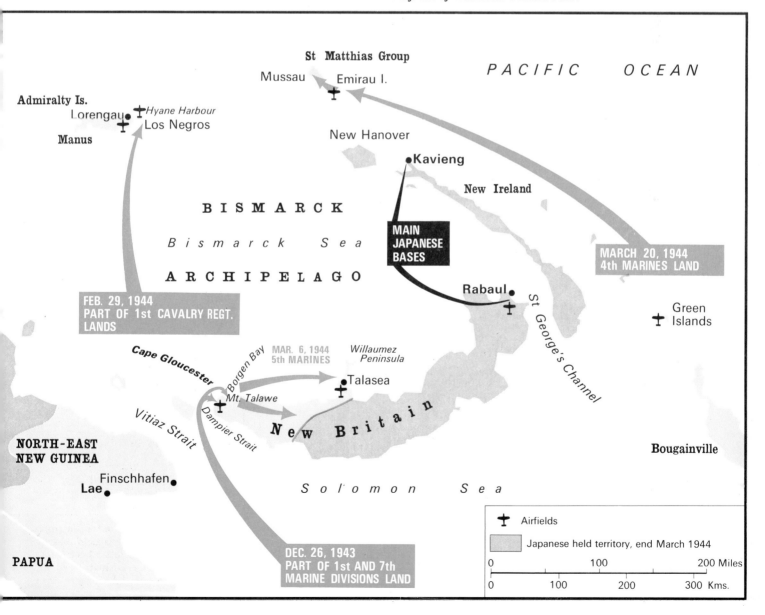

The Battle for the Marianas

Saipan, Tinian and Guam formed the main Japanese defences in the Marianas, 1,000 miles north-west of Eniwetok in the Marshalls (map 1). 530 vessels and 127,000 men formed the largest amphibious force seen in the Pacific, deployed to attack the Japanese XXXI Army in the Marianas.

On June 15, 1944, after prolonged bombardment, the first landings were made on Saipan by 2nd and 4th Marine Divisions (map 2). They achieved a beach-head against stiff opposition and on June 17 the reserve 27th Infantry Division was committed. Effective Japanese resistance did not end until July 9, after a fanatical counter-attack had failed on July 7. Almost the entire garrison of 27,000 was killed.

On July 24–25, 2nd and 4th Marines launched their attack on Tinian (map 2). After surviving another suicidal counter-attack, they cleared the island by July 31. Meanwhile on Guam, a combined Marine and Army assault on July 21 had established two beach-heads, each side of the Orote Peninsula (map 3). A Japanese counter-attack failed to wipe these beach-heads out on the night of July 25–26. Effective Japanese resistance ended on August 10, after 10,000 Japanese had been killed. But the mopping-up operation continued for a long time. The last Japanese to surrender on the island did so in 1960.

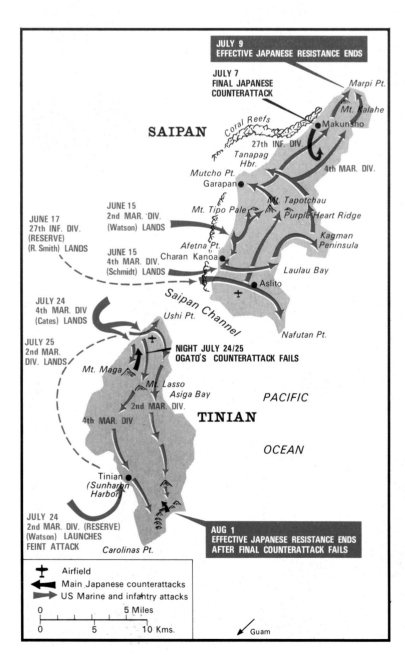

Above: (1) The Pacific, July–August 1944. The capture of the Marianas provided bases from which naval and air forces could cut the lines of communication to Japan's southern empire and undertake heavy and continuous bombing of Japan itself.

Left: (2) The attacks on Saipan and Tinian in the Marianas, June–July 1944. Saipan was attacked first because it would cut off Japanese forces on the other islands from the homeland.

Below: (3) The attack on Guam, July–August 1944. Sheer cliffs and coral reefs around much of the island meant that landings could only be made either side of the Orote Peninsula, where the Japanese were in waiting for the marines.

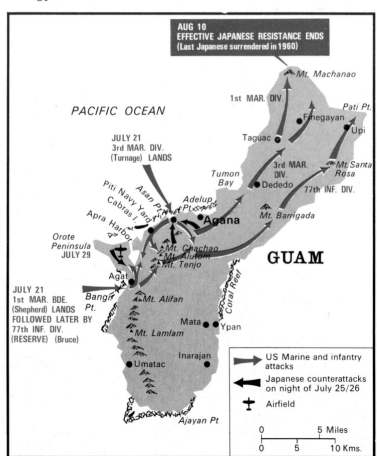

Above: Beginning the massive amphibious operation, the first wave of troops hits the tiny beaches of northern Tinian.

Below: Sustained tank-infantry pressure, coupled with intensive air, artillery and naval gunfire, cleared Guam in three weeks.

The Battle of the Philippine Sea

The US finally destroyed Japanese naval air power in the last great carrier battle of the war. Despite their losses, the Japanese still attempted to deploy their carriers in the summer of 1944 to stop the Americans landing on the Marianas. US control of the islands would cut the Japanese empire in half, isolating the homeland from the Philippines and south-east possessions.

The first US landings in the Marianas were made on June 15, 1944: the Marines landed on Saipan. On June 16, US submarines reported that the Japanese First Mobile Fleet under Ozawa and a Southern Force under Ugaki were rendezvousing off the Philippines, preparing to attack (map 1). The Japanese had five heavy carriers, four light carriers, five battleships, 11 heavy cruisers, two light cruisers and 28 destroyers. Mitscher's US Task Force 58 had in opposition a massive total of seven heavy carriers, eight light carriers, seven battleships, eight heavy cruisers, 13 light cruisers and 69 destroyers. The Japanese split their force into two groups, with the light carriers in Force 'C' ahead of the Main Body (map 2). Mitscher divided his force into four carrier task groups and one battleship task group (map 3).

Ozawa's scouting planes sighted Mitscher's force on the morning of June 19. The Japanese immediately launched strike aircraft at 0830 hours and 0900 hours (map 4). Mitscher's radar, now used to better effect than the American radar had been used during the naval actions off Guadalcanal, warned of the attack. US fighters were sent up to intercept the Japanese planes more than 50 miles before they reached the American carriers. More than 200 Japanese aircraft were shot down at a cost of only 23 US planes.

US submarines had meanwhile located Ozawa's Main Body. The Japanese carrier *Taiho* was attacked at 0900 hours and sunk. The carrier *Shokaku* was hit at 1220 hours and sank four hours later. Another strike sent out by Ozawa headed off in the wrong direction, towards Guam. This too was intercepted by US fighters and largely destroyed.

On June 20, Task Force 58 turned to pursuit. Mitscher found the Japanese in the afternoon. He made an air strike at 1624 hours (map 5). Two hours later, the retreating Japanese carrier *Hiyo* and two oilers were sunk. Losing more planes, Ozawa withdrew toward Okinawa. His task completed, Mitscher eventually turned back to the Marianas.

The battle came to be known as 'The Great Marianas Turkey Shoot', from the number of Japanese aircraft shot down. Between 300 and 400 were destroyed, with an attendant loss of air crews which was disastrous for the Japanese. Though many of the Japanese carriers were intact, such irreparable damage discredited the apparent strength of the Japanese navy. Critics complained that the Battle of the Philippine Sea was solely an air victory; but the Japanese navy was now a defeated force.

Left: For the Americans, the battle on June 19 was a defensive action, in which they waited for the Japanese planes to attack and then destroyed them in aerial battles before they reached the US carriers.

Below: On June 20, Mitscher took the initiative. His planes attacked and sank the carrier Hiyo *and seriously damaged two others.*

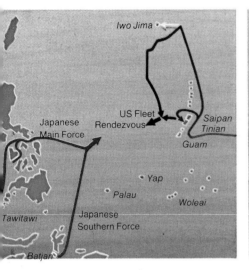

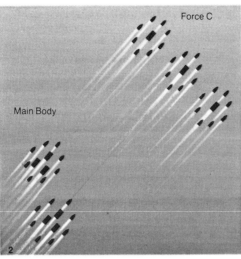

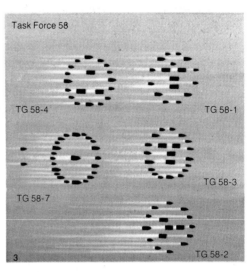

Above: (1) The Japanese main force under Ozawa and the Southern Force under Ugaki rendezvous prior to their attack on Mitscher's Task Force 58, which was protecting the landings on the Marianas. US submarines sighted the Japanese forces on June 16, the day after the landings began.

Above: (2) Ozawa split his force into two groups, with his light carriers in Force 'C', about 100 miles ahead of his Main Body. It was he who took the initiative and launched the first air strikes.

Above: (3) Mitscher divided his US Task Force 58 into four carrier task groups, manoeuvring about 12–15 miles apart, with a separate battleship task group, TG 58–7. He had the advantage of radar and was able to detect the Japanese air strike.

Below: (4) June 19, 1944. The Japanese launched their strike aircraft at 0830 hours and 0900 hours (along the lines of the top two pink arrows – A). US radar gave warning of the attack and American fighters (white arrows – B) intercepted the Japanese 50 miles from their targets. Meanwhile, US submarines attacked the carriers Taiho (C) and Shokaku (D). Another strike sent out by Ozawa (lower pink arrow) flew toward Guam and was also intercepted by US fighters.

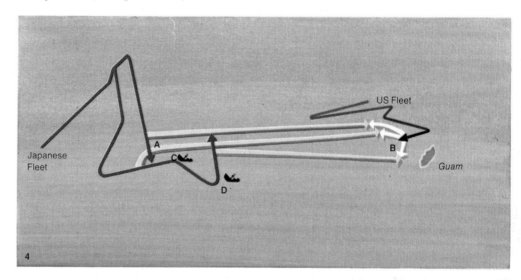

Below: (5) June 20, 1944. The Japanese withdrew and Mitscher's Task Force took the initiative. Mitscher launched an air strike at 1624 hours (E), which sank the carrier Hiyo (F) and two oilers; it also damaged two other carriers. Ozawa sailed on toward Okinawa, while Mitscher turned back to the Marianas. 'The Great Marianas Turkey Shoot' was over.

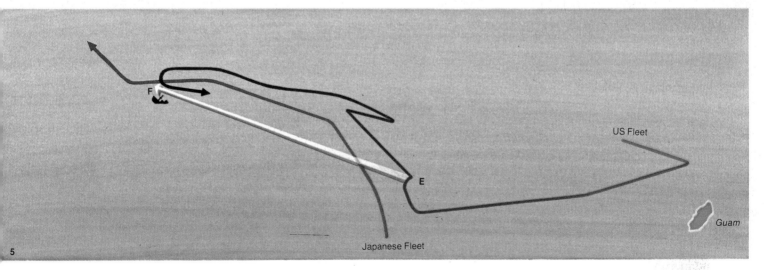

Clearing the Philippines

The Philippines were the next Pacific target, defended by some 350,000 Japanese troops under the command of Yamashita. A vast amphibious armada carrying 200,000 men of Krueger's US 6th Army sailed towards the eastern shore of Leyte in autumn 1944 (map 1). On October 20, Sibert's 10th Corps and Hodge's 24th Corps landed and established a beach-head against light opposition from XVI Division of Suzuki's XXXV Army (maps 1 and 2).

Japanese battleships and carriers attempted to draw off the US fleets from their support of the landings (map 1) but in a series of engagements in the Battle of Leyte Gulf, between October 23 and 25, Japanese sea power was shattered. Between October and December, 10th Corps moved north slowly and 24th Corps swung south and then west to attack Ormoc, the Japanese stronghold, which fell on December 10. The two corps linked up and in a series of overland and amphibious operations forced the end of Japanese resistance in Leyte by December 25, 1944.

Having secured Leyte, Krueger's 6th Army moved north to Luzon, which saw the largest battle in the Pacific War. On January 9, 1945, US 1st and 14th Corps landed without opposition in the Lingayen Gulf (map 3). 1st Corps fought off the bulk of Yamashita's forces in the north of the island, while 14th Corps moved south towards Manila. In the last few days of January, task forces were dropped north and south of Manila but the battle for Manila itself went on until March 3–4 and concluded with desperate street-by-street fighting for the old walled city where more than 16,000 Japanese died.

On February 16, airborne troops landed on Corregidor. Supported by an amphibious landing from Bataan, they cleared the fortress by the end of the month. Fort Drum, the 'Concrete Battleship' that guarded Manila Bay, fell on April 13. The bulk of US 6th Army then turned against the mountain fortresses of Yamashita's army. The Japanese commander still had a force of some 50,000 when he surrendered at the end of the war, on August 15. More than 190,000 Japanese were killed in the fight for Luzon; nearly 8,000 Americans died.

Above: (1) Operation SHO (Victory): the Japanese naval threat to the US landings which resulted in the Battle of Leyte Gulf.

Right: (3) The assault on Luzon, the largest island campaign of the war.

Below: (2) The assault on Leyte, October–December 1944, was the real beginning of the Philippines campaign.

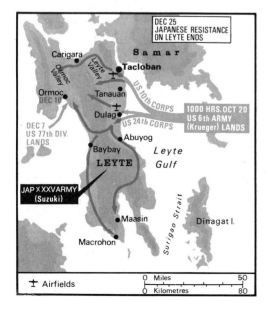

Eichelberger's 8th Army conducted a series of amphibious, island-hopping operations to isolate and mop up the remaining elements of XXXV Army in the central and southern Philippines (map 4). These forces were concentrated on Mindanao, where Suzuki put up stiff resistance inland until the end of the war.

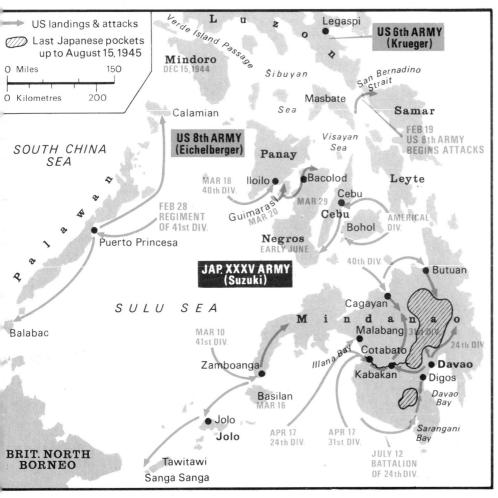

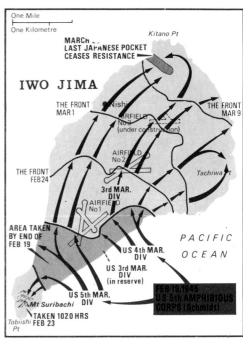

Above: (5) The battle for Iwo Jima, February 19–March 26, 1945. Iwo Jima was essential to Allied strategy, as a fighter base, an emergency bomber landing base and as a traditional part of Japanese territory. Its capture would be both a physical and psychological blow to the Japanese.

Left: (4) Eichelberger's 8th Army clearing the central and southern Philippines in the first half of 1945.

Below: (6) The battle for Okinawa, April–June 1945. The main Japanese defences were on the Shuri Line in the south.

Iwo Jima and Okinawa

While US 6th Army was fighting for control of Luzon, in the Philippines, US 5th Amphibious Corps was preparing for its landings on Iwo Jima and the bloodiest fight in Marine Corps history (map 5). The barren, eight-mile-square island was held by a Japanese garrison firmly entrenched in a honeycomb of gun emplacements, tunnels, pillboxes and caves.

On February 19, following a prolonged aerial and naval bombardment, US 4th and 5th Marine Divisions (with 3rd in reserve) landed in the south. They met no resistance in the first few minutes and were then suddenly subjected to fierce co-ordinated fire. It was just too late. They had already won their foothold. 30,000 Marines had landed by the end of the day and within four days they had raised their flag on Mt Suribachi in the south. The fight for the northern end of the island continued bitterly for another month. The last Japanese pocket did not cease resistance until March 26, by which time nearly 7,000 Americans had died, as had all but 1,000 of the 23,000-strong Japanese garrison.

The final preliminary before the invasion of the Japanese homeland was Okinawa, in the Ryukyu group (map 6). Ushijima's XXXII Army defended the island against Buckner's US 10th Army, which attacked on April 1. The Americans quickly cleared the northern end of the island but the main network of Japanese defences was in the south. Hodge's 24th Corps ran up against the strongly defended Shuri Line on April 9. On May 3–4 the Japanese conducted a suicidal counter-attack but it was not until the end of May that Buckner broke the line. Resistance did not end until June 21–22. American losses numbered nearly 7,500 dead. The final count of Japanese dead was never accurate, for many thousands were believed trapped in their underground caves, but it was thought to be some 100,000.

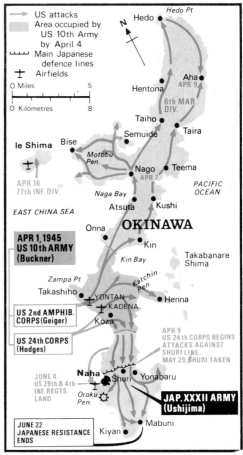

Leyte Gulf: the Naval Actions

Operation 'SHO' (Victory) was planned as a desperate endeavour to combat the US invasion of the Philippines by throwing in the last Japanese battleships and carriers. The Japanese Combined Fleet was already moving to the attack when US troops landed in Leyte Gulf on October 20. Ozawa's Main Body, with four carriers but virtually no planes, was to act as a decoy to lure Halsey's powerful US Third Fleet away from the landings, while Kurita's I Striking Force, including the giants *Musashi* and *Yamato* among its battleships, sailed through the San Bernadino Straight to attack Kinkaid's US Seventh Fleet, which was covering the landings. A smaller and slower Japanese force under Nishimura, followed by Shima's II Striking Force, was to sail through the Surigao Strait to attack from the south (see map 1, previous page).

Contact was made between the opposing fleets on October 23 (map 1, this page). US submarines sighted Kurita's force and sank two heavy cruisers. Kurita continued into the Sibuyan Sea, where planes from Mitscher's Task Force 38 (with the carriers from Halsey's Third Fleet) sank the *Musashi* on October 24. Nishimura was also attacked by aircraft. Mitscher's carrier *Princeton* was sunk by land-based Japanese planes from Luzon. At this point, Halsey concentrated his fleet to counter Ozawa, leaving Kinkaid's Seventh Fleet to protect the landings.

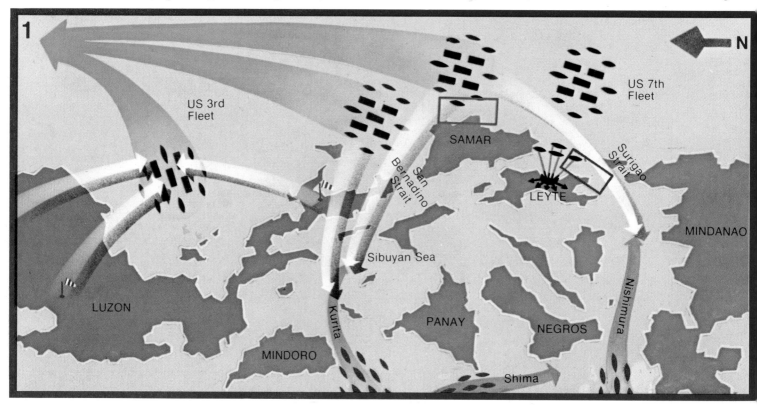

Above: (1) Phase One: Battle of Sibuyan Sea, October 24. Kurita runs into Mitscher's carrier planes. (Boxes show maps 2 and 3).

Below: (2) Phase Two: Battle of Surigao Strait, October 25. Nishimura is destroyed by Oldendorf's torpedoes and gunfire.

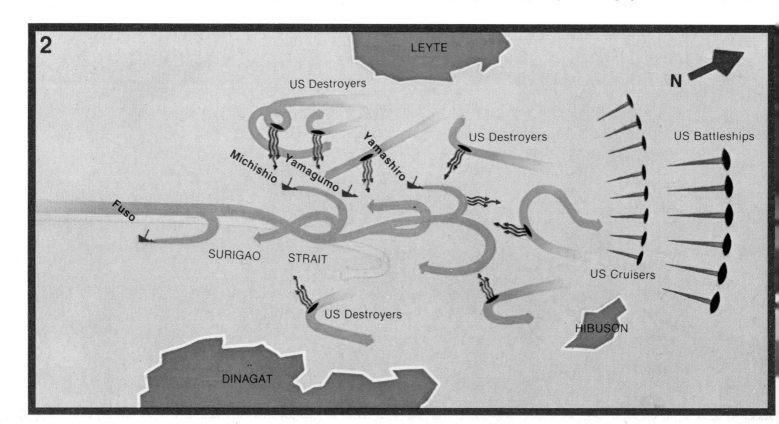

In the second phase (map 2), Nishimura approached in line ahead through the Surigao Strait. In the early hours of October 25, US destroyers launched torpedo attacks from both sides of the strait and sank the battleship *Fuso*. Nishimura then ran into the cruisers and battleships of Oldendorf's Task Group 77, from the US Seventh Fleet, which successfully crossed the Japanese 'T' in a classic naval manoeuvre. Nishimura's force was virtually destroyed and he himself went down in the *Yamashiro*. Shima arrived too late to be of any help.

Kurita, meanwhile, had passed undetected through the San Bernadino Strait and was sailing down the east coast of Samar. At daybreak on October 25, he surprised Sprague's small carrier force from the Seventh Fleet (map 3). Pursued by Kurita's cruisers, Sprague barely escaped but Kurita suddenly turned back, believing the opposition to be stronger than it was. Sprague was then hit by kamikaze attacks from landbased planes (long white arrow, map 3) and lost the carrier *St Lô*.

To the north, Mitscher's planes caught and sank three of Ozawa's carriers on October 25 (map 4). Halsey was about to bring his big guns to bear on Ozawa when he was called back by Sprague's crisis. Kurita had gone by the time he returned. Ozawa lost one more cruiser to Mitscher before escaping. In sum, the Japanese lost four carriers, three battleships, six heavy and four light cruisers, and 11 destroyers.

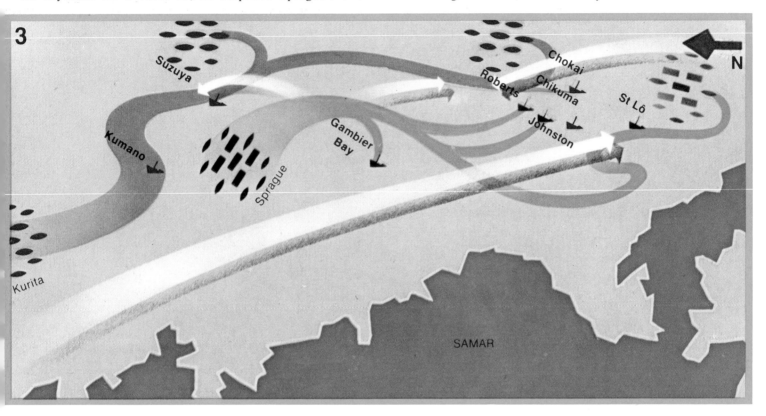

Above: (3) Phase Three: Battle off Samar, October 25. Sprague surprised by Kurita's I Striking Force but Kurita withdraws.

Below: (4) Phase Four: Battle of Cape Engaño, October 25. Halsey and Mitscher attack Ozawa. Halsey forced to withdraw.

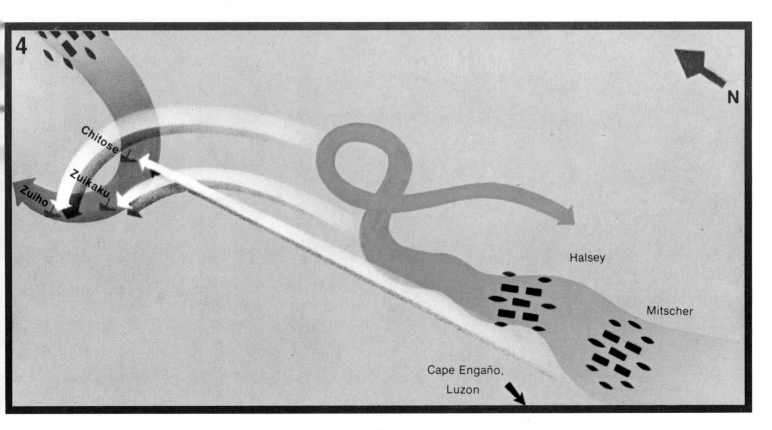

The Arakan Offensives

The Pacific War was only one aspect of the war in the Orient. There was also the continued struggle for Burma. The humiliating retreat by the British from Burma in early 1942 had badly shaken the morale of the troops, now in India. It was therefore with the hope of restoring morale by achieving local success that a counter-offensive was planned in Arakan (map 3). The aim was to take the Mayu Peninsula and the airfields at Akyab, from which the Japanese could threaten Chittagong and even Calcutta.

On September 21, 1942, 14th Indian Division advanced from Chittagong to a base at Cox's Bazaar (map 1). As 14th Division reached the Buthidaung-Maungdaw Line, the Japanese prepared to outflank them through the jungle. There was stalemate

around Donbaik and Rathedaung between January and March 1943. It was not until March 29 that the Allies retreated under threat of another flanking attack. The Japanese had regained Maungdaw and Buthidaung by May 4. The unfortunate British foray was over.

Undeterred by this reverse, Slim ordered a second attack in December 1943 (map 2). Christison's 15th Corps was halted along the same line from Maungdaw to Buthidaung and, on February 4, 1944, the Sakurai Force outflanked Briggs' 5th and Messervy's 7th Indian Divisions, severing communications. Slim continued to supply them by air and after fierce fighting they contacted each other on February 24 and in turn trapped the Japanese. Between March and April, 15th Corps broke the Maungdaw line and was about to resume its advance on Akyab when it was forced to send reinforcements to Imphal.

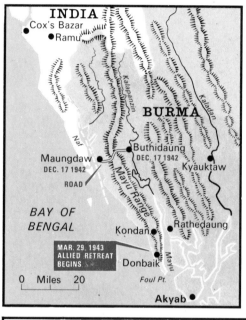

Right: General Slim, commander of the Allied ground forces operating against the Japanese in Burma. He refused to allow 5th and 7th Indian Divisions to withdraw after they were surrounded by the Japanese in February 1944. They eventually broke the Japanese line.

Left: (1) The first Arakan campaign, September 1942–May 1943, was intended to raise morale but ended disastrously.
Below: (2) The second Arakan campaign, December 1943–April 1944, met and held a full-scale Japanese counter-offensive and achieved an important psychological victory over the Japanese.

Below: (3) Akyab, in Arakan, provided an air base from which the Japanese could raid Chittagong and Calcutta.

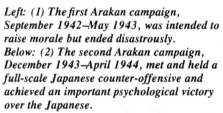

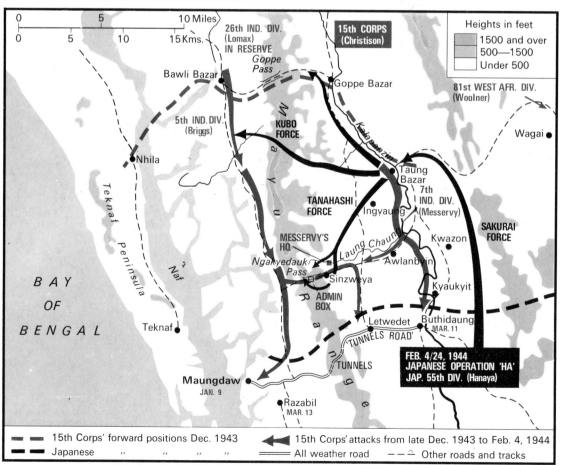

The Chindit Operations

To the north of Arakan, a more unorthodox campaign was being waged behind enemy lines by Colonel Orde Wingate. On February 14–15, 1943, two groups of Wingate's Chindits, guerilla troops, crossed the Chindwin into Burma to harass Japanese communications (map 1). Resistance stiffened as the Chindits advanced into a triangle between the Schweli and Irrawaddy rivers and on March 24 Wingate was ordered to return to India after suffering heavy losses both from disease and attack.

The final major Chindit operation was to complement Stilwell's advance with the Chinese Army in India (CAI) and Merrill's Marauders to Myitkyina (map 2). Calvert's 77th Brigade was airlifted behind enemy lines to cut off Japanese supplies but on March 25 Wingate was killed in an air crash and the Chindits were subsequently used as conventional troops. Myitkyina was taken on August 3–4 and the last Chindits left India on August 27.

Left: Colonel Orde Wingate, one of the most unorthodox British officers of the war, persuaded Churchill to back his ideas for taking the fight behind enemy lines.

Below left: (1) The first Chindit operation, February–March 1943, which suffered heavy losses in the triangle east of the Irrawaddy.

Below right: (2) The final Chindit Operation, to complement Stilwell's advance to Myitkyina, February–August 1944.

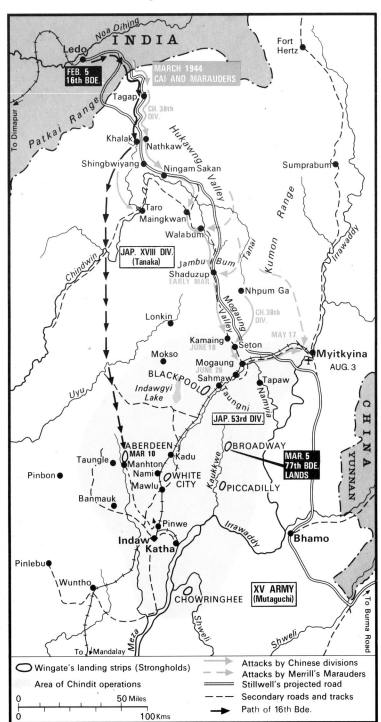

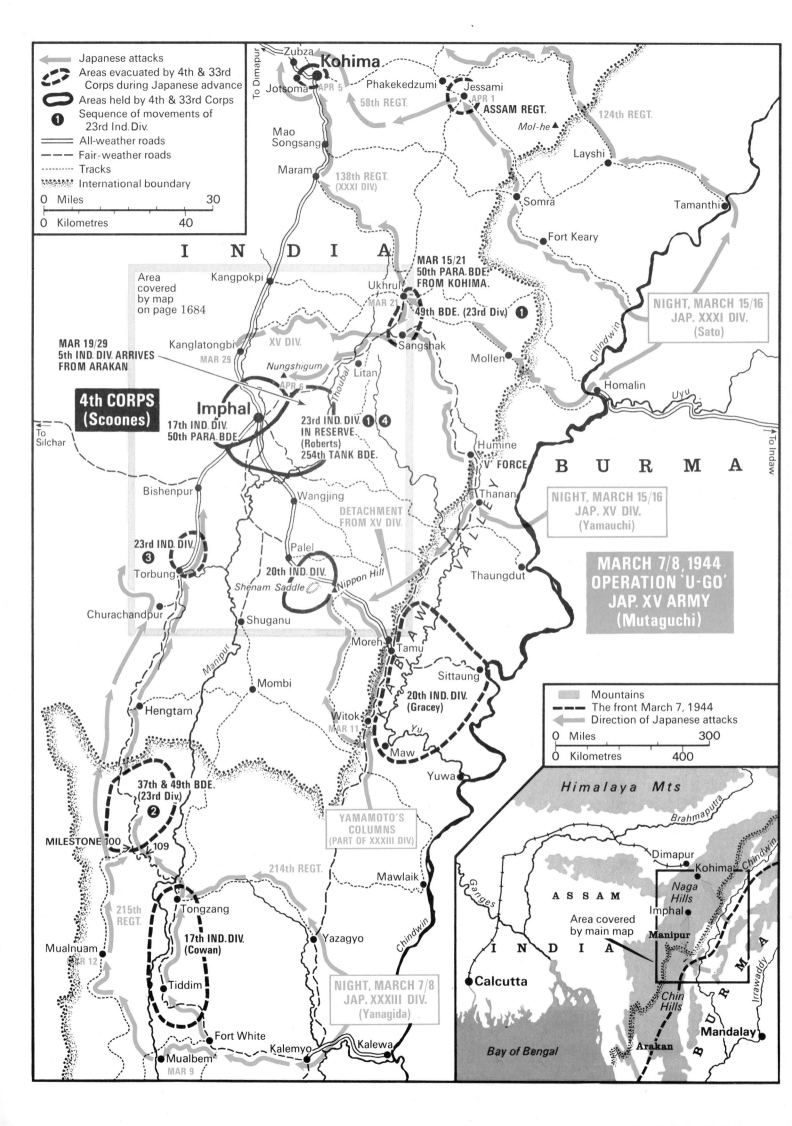

Japanese attacks
Areas evacuated by 4th & 33rd Corps during Japanese advance
Areas held by 4th & 33rd Corps
Sequence of movements of 23rd Ind. Div.
All-weather roads
Fair-weather roads
Tracks
International boundary

0 Miles 30
0 Kilometres 40

To Dimapur
Zubza
Kohima
Jotsoma APR 5
Phakekedzumi
Jessami APR 1
ASSAM REGT.
124th REGT.
58th REGT.
Mol-he ▲
Mao Songsang
Layshi
Maram
138th REGT. (XXXI DIV.)
Somra
Fort Keary
Tamanthi

I N D I A

Area covered by map on page 1684
Kangpokpi
Ukhrul
MAR 15/21
50th PARA. BDE.
FROM KOHIMA.
MAR 21
49th BDE. (23rd Div.) ①
Sangshak
NIGHT, MARCH 15/16
JAP. XXXI DIV.
(Sato)

MAR 19/29
5th IND. DIV. ARRIVES
FROM ARAKAN
Kanglatongbi
MAR 29
XV DIV.
Nungshigum ▲
APR 6
Litan
Thoubal
Mollen
Chindwin
Uyu
To Indaw

4th CORPS
(Scoones)
Imphal
17th IND. DIV.
50th PARA. BDE.
23rd IND. DIV. ① ④
IN RESERVE
(Roberts)
254th TANK BDE.
Humine
V' FORCE

To Silchar

Homalin

B U R M A

Bishenpur
Wangjing
Thanan
NIGHT, MARCH 15/16
JAP. XV DIV.
(Yamauchi)

23rd IND. DIV.
③
Torbung
DETACHMENT
FROM XV DIV.
Palel
20th IND. DIV.
Shenam Saddle
Nippon Hill
Thaungdut

MARCH 7/8, 1944
OPERATION 'U-GO'
JAP. XV ARMY
(Mutaguchi)

Churachandpur
Shuganu
Moreh
Tamu
Sittaung
20th IND. DIV.
(Gracey)

Manipur
Mombi
Hengtam
Witok
MAR 11
Yu
Maw
Yuwa

37th & 49th BDE.
(23rd Div.)
②
MILESTONE 100
109
214th REGT.
Mawlaik
YAMAMOTO'S
COLUMNS
(PART OF XXXIII DIV.)

Mountains
The front March 7, 1944
Direction of Japanese attacks

0 Miles 300
0 Kilometres 400

Himalaya Mts

Brahmaputra

215th
REGT.
Tongzang
17th IND. DIV.
(Cowan)
Yazagyo
Ganges
Dimapur
Kohima
Chindwin
Naga
Hills
Imphal
Manipur

Mualnuam
MAR 12
Tiddim
Chindwin
NIGHT, MARCH 7/8
JAP. XXXIII DIV.
(Yanagida)

A S S A M

I N D I A

Area covered
by main map

Calcutta

Irrawaddy

Fort White
Kalemyo
Kalewa
Mualbem
MAR 9

Bay of Bengal

Chin
Hills

Arakan

B U R M A

Mandalay

The Attack on Imphal and Kohima

By the end of 1943, the Japanese knew that the Allies were preparing for a major counter-offensive in Burma. General Kawabe, Commander of the Japanese Burma Area Army, determined to forestall an invasion by launching Mutaguchi's XV Army in a limited offensive against Imphal and Kohima, the Allied forward supply bases in India (map 1). It was essential to the Japanese to seize Imphal quickly, as a supply base for their own attack on Kohima. It was equally vital for the Allies to hold both towns. Only by holding Imphal could Slim pin down the Japanese in the south and cut their communications with Kohima and only by holding Kohima could he hope to keep the road open for supplies to beleaguered Imphal. Slim's plan was to hold Imphal while defeating the Japanese attack on Kohima.

Operation "U-GO" opened on the night of March 7–8, 1944. The Japanese XXXIII Division cut off 17th Indian Division in the south, while XV and XXXI Divisions crossed the Chindwin farther north and attacked Imphal and Kohima. Taken by surprise by the speed of the attack, the outlying Allied forces managed to withdraw to Imphal and Kohima in good order but by April 4–5 both towns had been cut off and were being supplied by air, while 33rd Corps made preparations for relieving them.

Scoones' 4th Corps concentrated on holding on to the forward position at Imphal (map 2), where the battle developed into a desperate struggle. During April, May and June, 4th Corps withstood repeated heavy attacks by XXXIII Division from the south, while attempting to thrust north up the road to Ukhrul against XV Division. Supplies and reinforcements were flown in by Slim throughout the fighting to sustain the defenders of Imphal but both the Allies and the Japanese suffered severely from shortages of food. The battle for Kohima was raging at the same time and it was not until June 22 that units of 4th Corps from Imphal and Stopford's 33rd Corps from Kohima met at Milestone 107 and the long, desperate siege was relieved. The Japanese were defeated by problems of supply and Allied endurance.

Above: General Kawabe, Commander of the Japanese Burma Area Army, who determined to launch a limited offensive against Imphal and Kohima to thwart Allied plans for an offensive into Burma in 1944.

Left: (1) Operation "U-GO", the Japanese offensive against Imphal and Kohima, March 1944. Inset map shows the area of operations. The Allied position in India would certainly have become untenable if Imphal had fallen to the Japanese.

Right: (2) Imphal was cut off by Japanese XXXIII and XV Divisions in the first week of April 1944, but 4th Corps managed to hold off the Japanese attacks for the best part of three months. Relief came from Kohima in late June.

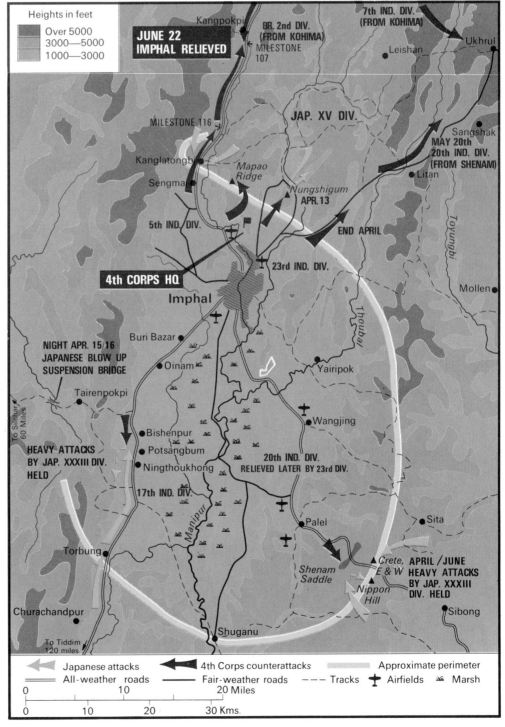

The Relief of Kohima

By holding on to Imphal, 4th Corps prevented the Japanese from bringing up the supplies and men necessary for them to break through the Allied defences at Kohima (map 1). Sato's XXXI Division surrounded Kohima and captured Jail Hill on April 6, 1944, and on April 7 the Japanese cut the relief road from Dimapur, whence Stopford's 33rd Corps was hastening. The garrison on Kohima Ridge was completely besieged.

Kohima was in a perilous situation for nearly two weeks, threatened constantly by collapse and only supported by American and British fighter planes and medium bombers, which kept up a steady harassment of the Japanese. Pushing on ahead of Stopford's 33rd Corps, 2nd Division's 5th Brigade destroyed the Japanese strongholds at Zubza on April 14 and relieved 161st Indian Brigade at Jotsoma. 5th Brigade then advanced rapidly to relieve Kohima itself on April 18 and to reinforce the garrison but this was only the beginning of the bitter struggle. The Japanese were firmly dug into strong defensive positions that the Allies were unable to break.

On the night of April 22–23, 5th Brigade began a left hook to drive the Japanese outposts off Merema Ridge and to attack Firs Hill and Naga Village. At the same time, 4th Brigade began a right hook from the south and took GPT Ridge on May 4. Additional attacks by 6th and 33rd Brigades on Kohima Ridge at first met with failure. Fierce resistance prolonged the fighting throughout May, as the Japanese held fanatically to their fine defensive line along the ridge from Gun Spur to Aradura Spur (map 2). Allied attacks on these two spurs towards the end of May were repulsed by the Japanese and it was not until June 1 that an attack by 7th Indian Division breached the Japanese positions at the northern end of the ridge. Forced from their stronghold, the remnants of XXXI Division withdrew from the ridge. On June 6, 2nd Division advanced south to the relief of Imphal, although it did not finally make contact with 5th Indian Division advancing north out of Imphal until June 22.

Supplies had played a vital rôle in the battle for Imphal and Kohima. The Japanese supply lines were never secure, so long as Imphal remained untaken. For much of the battle and when in retreat, the ordinary Japanese soldier suffered greatly from lack of sufficient food and equipment. After their defeat, the withdrawal back to the Chindwin Valley was a long and painful one for Japanese XV Army.

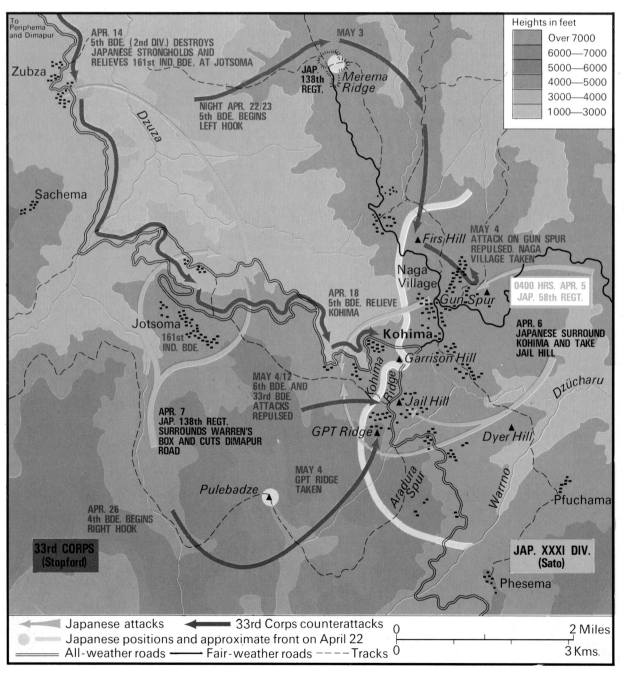

Left: (1) The battle to relieve the besieged garrison of Kohima, April–May 1944. Kohima was completely surrounded from April 6–18, when it was relieved by 5th Brigade of 33rd Corps' 2nd Division. But the bitter struggle for Kohima Ridge continued throughout May, before the Japanese were finally forced off their defensive positions and the victors of Kohima could hasten south to relieve their colleagues

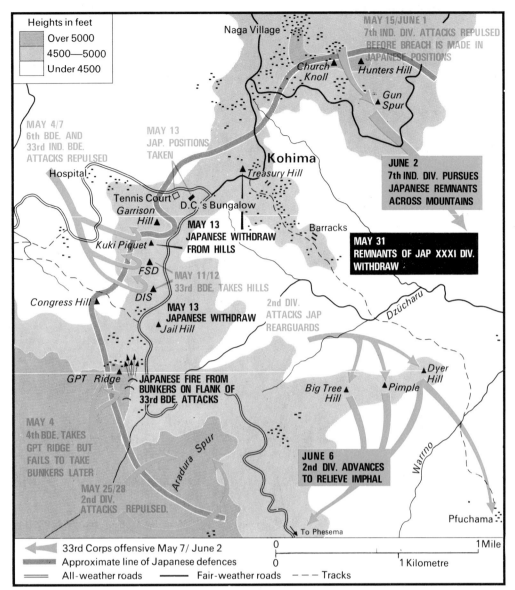

Heights in feet
Over 5000
4500—5000
Under 4500

Naga Village

MAY 15/JUNE 1
7th IND. DIV. ATTACKS REPULSED
BEFORE BREACH IS MADE IN
JAPANESE POSITIONS

Church Knoll
Hunters Hill
Gun Spur

MAY 4/7
6th BDE. AND
33rd IND. BDE.
ATTACKS REPULSED

MAY 13
JAP. POSITIONS
TAKEN

Kohima

Treasury Hill

JUNE 2
7th IND. DIV. PURSUES
JAPANESE REMNANTS
ACROSS MOUNTAINS

Hospital

Tennis Court
Garrison Hill
D.C.'s Bungalow

MAY 13
JAPANESE WITHDRAW
FROM HILLS

Barracks

MAY 31
REMNANTS OF JAP XXXI DIV.
WITHDRAW

Kuki Piquet

FSD

MAY 11/12
33rd BDE. TAKES HILLS

Dzücharu

Congress Hill

DIS

MAY 13
JAPANESE WITHDRAW

Jail Hill

2nd DIV.
ATTACKS JAP
REARGUARDS

Dyer Hill

GPT Ridge

JAPANESE FIRE FROM
BUNKERS ON FLANK OF
33rd BDE. ATTACKS

Big Tree Hill
Pimple

MAY 4
4th BDE. TAKES
GPT RIDGE BUT
FAILS TO TAKE
BUNKERS LATER

Aradura Spur

JUNE 6
2nd DIV. ADVANCES
TO RELIEVE IMPHAL

Warrno

MAY 25/28
2nd DIV.
ATTACKS REPULSED.

Pfuchama

To Phesema

33rd Corps offensive May 7/ June 2
Approximate line of Japanese defences
All-weather roads   Fair-weather roads   Tracks

0   1 Mile
0   1 Kilometre

Right: (2) The desperate fight by Stopford's 33rd Corps to break through the Japanese positions on the central sector at Kohima involved some of the most bitter fighting of the war. One Japanese major remarked that, 'it will go down as one of the greatest battles in history'. The Japanese supply lines were inadequate for a long, static battle and it was on the question of supply that the fortunes of the battle finally turned. According to some Japanese, it was the deliberate and treasonable withdrawal of Sato's XXXI Division from the battle-front in order to avoid annihilation that was the immediate cause of the Japanese collapse.

Below: The battle for Imphal. Troops of 1/17th Dogra Regiment prepare to attack Nungshigum, just north of Imphal.

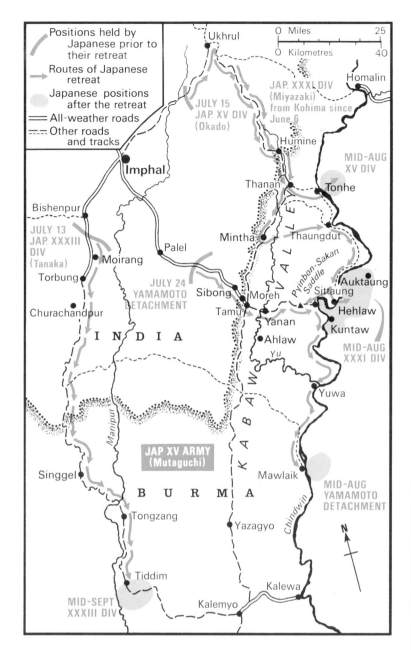

Left: (1) The retreat of Japanese XV Army after the failure of their offensive against Imphal and Kohima. By mid-August 1944 they were behind the Chindwin once again.

Below: (2) Slim's advance on Mandalay and Meiktila, December 1944–February 1945. By skilfully preserving the appearance that his main attack was against Mandalay, Slim surprised the Japanese with 4th Corps at Meiktila.

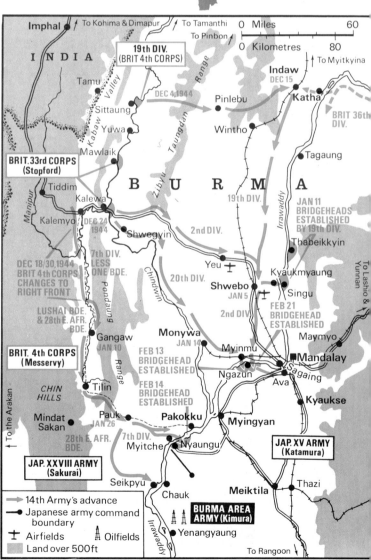

Mandalay and Meiktila

The Japanese withdrew into Burma after Kohima, hoping the Allies would over-extend themselves in pursuit (map 1). Kimura replaced Kawabe and Katamaru replaced Mutaguchi. On November 19, 1944, Slim's 14th Army began to advance over the Chindwin, with 4th Corps crossing at Sittaung and 33rd Corps farther south at Mawlaik and Kalewa (map 2). Kimura hoped to lure 14th Army to destruction north of Mandalay, as it crossed the Irrawaddy. Slim, alerted, secretly switched 4th Corps south of 33rd Corps, leaving 19th Indian Division in the north as a decoy. 19th Division attacked across the Irrawaddy in mid-January 1945 at Thebeikkyin and Kyaukmyaung and 33rd Corps nearer Mandalay on February 12–13. Slim slipped Messervy's 4th Corps across the Irrawaddy at Nyaungu, 100 miles south of Mandalay, on February 13. Taking the Japanese completely by surprise, Cowan's 17th Indian Division seized the strategic railroad junction of Meiktila by the beginning of March (map 3). Kimura sent all his reserves from Mandalay to retrieve Meiktila, and fighting raged throughout March. Meanwhile 33rd Corps kept the remaining Japanese forces pinned down at Mandalay. 19th Division had taken the city by March 20. The defenders of Meiktila held out stubbornly until relieved by 33rd Corps. Realizing his position was hopeless, Kimura withdrew east through Thazi.

Above: Major-General Cowan, Commander of 17th Indian Division, charged with the capture of Meiktila, which he accomplished by March 3. Japanese counter-attacks cut off the division in Meiktila, forcing 14th Army to supply the garrison by air for three weeks.

Above: Lieutenant-General Honda, Commander of Japanese XXXIII Army, who led the Japanese attempt to recover Meiktila, was thwarted by the ability of Allied air power to keep the garrison well-supplied. Honda admitted defeat on March 29 and his forces retreated east.

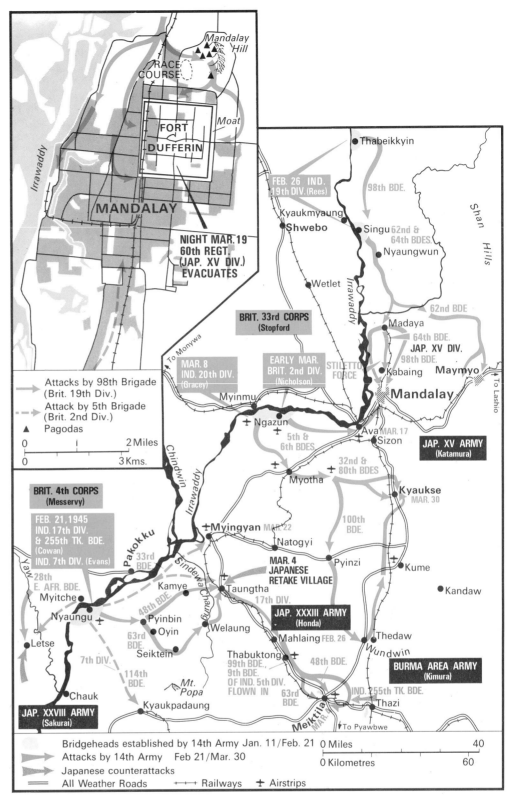

Left: A Beaufighter strike hits a Japanese supply train. Meiktila was a vital railroad junction in central Burma and supplies were the essential key to the battle for the Allied recovery of Burma. By switching the emphasis of the battle from Mandalay to Meiktila, Slim had caught the Japanese on the wrong foot. They could not afford to ignore the importance of Meiktila and so they were prepared to leave Mandalay relatively unprotected in order to throw in their full strength at Meiktila.

Above: (3) The Battle for Meiktila and Mandalay, February–March 1945. Messervy's 4th Corps achieved their surprise crossing of the Irrawaddy almost completely unopposed. The Japanese had been led to believe that they were still in full strength in the north with 19th Indian Division. With the capture of Meiktila by Cowan's 17th Indian Division, the Japanese were forced to turn their attention south and leave Mandalay exposed to 33rd Corps and 19th Division.

The Race to Rangoon

When 19th Indian Division and 33rd Corps finally took Mandalay in late March 1945, they were joined by 36th Division, which had been operating in northern Burma with the Chinese armies. Having taken Myitkyina in early August 1944 (see page 173), Stilwell had planned a grand pincer movement between his Northern Combat Area Command (Chinese New 1st and 6th Armies) and the Chinese Y Force to reopen the Burma Road (map 2). A command crisis replaced Stilwell with Sultan but the basic plan remained. Chinese Y Force advanced from the north-east, while 6th Army advanced through Shwegu (November 7) and 1st Army advanced through Bhamo (December 15), after determined opposition by the Japanese. 36th Division meanwhile advanced on the left flank of 6th Army. On January 27, 1945, Chinese Y Force and 1st Army met at Mongyu and the advance then continued down the Burma Road to Lashio (March 7) and Kyaukme (March 31).

At much the same time, Christison's 15th Corps had begun its final Arakan campaign, on December 12, 1944 (map 3). Kimura had already stripped the defences of Arakan to a minimum to draw off reinforcements for Mandalay, where he was determined to fight a decisive battle. As a result, Akyab fell to 15th Corps on January 4, 1945, and Ramree fell on February 9. Mountbatten immediately ordered the construction of an all-weather airstrip at Kyaukpyu (map 1).

By the end of March 1945, therefore, northern Burma had been reopened, Arakan was in Allied hands, and so were Meiktila and Mandalay. Slim ordered an immediate advance from Meiktila to Rangoon, before the monsoons made progress impossible (map 4). One force advanced down the Irrawaddy towards Prome, which was taken on May 2–3 by 20th Indian Division. The other, faster force, moved down the railway through Toungoo to Pegu. Often outstripping the retreating Japanese, 17th Indian Division seized Pegu on May 2, the day after the monsoon broke. But both these forces were beaten to Rangoon by 26th Indian Division, which was brought round from Arakan by sea and made an amphibious landing south of Rangoon on May 2. Rangoon was occupied by 26th Division the next day, with the mainland forces still 28 miles to the north. The remaining Japanese held out in pockets inland, isolated by the monsoon, or retreated into Thailand.

Above: British guns pound the walls of Mandalay.

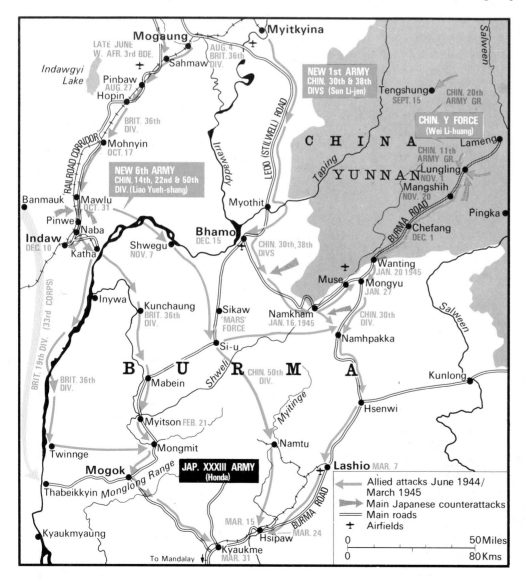

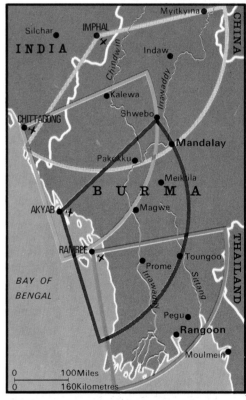

Above: (1) Air superiority played a vital part in the recovery of Burma. Imphal, Akyab and Ramree, added to Chittagong, extended Allied air cover south and east.

Left: (2) The re-opening of the Burma Road as Chinese armies and 36th Division advance in northern Burma. The advance of 19th Indian Division towards Mandalay is shown on the left of the map.

Above: A lash-up bamboo bridge in Burma, for men and mules only. The Allied battle of supply was a mammoth undertaking as the front widened and extended to the south.

Below: A British fighting patrol, carried in local craft across the flooded fields, probes for signs of Japanese resistance in Burma.

Right: (3) The final Arakan campaign by Christison's 15th Corps, December 1944–February 1945. This provided a base for the long-range operation by 26th Indian Division, who took Rangoon on May 3.

Below: (4) Advance of 14th Army from Meiktila south to Rangoon, March–May 1945. It was a race against the monsoon and the Japanese.

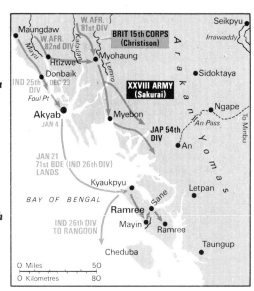

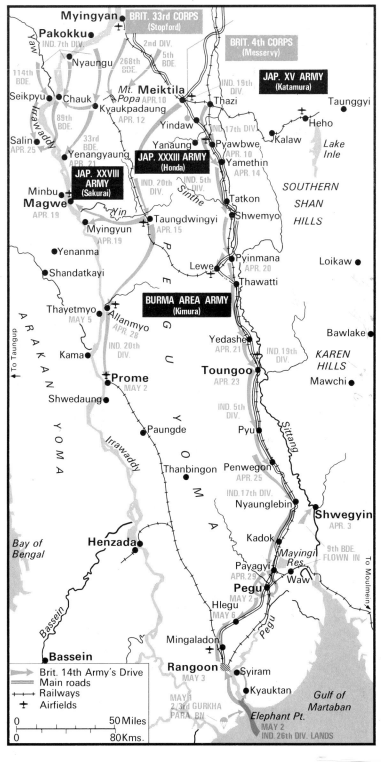

The War in China

Japan's expansion began in the 19th century and quickly included Formosa, Korea and Manchuria (map 1). Alarmed by a temporary truce between the Chinese Nationalists and Communists, the Japanese invaded China itself from the north on July 7, 1937. The planned link-up with a second force landing at Shanghai, which met unexpected resistance, did not occur for another year, after which the extension of Japanese occupation continued slowly.

American interest in the struggle grew during 1940. Supplies were sent in to China at first along the Burma Road and then 'over the hump', by plane across the mountains. Stilwell acted as military adviser and chief-of-staff to Chiang Kai-shek. Chennault's 'Flying Tigers', already in China, were built up into a new US 14th Air Force.

Goaded by the increasing success of US air operations, the Japanese launched a major ground offensive to capture the air-fields. At the end of May 1944, XI and XXIII Army attacked from Hankow and Canton (map 2). Chinese resistance crumbled before the attack and 14th Air Force were unable to check it. The Japanese offensive linked forces in northern China with those in Indo-China and continued to the spring of 1945, when the threat from Russia towards Manchuria forced the Japanese to shift much of their strength to the north. The Chinese subsequently cut the corridor to Indo-China but the general situation changed little until the end of the war.

Left: Chiang Kai-shek, leader of the Chinese Nationalist Government. His country was simultaneously threatened by the Japanese and split from within by the Communists. His armies were trained by US General Stilwell, with whom he eventually quarrelled.

Right: Mao Tse-tung, leader of the Chinese Communists, rivals for power within China, whose unsteady truces with the Nationalists barely lasted out the war. Civil War resumed once the Japanese threat was removed.

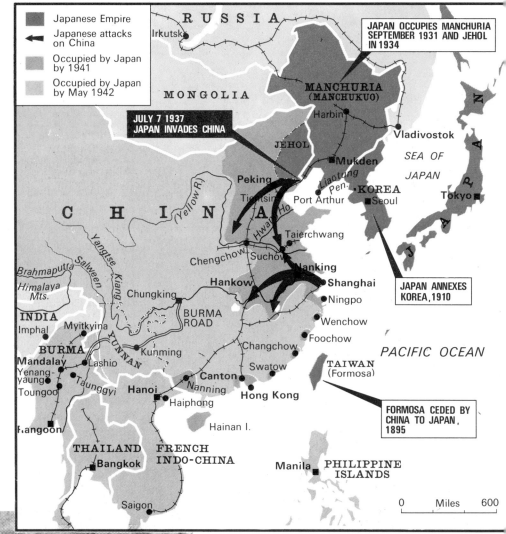

Above: (1) Japanese encroachments on Chinese territory before and after the invasion of 1937. When the Japanese attacked, Chiang Kai-shek's National Government Army consisted of about two million ill-equipped and poorly trained troops. The Chinese Communist guerrillas in north-west China had about 150,000 troops, nominally supporting Chiang Kai-shek against the Japanese.

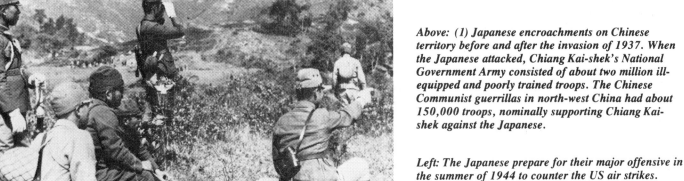

Left: The Japanese prepare for their major offensive in the summer of 1944 to counter the US air strikes.

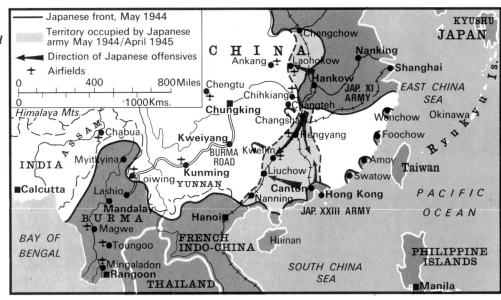

Right: (2) The Japanese offensives in the summer of 1944, which over-ran the US air fields. Further small offensives were launched in the first few months of 1945, mainly to consolidate the gains of the previous year, before the Japanese were forced to deploy their strength in the north.

Legend:
— Japanese front, May 1944
▨ Territory occupied by Japanese army May 1944/April 1945
◄— Direction of Japanese offensives
✝ Airfields

0   400   800 Miles
0   1000 Kms.

Below: Chinese troops march to meet the Japanese challenge. They were trained and supplied by the Americans. Chennault managed to get the bulk of the supplies coming 'over the hump' for his gradual build-up of air power in China. Stilwell objected strongly, insisting that the land forces were more important.

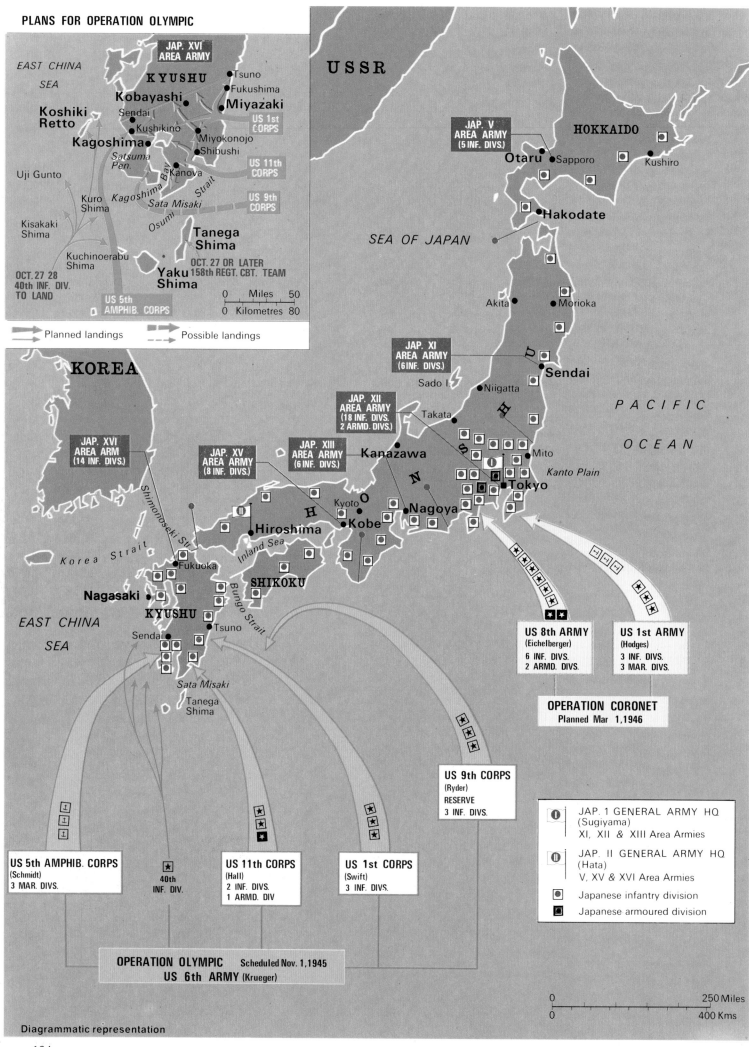

PLANS FOR OPERATION OLYMPIC

JAP. XVI AREA ARMY

EAST CHINA SEA

KYUSHU

Koshiki Retto

Kobayashi
Sendai
Kushikino
Kagoshima
Miyokonojo
Shibushi

Tsuno
Fukushima
Miyazaki

US 1st CORPS
US 11th CORPS
US 9th CORPS

Uji Gunto

Satsuma Pen.
Kagoshima Bay
Kanova
Sata Misaki
Kuro Shima
Osumi Strait

Kisakaki Shima

Kuchinoerabu Shima

OCT. 27 28
40th INF. DIV.
TO LAND

Tanega Shima

Yaku Shima

OCT. 27 OR LATER
158th REGT. CBT. TEAM

0 Miles 50
0 Kilometres 80

US 5th AMPHIB. CORPS

→ Planned landings   ⇢ Possible landings

USSR

HOKKAIDO

JAP. V AREA ARMY (5 INF. DIVS.)
Otaru • Sapporo
Kushiro

SEA OF JAPAN

Hakodate

Akita • Morioka

JAP. XI AREA ARMY (6 INF. DIVS.)

Sado I.
Niigatta
Sendai

PACIFIC OCEAN

KOREA

JAP. XVI AREA ARM (14 INF. DIVS.)

JAP. XV AREA ARMY (8 INF. DIVS.)

JAP. XII AREA ARMY (18 INF. DIVS. 2 ARMD. DIVS.)

JAP. XIII AREA ARMY (6 INF. DIVS.)

Takata
Kanazawa

Mito
Kanto Plain

Tokyo

Kyoto
Kobe
Nagoya

Shimonoseki Str.

Hiroshima

Korea Strait

Inland Sea

Fukuoka

Nagasaki •

KYUSHU
SHIKOKU

Bungo Strait

EAST CHINA SEA

Sendai
Tsuno

Sata Misaki

Tanega Shima

US 8th ARMY
(Eichelberger)
6 INF. DIVS.
2 ARMD. DIVS.

US 1st ARMY
(Hodges)
3 INF. DIVS.
3 MAR. DIVS.

OPERATION CORONET
Planned Mar 1,1946

US 9th CORPS
(Ryder)
RESERVE
3 INF. DIVS.

US 5th AMPHIB. CORPS
(Schmidt)
3 MAR. DIVS.

40th INF. DIV.

US 11th CORPS
(Hall)
2 INF. DIVS.
1 ARMD. DIV

US 1st CORPS
(Swift)
3 INF. DIVS.

OPERATION OLYMPIC   Scheduled Nov. 1,1945
US 6th ARMY (Krueger)

JAP. 1 GENERAL ARMY HQ (Sugiyama)
XI, XII & XIII Area Armies

JAP. II GENERAL ARMY HQ (Hata)
V, XV & XVI Area Armies

▣ Japanese infantry division

◼ Japanese armoured division

0 250 Miles
0 400 Kms

Diagrammatic representation

184

Victory in the Orient

After conflicting plans for the invasion of Japan had been aired in the first half of 1945, preparations were made for Operations Olympic and Coronet (map 1). Olympic was scheduled for November 1, 1945, to land Krueger's 6th Army on Kyushu (map 2). Coronet was scheduled for March 1, 1946, to land 1st and 8th Armies on Honshu. Two Japanese army groups, or 'general armies', stood ready to defend the homeland, one based on Tokyo, the other on Hiroshima.

It was President Truman who had to take the decision to shorten the war by dropping the first offensive atomic bomb on Hiroshima, an important military HQ and supply depot, on August 6, 1945. The bomb exploded over the centre of the city, destroying two-thirds of Hiroshima. When Japan ignored another surrender ultimatum, a second bomb was dropped on Nagasaki, a seaport and industrial town north of Sendai, on the extreme west coast of Kyushu, on August 9. Japan immediately surrendered unconditionally. A general cease-fire came into existence on August 15 and the official surrender was signed on September 2 aboard the USS *Missouri* in Tokyo Bay.

Russia only entered the war against Japan after the dropping of the Hiroshima bomb. War was declared on August 8 and the Soviet armies invaded Manchuria on August 9, anxious to seize what territory they could before Japan surrendered (map 3). They achieved a swift and decisive victory. In nine days, Yamada's Kwantung Army was completely overwhelmed. Written confirmation of Japan's surrender to the Allies did not reach Yamada until August 17. Negotiations with the Russians began on August 18 and the surrender document was signed the next day. Russia had gained a last-minute triumph which, while contributing nothing to the Allied victory over Japan, brought the Soviet Union a vast addition of territory.

Right: Various estimates have been given for the number killed by the atomic bombs on Hiroshima and Nagasaki. The lowest reasoned figures for immediate deaths are approximately 40,000 in Nagasaki and 80,000 in Hiroshima. Higher estimates, including those who died later as a consequence of the bombs, rise to two or three times those figures. The Tokyo fire-raid by the Allies on the night of March 9–10, 1945, is estimated to have killed more than 80,000 people and to have wounded more than 100,000 people. But the density of deaths per square mile was only one-third or one-quarter as high as in Nagasaki and Hiroshima.

Above: (1) The conflicting plans of the American naval and military forces for the final attack on Japan. Nimitz favoured a prolonged bombardment from the mainland of China. But MacArthur's plan for a direct assault, at least on Kyushu, was given priority. These plans would have stretched the war through the first half of 1946 and quite possibly even longer.

Left: (2) The plans for Operations Olympic (November 1, 1945) and Coronet (March 1, 1946), in the projected final assault on Japan. If Japanese resistance on the Pacific islands was anything to go by, loss of life on both sides would have been very high indeed; far higher than the numbers killed by the bombs dropped on Hiroshima and Nagasaki.

Right: (3) The Soviet invasion of Manchuria in August 1945. Stalin raced against time to gain new land in Eastern Asia before the end of the war.

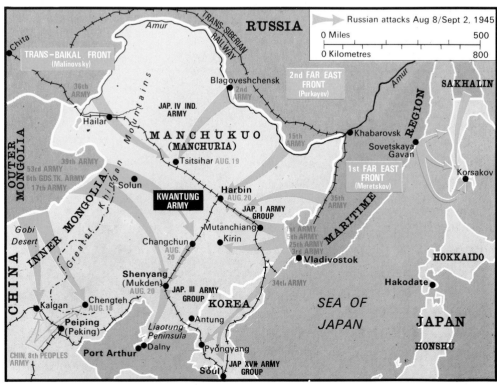

Bibliography

Of the many books available on the subject of the Second World War, the following are highly recommended: Basil Collier, *A Short History of the Second World War* (1967); J. F. C. Fuller, *The Second World War, 1939–1945: A Strategical and Tactical History* (1945); B. H. Liddell Hart (ed.), *History of the Second World War* (1966–   ).

From the naval perspective: Stephen W. Roskill, *The War at Sea, 1939–1945*, 3 vol. (1954–61); Friedrich Ruge *Der Seekrieg, 1939–1945* (1954), translated as *Sea Warfare, 1939–1945; A German Viewpoint* (1957).

The war in the air: Charles K. Webster and Noble Frankland, *The Strategic Air Offensive Against Germany, 1939–1945*, 4 vol. (1961); Wesley F. Craven and James L. Cate (eds.), *Army Air Forces in World War Two*, 7 vol. (1945–50).

Useful as well are the series of books on various aspects of the conflict by Herbert Feis and the innumerable specialized texts published by H. M. Stationery Office, to be found in a well-stocked reference library.

Ed. note – For the *sense of the facts* in the Pacific sphere, Norman Mailer's *The Naked and the Dead* is recommended reading. Similarly, James Jones' classic *The Thin Red Line* is a harrowing account of what war meant for the rank and file soldier at Guadalcanal.

Acknowledgement

Thanks are due to the Imperial War Museum for pictures previously reproduced in Purnell's *History of the Second World War*.

Index

(Indexed by E. I. Mulligan)